# Managing and Working in Project Society

In this book, leading authorities on project organizing explore the
growing deployment of projects and other types of temporary
organizations, with a focus on the challenges created by projectification. The way projects are coordinated and handled influences the
success of innovation and change within organizations and is critical
for strategic development in our societies, yet it is often at odds with
the institutions of traditional industrial society. Drawing on both
theoretical perspectives and real-world cases, this book sheds light on
the transformation toward a project society and explores the effects,
opportunities, and conflicts it has created. As change continues, the
authors make a case for renewing institutions and mind-sets and
provide a foundation from which to discuss societal changes for the
future. This is an invaluable book for researchers and students in
project management and organizational theory programs, as well as
professionals involved in the management of projects.

ROLF A. LUNDIN is Professor Emeritus of Business Administration
at Jönköping International Business School and Courtesy
Professor-in-Residence at Umeå School of Business and Economics.
He has received several prizes and awards for his research on
projects and temporary organizations, including the 2014 PMI
Research Achievement Award. He has published widely, with a
concentration on temporary organizations, and has edited numerous
special issues of journals focusing on the area of projects. Currently,
his main focus is on innovative research on projects and temporary
organizations.

NIKLAS ARVIDSSON is Associate Professor and Head of the Department
of Sustainability and Industrial Dynamics at the Royal Institute of
Technology (KTH) in Stockholm. He also has long working experience
as a management consultant. His research is focused on innovation,
learning, and change in organizations and industrial systems, with a

particular interest in processes in which currently dominating ideas and practices are being replaced by new ones.

TIM BRADY is Professor of Innovation in the Centre for Research in Innovation Management at Brighton Business School, the University of Brighton, and Visiting Professor in the Department of Industrial Engineering Management at the University of Oulu, Finland. He was a member of the Rethinking Project Management network funded by the UK Engineering and Physical Sciences Research Council and Deputy Director of the Complex Product Systems (CoPS) Innovation Centre funded by the UK Economic and Social Research Council. His current research interests include the development of new business models for infrastructure, the management of complex projects and programs, and learning and capability development in project-based business.

ESKIL EKSTEDT is Professor in Business Administration and Associate Professor in Economic History at the University of Uppsala. He was the founding editor of the Scientific Publication series *Work Life in Transition* and the project leader of several major research programs dealing with knowledge formation and organizational and local economic development. His research has focused on knowledge formation, temporary organizations, and structural change of business and work life.

CHRISTOPHE MIDLER is Professor of Innovation Management at École Polytechnique and Research Director at the French National Research Council (FNRS). He has received many prizes and awards for his research on project organizing, among them Doctor Honoris Causa at Umeå University, Sweden, and the 2013 PMI Research Achievement Award. His research topics include project management and innovation management in relation to organizational theory and strategy, exploring them in various industrial contexts.

JÖRG SYDOW is Professor of Management and Chair for Inter-firm Cooperation at the School of Business & Economics, Freie Universität Berlin, and a Visiting Professor at Strathclyde Business School in Glasgow. He is a founding coeditor of two leading German academic journals, *Managementforschung* and *Industrielle Beziehungen*, and is a member of several editorial boards. His current research interests are management and organization theory, inter-organizational relations and networks, innovation and project management, and industrial relations.

# Managing and Working in Project Society

## Institutional Challenges of Temporary Organizations

ROLF A. LUNDIN
*Jönköping International Business School*

NIKLAS ARVIDSSON
*Royal Institute of Technology in Stockholm*

TIM BRADY
*CENTRIM, University of Brighton*

ESKIL EKSTEDT
*University of Uppsala*

CHRISTOPHE MIDLER
*CRG, École Polytechnique in Paris*

JÖRG SYDOW
*Freie Universität Berlin*

CAMBRIDGE
UNIVERSITY PRESS

# CAMBRIDGE
UNIVERSITY PRESS

University Printing House, Cambridge CB2 8BS, United Kingdom

Cambridge University Press is part of the University of Cambridge.

It furthers the University's mission by disseminating knowledge in the pursuit of education, learning and research at the highest international levels of excellence.

www.cambridge.org
Information on this title: www.cambridge.org/9781107077652

First published 2015

A catalogue record for this publication is available from the British Library

Library of Congress Cataloguing in Publication data
Lundin, Rolf A.
Managing and working in project society : institutional challenges of temporary organizations / Rolf A. Lundin, Niklas Arvidsson, Tim Brady, Eskil Ekstedt, Christophe Midler, Jörg Sydow.
    pages   cm
ISBN 978-1-107-07765-2 (hardback)
1. Project management.   I. Title.
HD69.P75L86   2015
658.4'04–dc23

                                          2014049480

ISBN 978-1-107-07765-2 Hardback

# Contents

# Figures

# Preface: contents in a nutshell

The projectification of business and working life is ongoing and strong. This movement goes beyond traditional project-organized sectors such as construction, consultancy, media, and entertainment. Project thinking is spreading to most parts of society, including industrial enterprises, governmental organizations, educational institutions, and volunteer groups. Not only do people relate to projects and to project organizing in their working lives, but they even speak and think of their daily activities in project terms. When faced with an institutional context shaped and embedded by an earlier, now by-and-large foregone Industrial Society, a shift toward Project Society can lead to frustration, and problems may appear as a result of this imbalance. Our own and others' empirical research and observations suggest this is what is happening. We therefore aim to develop an understanding of the implications for management and work related to the projectification process. We discuss how the process will challenge the institutional framework once molded in the traditional Industrial Society and what this might lead to. By using the term "Project Society," we are pointing out specific changes in the organization of work and business activity as an important part of the overall transition from the Industrial Society without denying the continued importance of producing goods and services, the rapid and widespread diffusion of a revolutionary technology – the Internet, and the spread of knowledge discussed by other scholars. Indeed, the evolution of Project Society has been alluded to in other contexts, but the movement has accelerated and will continue to do so since it is facilitated by modern information and communication technology and knowledge formation through the Internet.

This monograph is about the ascendance of projects and temporary organizations in society. The antecedents and consequences of this trend are its subject, but the particular focus is on the way that business, management, and work are being projectified. Our stance is that despite recent attempts to revive it under the notion of the Fourth Industrial Society or Industry 4.0, Industrial Society with its institutional setting represents a historic era that is diminishing in importance over time. The projectification trend is strong and is dominating business in today's economic realities. This change is occurring at the same time that the institutions of traditional Industrial Society are promoting sustainability and predictability, thereby creating tensions and conflicts that generate ambiguities, paradoxes, and an interesting future. The examples provided predominantly come from industry and industry-related activities since these jointly manifest some of the most important structural changes in our society. But the trend is also present in other parts of society that have an impact on individuals. The theoretical framing for the book is based on the advances made in research on projects and other forms of temporary organizations.

From studies and experience in various contexts, the authors have learned that projectification is widely accepted as a means of handling both old and new problems in the economic realm. This is particularly true in project-based organizations where projects are considered to be "natural." However, project work is invading many fields of management and work. At the same time, prevailing institutions often seem poorly adapted to the projectification process and eventually need to be replaced by other institutions.

The normative message is that there is a need to prepare for the emerging Project Society, and this monograph provides a theoretical apparatus for analyzing projects and projectification in a broad range of contexts. Project managers, managers in large professional organizations, public authorities, leaders of educational institutions, politicians, leaders of trade unions and social movements, and, not least, researchers need to prepare for this shift in the predominant ways of thinking. The development is global!

The scope of the analysis includes all varieties of project work, from the traditional to the emerging, and concludes that projects or temporary organizations more generally have become the preferred organizational form for efficiency and flexibility in industry and elsewhere. The sites of this shift in approach encompass project-based organizations, project management, and project work in traditional organizations as well as in project networks that typically cut across organizational boundaries. This monograph – in contrast to books on project management as a technique – adopts a variety of complementary analytical approaches, ranging from the macro level of projectification in society and institutions to transformations of work and management practices at the meso level; occasionally, it also addresses these issues at the level of individuals, including project managers and project entrepreneurs. Moreover, it takes context and history into account. Even though it is heavily based on data about ongoing changes in industry, services, and the public sector, the tenor of the monograph is conceptual. Its goal is to raise awareness of the trend toward managing by project and working within projects in most areas of society and the implications of this for not only practitioners who are heavily involved in project management and project work but also those undertaking research on temporary organizations in different contexts.

This book presents and interprets the historical evolution of projects and organizational forms supporting projects. Given our main concerns with management, work, and institutions in a project society, our presentation of the evolution has at least face validity and is convincing when we talk with other people as well as in our own discussions. Some elements could be described in more detail, for instance, the role of the arms race, nuclear power, aircraft, and space ventures, so we have made a choice. Our somewhat unorthodox and broad approach to understanding the project society means that other approaches and historical accounts that are more limited in their focus are left aside. But in our minds, this is the strength of our book.

Project Society is not an end point in history even if the label itself might provide a temptation to think of it in that way. We believe that it is merely a characteristic of a special phase of developments. The social nature of society means that it can only be understood as a process that will produce other foci for attention in the future.

# Acknowledgments

The work on this book was initiated by the authors based on our shared interests, expectations, and concerns about the effect of projectification on society. The word itself did not exist in the English language, but as far as we know, it was imported from the French by one of the coauthors of this book, Christophe Midler, who introduced it as a description of what had occurred in his study on how innovation work was reorganized by a French car manufacturer. That study constitutes an example of how a traditional manufacturing firm adapted to the idea of organizing its activities into project form.

From our vantage points, we realized that the development we have chosen to call projectification is in fact very strong. It has important implications not only in isolated cases but also for society at large. The movement toward what we have labeled Project Society has potentially far-reaching consequences. Managing and working in projects is now prescribed by supranational bodies such as the United Nations and the European Union, as well as being understood by many individuals to be a guideline in their own personal activities. Primarily, there seems to be a push toward projectification in business-related activities. Projectification on all these levels does not go uncontested, however, since it is not in line with prevailing institutions. Adaptations are needed and new institutions develop to accommodate it.

As researchers, each with our own take on project-based organizing, we realize that others in academia are studying projects and temporary organizations as empirically and theoretically interesting phenomena. And we already know that professional organizations such as the Project Management Institute (PMI), the International Project Management Association (IPMA), and others are active in this field, not to mention all those in practice who earn their living from working with and in projects. These facts have convinced us of the need to put a book of this type together for researchers, students, and practitioners alike.

The ideas proposed by us were welcomed by Cambridge University Press and in particular by the editor, Paula M. Parish. We thank you, your colleague Claire Wood, and all others so much for your encouragement and assistance. We also want to express our gratitude for the support received from our home universities and external funding bodies such as the National Institute of Working Life in Stockholm, which focused on the ongoing transformation of working life (now discontinued); the Jenz and Carl-Olof Hamrin Foundation; the German Research Foundation (DFG); the UK Research Councils; the Innovation Management Chair at École Polytechnique; and others that have enabled us to carry out the research that has provided the foundation for the ideas in this book. Also, we want to thank numerous colleagues for commenting on the manuscript in constructive ways. Among them in particular are Robert DeFillippi, Mats Engwall, Mark Hughes, Håkan Lindgren, Kurt Lundgren, Håkan Sjöholm, Anders Söderholm, Reinhard Wagner, Torbjörn Wenell, and the anonymous reviewers engaged by Cambridge University Press. Finally, we thank each other. Without the group of the six of us working together, this book would not exist!

# I  Project organizing and industrial organization – transformation dilemmas

## I.I THE TREND TOWARD PROJECTIFICATION

Projectification took a quantitative as well as a qualitative step forward from the mid 1960s, when the dominance of manufacturing began to be challenged by the rapid development of service companies and firms specializing in offering business support to manufacturing firms. The number of people directly engaged in manufacturing, particularly in the developed economies, started to decrease, compensated for by an increase in the number of people employed in supportive project-based business service companies and of self-employed professionals. In addition, much of the work in the manufacturing sector started to be managed in project forms of organization outside the traditional functional product-based industrial company. Beyond these project-based organizations, service activities inside traditional industrial organizations began to use projects in their knowledge-intensive activities, such as R&D. Some years later, in the first half of the 1990s, the focus on clusters and their role in establishing business opportunities (cf. Porter 1990) became a new field for entrepreneurial behavior and project organizing. Governmental authorities, such as the Invest in Sweden Agency (now Business Sweden), which was started toward the end of the previous century, fostered an action-oriented industrial policy facilitated by a diversity of projects. This is also true for the European Union (EU), as a major actor preoccupied with economic development, and for national institutions created to support innovation and regional efforts and to respond to EU demands for special structures.

The traditional way of approaching economic activity becomes obsolete in the emergent Project Society. The traditional organization model with the (e.g. car) factory as an archetype and as a dominating economic entity needs to be replaced. Projectification can also be seen in relation to the way we think and act. Actors going through a process of projectification of their activities may experience a "transformation dilemma" (Ekstedt et al. 1999). What are the characteristics of projects and project organizing and thinking? How does this organizational form differ from that of the traditional industrial organization? And how should institutions be changed to support managing and working in a projectified society? These types of questions are often difficult to respond to inside an organization and even more difficult to transfer to the institutions of the surrounding society. Nevertheless, they are at the heart of the transformation dilemma. Deep-rooted traditions and institutions make coping with a transformation difficult. Establishing a new organizational order and adapting to that new order do not come easily.

Projects can mean different things to different people and in different contexts. At a minimum, they seem, however, to have a specific perception of "time, task, and team" in common (Lundin and Söderholm 1995), while a fourth property of "transition" seems to be either neglected or debated (cf. Bakker 2010; Jacobsson et al. 2013a). Most of all, projects are considered to be temporary systems with an institutionalized termination or a form of temporary organization (Kenis et al. 2009), even if this feature is sometimes questioned (Müller-Seitz and Sydow 2011). For our purposes, we need to be a bit more precise, however, by indicating that a project ex ante specifies foci in terms of action to fulfill a task, time allotted, and assignment of responsibility to see that the task is fulfilled within the time specified and with the resources at hand. Ex post, as is well known, projects often do not meet the goals set in terms of responsibilities, task fulfillment, budget, and time frames (Pinto and Slevin 1998; Pinto 2002; Miller and Hobbs 2005; Priemus 2010; Flyvbjerg 2011), but this does not seem to affect the proliferation of projects.

One of the main reasons we are studying projects – regardless of the context in which a project is situated – is that they are constituted by action. Although it is likely to be the action that is linked to a particular project, the temporary system or organization is also characterized by (temporary) structures. Composed of rules and resources, these structures enable and constrain project actions by which they are, at the same time, either reproduced or transformed (Giddens 1984). Importantly, projects are embedded in an environment of more or less permanent organizations and in an institutional context, providing project managers as well as project workers with additional resources and constraints for action. Given this, we will highlight the importance of the institutional context in which project-based action is situated.

Project management is a performance-oriented practice aiming at the constitution, coordination, and control of activities within a project (Blomquist et al. 2010). Thereby, the roles of managers and subordinates in such temporary systems are different from those of traditional industrial organizations. Project leaders have limited responsibility for long-term resource management (including that related to employees). Their leadership is focused on project results, while the administration and development of personnel are to a great extent left to line managers of permanent organizations or other institutions. The training of project managers mostly takes place on the job even if it is increasingly complemented by formal courses or certificates from professional organizations. Experience in project management has become a critical resource in most organizations today, not only in project-based industries such as construction, consultancy, and media and entertainment but also in other industries and in public organizations.

Work in a project is guided by the task or the goal. In most cases, members of a project understand the meaning or the intent of the project organization, while it is common that members of the permanent organization understand only parts of its activities and goals. It is not unusual for project employees to feel a greater sense of belonging to their profession or the project itself than to the overall organization in which they are employed (Söderlund and Bredin 2005; Braun et al. 2013). The ties to a specific workplace are often rather weak. The rules governing the project members are related to the quality and standard of what the project will accomplish and not so much about the regulation of the activity itself. The connections to supporting work-life institutions may therefore also be weak.

There are naturally vast variations among organizations referred to as "traditional industrial organizations," but some common characteristics make them an organizational family that is quite different from project forms of organization. They are generally characterized by flow-process operations such as assembly line production. They tend to be thought of as permanent organizations – one expects them to last forever. Their long life expectancy makes it possible to make heavy investments in machinery and buildings supporting large batch and mass production activity to achieve high returns to scale. The location of activities is often stationary, mostly in a factory. This has traditionally led to strong permanent organizations surrounded by a few weak and temporary forms; a classic example is the R&D department of a manufacturing firm that typically exhibits a project organization.

Managerial bureaucracies are developed to run these big and complex industrial organizations. A hierarchy of leaders handled decisions on multi-level bases. The decision orientation has a long tradition and is described in theoretical terms by classic studies such as that by Cyert and March (1963). The decision-oriented permanent organizations have strong mechanisms for long-term knowledge formation and activities. Their rhetoric also helps them strengthen their image and organizational brand, which enables them to create projects in and around a focal organization. Strong, supportive societal institutions such as professional associations, business schools, and other educational organizations nurture the managers and leaders of these traditional industrial organizations.

Work in traditional industrial organizations is characterized by specialization and an extensive division of labor. Surrounding institutions, for example, unions, mirror the rough division between blue-collar and white-collar workers. Employment relations are often regulated and linked to the supportive institutions. An intimate interaction between those organizations and the political and legal systems develops along the lines of the divide between Capital and Labor – a most important institutional divide. The rules have necessarily been adapted to activities taking place at specific locations. The workplace is therefore also a focal point for work-life legislation.

In sum, industrial organization is the child of the transformation from an Agrarian Society to an Industrial one, while project organization is the child of the transformation from an Industrial Society to the society of today, no matter whether this is termed an "Information," "Knowledge," "Network," or "Project Society." Our next step then is to take a closer look into the historical context in which the traditional industrial form of organizing was born and formed. We examine why this form of organizing is challenged today, and we also ask whether the role of the traditional industrial organization has changed.

## I.2 THE ERA OF TRADITIONAL INDUSTRIAL ORGANIZATION

What is often referred to as traditional industrial organization started to develop under specific conditions around 150 years ago, while project organization has a much longer history. The traditional industrial organization developed to control new forces of energy such as steam and electricity that came into use, dramatically speeding up economic activities including transport and distribution, production, and consumption. We may ask to what extent those conditions prevail today. We think there has been a fundamental change in the surrounding context, but much of the thinking about organizations and organizing is still dominated by the context developed under the traditional industrial form of organizing. This occurred in part because this model of organization migrated to other parts of society, such as the public sector, even after its use declined in the industrial sector. Numerous versions of the traditional industrial model of organizing have developed, for example, the Anglo-Saxon or the Nordic management models or others based on stakeholder participation (e.g. unions or work councils) such as the Rhineland model or the Southern European model. The Anglo-Saxon model stresses that shareholders' interests are taken care of by top management; the Rhineland model provides institutions for high worker involvement in business policy (Allertz 2009). But all these models belong to the same family, a form of organizing we compare to quite a different one, that is, project organizations.

The formal and informal management models and contracts of work developed incrementally under the influence of institutions created in a specific historical period – that of the Industrial Revolution. The first signs of the revolution are found in eighteenth-century England. During the next century, it diffused to the United States, continental Western Europe, and Japan and reached its peak – measured by the relative share of people directly working in manufacturing – in the 1960s and 1970s. In other parts of the world, especially China, the number of people directly working in manufacturing continued to grow (Cameron and Neal 2003). Breakthroughs in energy technology – first steam power and later electricity – formed the basis of the industrial revolutions and associated developments in other fields such as mechanical engineering, metallurgy, chemistry, biology, medicine, transportation, and a wide variety of other technological areas and led to new forms of production, consumption, and social organization that together formed the Industrial Society (Castells 1996).

Historians have discussed at least three distinct phases in the development of the Industrial Society (Stine 1975; Finkelstein 1986; Magnusson 1999; McCraw 2005). The First Industrial Revolution occurred with the increased use of steam energy in the transport and textile sectors. The Second Industrial Revolution was connected to the spread of electricity, on the one hand to millions of homes, supplying them with electric lights and refrigerators, and on the other by equipping the manufacturing and transport sectors with electric and internal combustion engines. The Third Industrial Revolution came with the breakthrough of modern information technology supporting and controlling areas such as process industries, offices, and leisure time. The latest manifestation of this technology-driven development is the Internet, which is involved in most human activity today. The First Industrial Revolution can be connected to the birth and formation of traditional industrial organizations. This organizational form then matured and spread to most activities and economic branches after the Second Industrial Revolution. This was also a period when industrial thinking and institutions supporting the Industrial Society were developed and diffused to all parts of the economy. This book focuses on how the traditional industrial organization loses its dominance and becomes part of a projectified society during and after the Third Industrial Revolution. The transformation to this society is facilitated by modern information technology (IT) not least when it comes to planning and running complicated projects and other types of temporary organizations.

The technological innovations of the First Industrial Revolution were speeding up the entire societal processing system: "Never before in history had it been necessary to control processes and movements at speeds faster than those of wind, water and animal power – rarely more than a few miles per hour" (Beniger 1986: 218). The use of the new technologies subsequently created crises of control in the systems of production, distribution, and consumption. The steam engine increased the speed of trains to many times that of other forms of transport, but the lack of adequate control systems led to deadly accidents. The general public feared using railroads for personal transportation. As a response to this "safety crisis," private railroad companies in the United States started to build bureaucratic organizations for supervision. Timetables were introduced. The business historian Alfred Chandler suggests that the Western Railroad created "the first modern, carefully defined, internal organizational structure used by an American business enterprise" (Chandler 1977: 97). He also argues that the organizational models used for safety in railroad companies became role models for building efficient organizations when the industrial enterprise grew to be of comparable size and complexity (Chandler 1962).

This organizational model of bureaucratic control diffused to other locations such as railway stations and ports, where timetables and other control systems were established to regulate and supervise transportation activity. Prior to the Industrial Revolution, the organizing of transport and distribution was much more project-like. Each voyage of a sailing ship could be seen as a separate project. It was not unusual for the captain of the ship to be responsible for obtaining appropriate cargo as well as the crew for each trip. At the destination, he had to act as a businessman selling the cargo for profit. The captain was a de facto project manager with responsibility for the performance of the business and for hiring and leading the project members. With the emergence of steamships and timetables, a much more diversified division of labor developed. The captain of a vessel became responsible mainly for the safety of the ship and its cargo and crew at sea.

The second part of the nineteenth century saw the development of numerous innovations to control the processing in the metalworking sector. The Bessemer process increased the speed of steel production. Shop order account systems were developed to control material flows through factories. Carnegie steel plants were explicitly designed to facilitate fast throughputs (Temin 1964). Metcalfe (1885) published a book on cost control in factories. Records on the use of employees' time were introduced. At the end of the century, these processing technologies spread to the production of food (e.g. the cannery industry), soap, cigarettes, matches, and photographic film (Beniger 1986). The industrial organizations adopted hierarchical decision systems not too different from those in the military or the church – the only organizations of a comparable size at that time.

The control crises in the last part of the nineteenth century that resulted from the tremendous increase in speed were most evident in the previously mentioned industries. However, the industrial form of organizing never became dominant in all sectors of the economy. For example, in construction and shipbuilding, the older project form persisted, a way of organizing that has not only survived until today but characterizes Project Society. A project-organized naval shipbuilding industry could be found in many countries long before the Industrial Revolution (Glete 2002). Agriculture, the activity in which most people were occupied up to the first half of the twentieth century (although there are large variations between countries), was mechanized without transforming to an industrial form of organizing. In addition, the industry-like experiment by the Soviet kolkhoz system was far from a success. Arguably, agriculture activity in general resembles neither the traditional industry model, with the possible exception of large-scale livestock breeding, nor the project model. But recurrent activities are project-like in that they are time limited and with specific outcomes, for example, seasonally determined activities that include preparing the soil, sowing, harvesting, and post-harvest festivity. Festivals in wine-growing areas still mark the end of the season; in a similar way, house builders celebrate when the roof of a house is put in place. The celebration or festival is a way of acknowledging that a project or a specific activity has finished and an objective has been accomplished. In project terminology, it represents a milestone.

The traditional industrial organization was designed to respond to the control crises of early industrialization. The ongoing development included a series of organizational innovations starting from that first step of the carefully defined internal organization of the Western Railroad in 1842. From the middle of the century, the railroads employed more accountants and auditors than any governmental agency in the United States. The companies also started to use line managers and staff executives for positions in the organization in many industries. Bureaucracies with operating departments (e.g. in billing, sales analyses, and inventory) controlled by a hierarchy of salaried managers grew in scope and complexity. Business education at the university level was introduced on a grand scale. In the United States, the Eastman Commercial College was founded in 1842. The Wharton Business School was established in 1881

(Beniger 1986). The business schools created in Germany focused initially on trade (and on difficulties in handling trade among all the small German states) and on accounting, but over time they developed into more academically focused institutions (Engwall and Zamagni 1998). The business school idea spread from Germany to Northern Europe. However, their development in the United Kingdom and in France differed. The Grandes Écoles in France originated in the eighteenth century and were designed to educate civil servants. The first business schools in the UK did not appear until the middle of the twentieth century, possibly as a response to the appearance of the weaknesses of industrialization. Nevertheless, the development of business schools as well as technical schools can be seen as having some roots in the Industrial Revolution.

At the turn of the twentieth century, leading members of the bureaucracies of big companies achieved such strong positions of power that the period from then on is often referred to as one of "managerial capitalism" (Chandler 1977). This organizational archetype was designed to offer long series of standardized products (Fordism) and services for mass consumption. The production units, the factories, employed more and more people organized in a hierarchical way, probably inspired by the organizational models of the armed forces and the church. At the peak of the Soviet empire, where the production system lacked appropriate incentives to rationalize, there were workplaces of as many as 100,000 employees (e.g. Nowa Huta in Krakow). In England, the origin of the First Industrial Revolution, with its abundance of cheap labor, the organization of the shop floor of the factories was very much influenced by the old guild system and handicraft with strong professions promoting "learning by doing," which resulted in many workers and managers being resistant to changes in the organizational order. In the United States, with its lack of trained blue-collar workers, investments in machines that replaced workers resulted in automation and productivity increases (Habakkuk 1962). The managerial methods of Frederick W. Taylor (1911) were introduced first to support the rationalization of manual work and later to handle and use the expensive machines in an efficient way. In France, Henri Fayol (1949) developed ideas on how to create an administrative organization that served to support the industrial achievements.

This general form of organizing has been continually refined and hardly challenged, at least not in a fundamental way, until recently. The long dominance of the industrial model has had a major impact on the institutions of the surrounding society. The labor market, the corporate legal system, and the educational system including research institutions are all in one way or another offspring of the models of traditional industrial organization – with significant implications for the transformation dilemma alluded to earlier. Institutions important for the future including trade unions, limited or stock companies, and compulsory/mandatory schools emerged in this period (McCraw 2005).

The preconditions for the dominance of the industrial organization model in Western Europe and the United States no longer apply: employment in the traditional industrial sector has declined dramatically. The control revolution introduced devices and organizational solutions whereby time and speed could be better handled. Machines have largely replaced humans directly involved in process activity. In process industries, such as paper and pulp, most of the non-automated work time consists of monitoring the process on screens (Ekstedt 1988; Zuboff 1988). The number of people directly working within the production process has declined dramatically, while the number of people working in marketing, sales, R&D, education, and other overhead functions has increased. This work is organized differently than in the traditional industrial organization; it occurs mostly as projects and other forms of temporary organization. A continuation if not acceleration of this trend is to be expected even if Project Society is termed Industry 4.0.

But changed conditions are not solely affecting the production side. During the heyday of the traditional industrial model, the aim was to produce for the "masses" – the growing middle class in the

United States, Western Europe, and Japan – and also seen more recently in newly developed countries such as China and India. The organizational innovations necessary for production took place concurrently with innovations in mass consumption and communication. This resulted in tremendous improvements in the standard of living for many people. A comparison of 1989 real GDP per capita to that from 1820 shows that after three industrial revolutions, real GDP per capita is 10 times greater in the UK, 15 times in Germany, 18 times in the United States, and 25 times in Japan (McCraw 2005: 10). However, one has to be aware that the spread of wealth and income has varied over time (Piketty 2014). The distribution reflects a u-curve, starting with huge variations between incomes, followed by period of decreasing differences and finally transforming to a period of increased spread again (Piketty 2014).

The technological development that once made mass production possible has now diversified enough to meet the demands of single individuals. Modern technology allows individuals, more often than not those who are self-employed, to get stronger positions in the market. The mass market has been transformed into a market of individuals. Dialogues between sellers and buyers, producers and consumers may lead to unique solutions and start new projects that involve both parties. In that way, technological development and new networks create new possibilities. Some also argue that a company could be seen as a system for the creation of knowledge and value for the customer (Barney 1991; Nonaka 1991; Kogut and Zander 1992; Wikström et al. 1992; Normann 2001); these efforts are generally organized as projects.

The shift from the Agrarian Society to the Industrial and from the Industrial to Project Society can be illustrated by using Torsten Hägerstrand's (1974) model of time geography. He states that all action takes place in both time and space dimensions. The individual is introduced into the "time-room" at the point of birth and leaves it at the point of death (Asplund 1985; Hägerstrand 1991). The time-room consists of different stations. In the Agrarian Society, most people both lived and worked at the same location, the farm. Work, training, education, and leisure time (to the extent that concept was known) were intertwined. Women participated in both reproduction and production: besides taking care of the household, they worked with production processes related to the output of the animals and the fields.

The shift to the Industrial Society has other time/space dimensions that separate and define activities much more precisely than in the Agrarian Society. The place and time for living and for working are separated for the industrial workforce. Work in the industrial organization occurs during a specific time at a specific place. Unions arose to deal with the length of time the employee should be present at the workplace. The division of labor became far-reaching; the time spent on different stations of the production process was successively measured in more and more detail in line with the well-known ideas of Frederick Taylor. A multi-level hierarchy and an institutional framework related to the industrial organization started to develop (Johansson 1977; Isidorsson 2001; Rosengren 2009).

However, not everyone was involved in the transformation to the industrial economy. Most women were still at home as in the Agrarian Society (Göransson 1988). But this has changed dramatically during the past decades. When many women entered separate organizations to teach and to care for children and the sick and the elderly, they also became part of an industrial model with an extensive division of labor. The similarities between the public service sectors and the private industrial sector have become even more apparent by the breakthrough of ideas denoted as New Public Management (Forsell and Jansson 2000; McLaughlin et al. 2002; Schedler and Proeller 2011).

More recent and future developments can also be analyzed in line with Hägerstrand's ideas. What will the time-room dimensions look like in the information-dense, knowledge-intensive, and networked Project Society? The absolute separation between work and home as experienced by employees in the traditional Industrial Society will probably disappear. Some work will take place at home as in the Agrarian Society, some in fixed workplaces as in the Industrial Society, but many new locales are likely to appear. Facilitated by mobile technologies such as smart phones and the Internet, project work is increasingly carried out at train stations and airports, on trains and aircrafts, or at conferences and in hotel rooms. Moreover, the "lifelong learning" of the old apprenticeship system may reappear in new forms, wherein unlearning and relearning are predominant. Learning, working, and leisure may be more and more intertwined. The time-room will be extended by new dimensions. It will be possible to be in one place and still participate in working processes in other places. The new technology enables people to engage in instant as well as distant project participation. The sharp borders between work, education, and leisure as characteristic of the Industrial Society are likely to disappear (Allvin et al. 2006).

One may argue that what we refer to as the traditional industrial organization is a form of organizing developed under specific circumstances in a unique historical setting. Before industrialization, the use of project-like or temporary organizations and organizing was common with fairly unique ventures and craft-based work quite different from the mass production of the Industrial Society but with similarities to modern project work of the twentieth and twenty-first centuries. In this book, we assume that Project Society, at least for the time to come, will, if not replace, at least complement the industrial organization, with regard to not only management but also work itself.

The transition from one period to another never happens in one single step, as thick sediments of what existed before might last for long periods. An example is the agriculture sector, in which only a small percentage of the labor force in Western Europe works today, but more than a third of the budget of European Union goes to this sector. However, its production is much larger than in the days when around 70 percent of all work took place there.

## I.3 TRANSFORMATION DILEMMAS — THE PURPOSE OF THE BOOK

This book is about transformation dilemmas not only for management and work but also for related institutions when we move from the Industrial Society and enter Project Society. The boundaries and the location of activities and organizations are changing when organizational solutions of a profoundly temporary nature are becoming increasingly common. New organizations with temporary forms and practices are becoming predominant, while many old organizations are transforming into new temporary forms. In addition, temporary arrangements between organizations to accomplish concrete as well as visionary goals are increasing. Old models of management and work organization are becoming obsolete in this new environment. The projectification process challenges institutions formed under the influence of the traditional industrial organization, but institutions do not change easily (Hodgson 1993; Sjöstrand 1993; North 2005; Scott 2008). So it might be appropriate to talk about "transitory institutions." Organizations and institutions related to management and work will undergo a profound transformation process as this transition to Project Society unfolds.

We argue that the driving force behind the projectification process is the development of a more diversified but unique and individual demand from consumers and companies, supplemented by technological and managerial know-how. The sophistication of demand and the differentiation and integration of supply are facilitated by the diffusion of modern information and communication technology, in particular by the Internet, and the opportunities that technical developments provide. But not all parts of the economy will transform. Activities with high returns to scale, such as component production and some rudimentary services, will keep to the industrial form. Industrial forms will always exist. Project Society represents the present direction of developments and (at least temporarily) a dominant form of organizing, not an end point!

The purpose of this book is to take a closer look at management and work in the projectification process and how the institutions of the surrounding society cope with the changed conditions. We discuss the characteristics of managing projects in different organizational and institutional environments and how management interacts with remaining permanent organizations. We also discuss the implications of projectification for work content and conditions. How does the project form change factors such as influence and responsibility for different actors? The way the projectification process challenges today's institutional framework for business and work is another important issue. How do project capabilities develop individually and in organizations or inter-organizational networks in comparison with strategic and functional capabilities in the traditional industrial organization?

What will happen to institutions formed by the Industrial Society when project activity becomes more and more influential? For example, what will happen to strong institutions linked to the workplace? In the industrial organization system, the employer has the right to organize the activity and the employee has certain rights concerning workplace conditions. Payment is often related to the time spent at the workplace. Much of the social partners' (e.g. the unions') engagement relates to this and to other conditions at the workplace (Ekstedt 2002). Will the workplace be replaced as a point of reference by the logic of project organization, a form of organization for which the work product is much more of a focus than the work process itself?

The workplace is only one of the institutional settings of the Industrial Society that will be impacted by projects and project thinking. What will happen to roles and rules of management and work in general when we enter successive stages of Project Society? Will today's corporate and labor laws be applicable? Will the content and organization of education be transformed? These kinds of questions are addressed in the rest of the book.

Chapter 2 discusses projectification trends and processes in more detail, using case studies and other empirical data from different countries. The chapter also scrutinizes how changes in organizing structures and processes influence the routes of projectification. We suggest that many "projectification machines" are at work today, with effects in different settings. By identifying three archetypal settings in which projects are used, and looking closely at these archetypes, the process of projectification becomes more evident. The first group consists of independent, permanent organizations in which most activities are run as projects providing income for the organization; the second includes permanent organizations implementing projects for specific development tasks and not directly for providing income; and the third involves projects in a network or interorganizational context. We refer to these three archetypes as project-based organizations (PBOs), project-supported organizations (PSOs), and project networks (PNWs) respectively.

Chapter 3 explains how project management differs from traditional management in these distinct contexts. Our discussion focuses on what the alternative archetypes look like and what implications they have for management and leadership given that projectification creates a new instrument for the manager/leader to use to control operations and employees. The dynamics of a manager's task change when the creation and termination of projects are added to the span of managerial work. In such cases, management itself tends to become a temporary rather than a permanent activity, depending on what the projects look like and how the project portfolio is set up. This creates new challenges for leadership as well as for the organizational context.

Chapter 4 characterizes work and employment regimes using theoretical notions of time and space. The forms they have adopted in each of the three project-oriented organizational settings relative to work in traditional organizational settings are compared. Project deadlines, budgetary constraints, and focus on individual or team performance in relation to customer service tend to create heavy workloads in project work. At the same time, there is often strong personal involvement and engagement among employees during project work, which tends to increase motivation and coping capacity. Some people will excel and prosper in a projectified economy; others may not. The question is how to be prepared for the new work situation. We discuss how these circumstances may impact people but also how this differs between the three archetypes. We also allude to how time pressures, changes in teammates, difficulties in recruiting a particular person for a project, changes of locality, and more direct responsibility for results affect the work situation of project members. In brief, we describe how the character of work is changing with Project Society.

Chapter 5 focuses on the effects of projectification on institutions and vice versa. Institutions are adapting to the new circumstances, but adaptation does not come easily; old institutions are challenged while Project Society gives rise to new ones. We see friction and tensions when projectification meets old institutions formed in the past, consisting of formal as well as informal rules and roles, tasked with stabilizing societal development. Even if institutions promote change, it happens extremely slowly, implying that institutions may act as a brake on the rise of a Project Society. This chapter discusses possible ways to develop and change the institutional framework governing Project Society. What happens when projects meet old institutions and how will institutions related to education, work life, employer issues, employment regulations, market regulations, and established processes for political decision making change? Will the pace and scope of projectification as well as the possibilities of friction differ in different cultures?

Chapter 6 discusses overall trends and relates them to present debates and theories of organizing in a Project Society. The chapter explains how the trend toward a Project Society has significant implications for theorizing organizations and inter-organizational networks in general and the management of and working in temporary organizations in particular. Above all and most obviously, the temporal dimension of management and work has to be taken much more seriously. While consideration of time and temporariness is decisive, the embeddedness of temporary organizations into more permanent structures has to be considered in these theoretical debates as well. The fundamental implication for theorizing projects and temporary organizations is a plea for process or practice theories that not only take past, present, and future into account but also are as sensitive to incremental and disruptive change as they are to stability and even hyper-stability of institutional project contexts. The implications of such theorizing for researching project-based organizing empirically are discussed.

# 2 Projectification trends and organizational archetypes

We can never know what to expect in the future. Nevertheless, the future is to a certain extent already here as the most important tendencies in the economy change incrementally and have a long-term impact on the society. Societal features that have been developed in the Industrial Society continue to impact Project Society, and some of the newer features in today's economy will most likely grow and become dominant tomorrow. This chapter describes the contexts in which three archetypes – project-based organizations (PBOs), project-supported organizations (PSOs), and project networks (PNWs) – and their different forms of governance (cf. Ahola et al. 2014) appear and how they contribute to projectification.

Although projects were likely used for major construction and civil engineering endeavors such as the Pyramids, the Great Wall of China, ancient Roman and Greek amphitheaters, European cathedrals, and the Suez Canal, it is only since the 1930s that they have emerged as a significant form of industrial organization. In the 1940s and 1950s, the most notable projects involved weapons system development such as the Manhattan Project (to develop the atomic bomb) and the Atlas and Polaris projects (to develop ballistic missiles). Project forms of organization were also used extensively in construction and civil engineering. The main argument in this book is that projectification took a quantitative as well as a qualitative step forward beginning in the mid 1960s, when, from this base in construction, civil engineering, defense, and aerospace, project forms of organizing and production spread to other sectors including power; petrochemicals; pharmaceuticals; oil and gas; computers and information systems; telecommunications; and creative industries such as advertising, film and television, research, and consultancy.

A survey by Whittington et al. (1999) of 3,500 European firms showed that use of project-based structures increased from 13 percent in 1992 to 42 percent in 1996. In a cross-sectoral survey of 200 firms from 30 countries, PricewaterhouseCoopers (PWC) found that these firms were running a total of 10,640 projects a year worth in excess of $4.5 billion (PWC 2004). Firms representing more than a quarter of this sample were running more than 100 projects each year. Moreover, the survey revealed great diversity in the use of projects as an organizational form, both in revenue-earning work and in organizational change: 73 percent of the firms had projects to implement IT change initiatives; 57 percent had performance improvement projects; 49 percent were conducting software development projects; 45 percent had projects for new product development, 43 percent for strategy deployment, 31 percent for construction, and 15 percent for research. Each of these types of project relates to some form of innovation – technological, business, or organizational. The PWC report states, "nowadays it is hard to imagine an organization that is not engaged in some kind of project activity. Over the past decade, organizations have been turning from operations to project management as part of their competitive advantage strategy" (PWC 2004: 4). The World Bank has estimated that approximately 21 percent of the world's GDP involves gross capital formation, most of which is accomplished through projects (World Bank 2009; Bredillet 2010). At around the same time, Deutsche Bank Research (2007) came up with a smaller figure for the German economy (2 percent) but forecast an increase to 15 percent by 2020. However, these more conservative estimates are based on a narrow definition of a project-based economy. A study based on a more comprehensive understanding, initiated and sponsored by the Deutsche Gesellschaft für Projektmanagement (GPM), is under way.

Research since 2000 has also suggested that projects are becoming more complex, larger, and more expensive and also increasingly widespread (Miller and Lessard 2000; Flyvbjerg et al. 2003b; Miller and

Hobbs 2005; Priemus 2010). Projects in one form or another represent a major proportion of international trade and business activities. Indeed, there has been a proliferation in not only the number and size of projects but also the range of project types. These include single- and multifirm projects and programs and national and international projects involving consortia such as systems integrators, customers, subsystem and component suppliers, software houses, and consultants – working together in temporary coalitions or networks of organizations that include strategic partnerships and alliances. Projects are used extensively for a whole range of tasks including achievement of organizational change, development of new products and services, process improvement, and implementation of IT and production technologies. Project management and project modes of organizing are increasingly used to deal with more complex business opportunities and problems, rapid technological obsolescence, shortening product life cycles, and cross-functional product development (Davies and Hobday 2005).

Several systematic ways to describe these developments have been proposed. Keegan and Turner (2002), for example, suggest two main types of organizations for which projects are important. Type 1 is those whose work consists primarily of projects and which sell their products and services on a project basis (see also Cohendet and Simon 2007; Cova et al. 2002; Hobday 2000; Archibald 2004). This includes firms in construction and civil engineering; defense and aerospace; engineering; power; petrochemicals; drug development; oil and gas; shipbuilding; information technology systems; telecommunications; and creative industries such as advertising, film and TV, and research and consultancy. The projects of type 2 firms are mainly operationally oriented, but projects are an important part of their overall activities.

Many authors refer to project-based firms or project-based organizations more broadly, but there are subtle differences in their definitions. Lindkvist (2004) suggests that a project-based firm is an organization that conducts most of its work in projects and/or has an emphasis on the project dimension rather than on the functional dimension of its organizational structure and processes. Gann and Salter (2000), by contrast, talk about project-based firms in the construction sector. Their main characteristics are that their design and production processes are organized around projects; they usually produce one-off or at least highly customized products and services, and they operate in diffuse coalitions of companies along the supplier–customer chain. These characteristics are similar to those possessed by firms producing complex products and systems (CoPS) such as aircraft, ships, or high-speed trains (Hobday 1998). CoPS suppliers use projects not just for managing all of their routine day-to-day business activities with customers but also for responding to new strategic opportunities such as supplying novel generations of technology, opening new markets, and achieving far-reaching organizational transformations. Hobday (2000) makes a distinction between "project-based organizations" and "project-led organizations." In project-based organizations, the knowledge, capabilities, and resources of the firm are built up through the execution of projects, and most of their internal and external productive activities are organized in projects. Project-led organizations consist of firms across all industries whose primary productive activity may be volume based or operations oriented that also carry out projects as an important part of their activity. Examples of project-based firms or organizations include construction and civil engineering; defense and aerospace; engineering; power; petrochemicals; pharmaceuticals; oil and gas; shipbuilding; information technology systems; telecommunications; creative industries including advertising, film, and TV; research services; consultancy services; and telecom services. Project-led organizations include all other organizations that provide goods and services such as consumer goods manufacturers, banking, financial services, government departments, universities, and hospitals, whose primary activity does not involve the sale and delivery of products but that undertake projects as an important part of their business activities. By including Hobday's (2000) project-led organizations in addition to those firms included in Lindkvist's (2004) definition, Artto and Wikstrom (2005) were able to extend the type of project activity to include both external production or customer delivery projects and internal development or capital investment projects.

Whitley (2006) has an elaborated, detailed, and subtle definition of project-based firms (PBFs), including a variation based on industrial sectors, regions, and countries. Whitley categorizes PBFs along two dimensions – separation and stability of work roles and singularity of goals and outputs. This leads to four types of PBFs, which he calls organizational, craft, precarious, and hollow. Organizational PBFs are characterized by low separation and low singularity; they produce multiple and varied outputs with different and changeable skills and roles; examples include strategic consultancies, innovative business service providers, and enterprise software suppliers. Craft PBFs exhibit high separation and low singularity; they produce multiple incrementally related outputs with distinct and stable roles and skills; examples provided by Whitley (2006) include London advertising firms, Danish furniture and machinery firms, and some IT consulting firms. Precarious PBFs exhibit low separation and high singularity; they produce risky and unusual outputs with changeable roles and skills; examples include some biotech firms, and Internet software firms such as Vermeer technology and many Silicon Valley firms. Hollow PBFs, the final category, exhibit high separation and high singularity; they produce single outputs and coordinate tasks through standardized, separate, and stable roles and skills; examples include firms involved in producing complex construction projects and feature films.

Our analysis has led us to illustrate the more extensive use of projects by examining more closely three organizational contexts of the economy in which projects are formed and increasingly used: (1) the expansion of project-based organizations or PBOs, that is, organizations delivering projects as their business (similar to Whitley's 2006 organizational and craft project-based firms),

(2) project-supported organizations or PSOs, that is, organizations increasingly making use of projects in the traditional, internal parts of their organization (similar to Hobday's 2000 project-led organizations), and (3) the extended use of project networks or PNWs, that is, the proliferation of interorganizational including interpersonal projects in various contexts. This chapter analyzes projectification in relation to these three archetypical forms.

Even if these archetypes share some basic properties, we argue that each is fundamentally different from the others in that each is dominated by its own distinct set of characteristics. In some sense, though, there is no absolute border between the three. PNWs, for instance, may include PBOs, PSOs, sometimes even individual actors and other temporary organizations. But if we take these three important archetypes of project-based organizing together with data on their diffusion in advanced economies, it is reasonable to argue that we are in the wake of a Project Society. Project-based organizing has already had a great impact on important parts of society, including work, management, and institutions and will no doubt continue to do so in the future. These archetypes provide particular social contexts with distinct implications for managing and working; nevertheless, individual projects within the archetypical groups might have similar characteristics. The stance taken vis-à-vis the three archetypes indirectly implies that we subscribe to the ideas of Wittgenstein on family resemblance ("Familienähnlichkeit") adapted to the project area by Jacobsson and coauthors (2013b) by introducing the archetypes rather than focus on definitions of projects per se and thereby use an alternative to traditional typology or taxonomy categorizations.

## The PBO context

Project-based organizations encompass many categories ranging from prime contractors with strong capabilities in project management and systems integration to small, specialized subcontractors that supply subsystems or components, software, or services (Davies and Hobday 2005). These organizations are found in a wide range of industries including consulting and other professional services (accounting, advertising, architecture, design, law, consulting, public relations), but also in cultural industries (fashion, filmmaking, video games, publishing), high technology (software, computer hardware, multimedia, e-commerce), and complex systems (construction, transportation, telecommunication, infrastructure). PBOs may play different roles in different projects – for example, a firm may be the prime contractor in one project and a subcontractor in another (Davies and Hobday 2005). Traditional PBOs such as those in the construction sector are still there, but the use of projects has diffused into areas including media, consulting, and IT-related activities where companies often are set up as PBOs. A new division of labor in the manufacturing sector also promotes the use of projects (Ekstedt and Sundin 2006). The long-run decrease of the relative number of people working in the manufacturing industry and the trend toward outsourcing have to a large extent been compensated for by an increase of the so-called business services, that is, companies supporting manufacturing activity by providing services on a contract basis.

The decrease in manufacturing employment started from the mid 1960s in the United States and Sweden, and then somewhat later in other parts of Western Europe. In Sweden, the decrease was totally compensated for by an increase of business service companies. In other words, a lot of the work in the manufacturing sector started to take place in PBOs outside the traditional industrial company. Many of these companies are service oriented and characterized as knowledge intensive. The extensive use of projects is often a response to highly differentiated and customized demand. Negotiations, dialogue, and interaction between customers and producers are becoming more and more common as the way of doing business (Hobday 1998).

In the context of PBOs, all activities are in some sense related to projects. The overhead functions of the organization are there to start, support, monitor, and finish projects, that is, to assist over the entire lifetime of the projects. Take, for instance, the employment and development of human resources, a traditional overhead function for most organizations. Running projects is the reason that PBOs exist and also the way for them to generate revenue and profits. There are explicit as well as tacit models of how to run projects. Most project members are well aware of how projects work and of their own role in the project, and, as the PBO is mainly made up of projects, this is true for almost all organizational members. The similarity between projects in PBOs leads to a certain degree of repetitiveness of regular project operations (Lundin and Söderholm 1995). One way to express this is the *renewal paradox* influencing how projects are handled: each time a new bread-and-butter project is started in a PBO context, there should be ample opportunities to reconsider the way projects are carried through and renew processes, but often repetition of behavioral patterns from the past dominates (Ekstedt et al. 1999: 7–8), sometimes even giving rise to hyper-stability or even lock-ins (see Chapter 3).

## The PSO context

The second context in which we notice an increase in the use of projects is inside traditional organizations. This tendency, the growth within project-supported organizations or PSOs, is related to the unprecedented spread of innovation-based competition. As global competition is now the rule in most industries, product life cycles are dramatically reduced as a result of aggressive strategies from competitors and systematic exploration of technology to increase product performances. Maintaining a permanent flow of new and differentiating products and services is needed to keep growth of mature markets on one side and to maintain competitiveness in relation to low-cost countries on the other. Impressive and costly development of design activities (such as R&D, marketing, and engineering design) is the tangible result of such a trend.

In those PSOs that can be categorized as producers of CoPS (Hobday 1998), the innovation process can be partitioned into three consecutive phases of project activity: (1) upstream research and development of technology, (2) new product development, and (3) downstream implementation. The international information and communication company Ericsson corporation, for example, typically delivers three types of projects that relate to this phased innovation process. R&D projects are carried out to develop each new generation of mobile communications technology, based on various technical and operational standards such as Global System for Mobile (GDM) and Code Division Multiple Access (CDMA). In turn, these technologies are taken and adapted for different market applications in product development projects in which Ericsson works with lead customers in what is called a First Office Application (FOA) development. Finally, it carries out numerous implementation projects for its customers, the mobile operating companies, in which it designs and installs mature product lines based on existing mobile network technology. One example of this sequencing of different projects is the development of a base station product for 2G networks based on the GSM standard (which Ericsson had been closely involved in developing with other companies in R&D projects). The three-year FOA project started in 1996 and involved working with Telia and Vodafone. Subsequently, the new generation base stations were offered as part of Ericsson's mature product line and used in the rollout of hundreds of implementation projects for a variety of mobile operators.

As in the first context (PBO), the projectification inside organizations is also promoted by an increase of service content in what many companies produce. Customers are becoming increasingly involved in creating products containing services. A lot of the business-to-business activity is also project organized. More often than not, new products as well are new services, not least because the increased involvement of single customers or entire communities requires novel processes, that is, process innovations regarding managing and/or working in PSOs. Ivory and Vaughan (2008) argue that such "transitional projects" offer a particular potential to depart from existing knowledge and capability paths, allowing for a reframing and reorientation of present activities (see also Ordanini et al. 2008). Again, Ericsson provides an example of this process. In 1995, Ericsson began an expansion into new markets for existing customers by offering a new type of turnkey project to meet customer demands for major outsourcing contracts (Davies 1997). Ericsson was asked by One2One (the UK mobile operator now owned by T-Mobile) to carry out a project to perform all the activities associated with designing and expanding its network across the UK; that is, it was expected to deliver a raft of services as well as mobile telecoms products. This "vanguard project" (Brady and Davies 2004) required new kinds of activity that Ericsson had not undertaken before, and it faced many problems in delivering the project. The market for this new type of project grew fast across Ericsson's various regional businesses and product divisions, and it had to develop new capabilities by learning from project-to-project and exploiting economies of repetition (Davies and Brady 2000) and recombination (Grabher 2005) as it moved from the first-of-a-kind turnkey project to the execution of a large volume of repetitive turnkey and other service-intensive projects (Brady and Davies 2004). Projectification has been the organizational approach to increase the innovation capabilities of the traditional organizations since the 1980s (Midler 1995).

Projectification of R&D activities varies among industries, cultures, and countries, but since R&D activities have expanded so strongly over the years, as demonstrated in Figure 2.1, overall projectification has increased. The sheer numbers point to a strong increase in projectification within companies. Most R&D activities are organized as projects even though the traditional habit of organizing such activities in the line prevails.

Figure 2.1 shows the constant growth of R&D expenditures in selected countries resulting from the growing importance of innovation-based competition in developed countries as well as high-speed development in emerging countries such as China. These statistics are underpinning the importance of projects as well as the efficiency and effectiveness of project management.

Last but not least, the transformation of traditional manufacturing companies is also linked to an expanding international division of

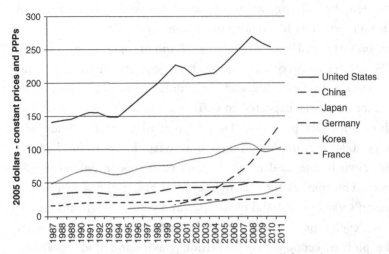

FIGURE 2.1. Evolution of R&D expenses from all firms. (Source: OECD Analytical Business Enterprise Research and Development Database in $ Constant Purchasing Constant Parity.)

labor, often referred to as globalization. Labor-intensive work is outsourced or offshored to companies with production units in low-cost areas of the world at the same time as service- and knowledge-dense activities, such as R&D, are still organized by the original company. Ericsson's reorganization at the beginning of this century illustrates this transformation. Developing from an integrated firm to an organizer of a global production network (and in this regard following Nike's model), the number of personnel in Ericsson as a classical PSO was reduced by around 50 percent. In the remaining parts, where development and marketing have an important role, the use of project organization became dominant. The manufacturing activity that was outsourced to international production companies including Flextronic, Solectron, and Emerson was characterized by a traditional industrial form of organizing. This was a new twist whereby outsourcing and offshoring were not only motivated by low labor cost but also by availability of talent (Lewin et al. 2009) and the increasing capabilities of providers of manufacturing services to develop new or at least to improve existing products (Ernst and Kim 2002).

In PSOs, the percentage of value created through projects is obviously lower and the relationship of economic activities to projects somewhat looser than in PBOs, but it is increasing in strength. Projects are more and more frequently used as a tool to accomplish internal as well as external goals, in particular in relation to innovation. Revenues and profits are only indirectly or partially a reflection of project activity. There is an ambiguity in this setting about the role of the projects and their relation to more permanent activities within a company. Project members are often unclear about their own role when it comes to the relation between the project and the permanent activity. A conflict of loyalty may occur. The increased use of projects in traditional organizations may therefore turn into a transformation dilemma (Ekstedt et al. 1999: 6–9) when the activities organized as projects meet with the traditional organizations. The transformation dilemma occurs when there is a misfit between the projects as a form of organizing and the traditional organizational setting. Renewal activities via projects or by other means are likely to be met with resistance.

## The PNW context

A third context in which the use of projects expands is in inter-organizational projects or project networks. Our point of departure here is that the traditional organization, illustrated by the stereotype of an industrial company, is challenged from the *inside* – from the increasing number of activities carried out in temporary organizations, that is, in projects. But one may also argue that the traditional organization is challenged from the *outside* – the company, the big one as well as the small one (even as small as one individual only), can be seen as part of a larger sphere (e.g. an ecology or system, a regional cluster, a knowledge block, or an interorganizational network or field). This sphere, which has to be delineated empirically, may consist of other companies; local, national, and international authorities; educational and research organizations; and so on. We argue, however, that these two main perspectives are related. Many projects are interorganizational and actually take place within a system or organizational field (see next section) characterized by more or less developed social relations and possibly also a common identity (Kenis and Knoke 2002). Our area of interest is to find out what the relations between the projects of this type of context and the system look like.

One possible, and very important, arrangement of relationships is captured by the notion of a project network that emphasizes the networked character of projects in the field (Bröchner et al. 1991; Jones 1996; Sydow and Windeler 1999; Windeler and Sydow 2001). The notion of project networks is used in many ways. For instance, Hellgren and Stjernberg (1995) were among the first in the international discourse using this notion to highlight the fact that several organizations are involved in carrying out a particular project. While this is a legitimate use of the term, we follow Sydow and Windeler (1999), who emphasize the particular coordinative capacity of this organizational form. This capacity results from the fact that organizations not only work together in carrying out a particular project but also have done so before. This past experience, together with the expectation that the collaboration will be repeated in the future, makes the coordination across projects in the network much easier (see also Windeler and Sydow 2001; Manning 2005).

Such project networks are more often than not embedded in wider regional or global networks of relations characterizing the field. The international division of labor is often performed in a way that certain areas, so-called industrial districts or regional clusters, are favored, while others are abandoned (Ekstedt and Sundin 2006). Resourceful areas of human capital are likely to be a suitable environment for creating projects. The best known is the phenomenon of Silicon Valley, where the open-mindedness of some people at Stanford University contributed to a creative environment (Saxenian 1994). Clusters like that can be seen as potential arenas for forming projects or project networks since interaction between actors with similar or complimentary specialties is facilitated (Tracey et al. 2014).

It is also common that public authorities such as local governments, universities, or EU agencies take an active part in forming inter-organizational projects in a wide range of areas, from huge construction endeavors to cultural events. In addition, the same institutions increasingly engage in developing clusters (Ketels et al. 2006). The joint activity of business companies, authorities, and universities is sometimes referred to as Triple Helix (Leydesdorff and Etzkowitz 1998). These activities are often carried out in projects (see also Chapter 5). Hence, it comes as no surprise that the project network organizational form is likely to continue to spread.

One such example can be found in the city of Brighton and Hove in the southeast of the UK. The cluster is made up of digital and IT companies that are considered "creative" as they are assumed to or actually come up with something novel and useful (Amabile et al. 1996). This is an important and growing area of interest in the UK – recent research by Nesta (an independent charity that works to increase the innovation capacity of the UK) showed that the sector employed some 1.35 million people in 2011 and contributed £69.9 billion to the UK economy (Bakshi et al. 2013). The creative economy (which includes people working in creative occupations in sectors outside the creative industries) accounts for almost 10 percent of UK employment – more than construction, advanced manufacturing, or financial services – and the sector grew four times faster than the overall UK economy between 2004 and 2010 (Sapsed et al. 2013). Research on this specific cluster estimated that around 1,500 firms were active in the creative and digital industries in the Brighton and Hove area. A survey (Sapsed et al. 2013) of these firms resulted in a final dataset of 501 responses. The firms in the survey employed 3,162 people in 2011 and generated sales of £231 million. The average firm employed 7 people, the median firm 2 people, and less than 1 percent had more than 100 employees. Around a third of the firms were working owners/sole traders (i.e. they employed no other people). Half the firms started operating in the past 10 years and a quarter in the past 5 years, so this is a relatively new and emerging cluster. The firms include service providers such as digital marketing and creative digital agencies that offer combinations of services such as search engine optimization, paid search advice, web design, digital marketing strategies, and increasingly social media; web portal firms that host sites and technology platforms; content companies that produce digital material to be viewed or interacted with on mobile devices, video game consoles, the web, or interactive TV; arts organizations that produce artistic works often subsidized by grants, sponsorship, and donations and bring these works to exhibitions, performances, and festivals. An interesting feature of two-thirds of the firms in this cluster is that they combine creative design and advanced technology in their work – a concept the researchers refer to as "fusion." The survey found that some sectors are more fused than others – for example, 94 percent of digital agencies, 80 percent of architecture and interior design firms, 78 percent of design services, and 67 percent of marketing services are fused (Sapsed et al. 2013). Fused firms in the cluster carry out coding related to technology as well as content production, rely on external collaborators for technology and creative inputs, and are reliant on both these areas of expertise to succeed in their markets. Firms in this sector benefit from having a critical mass of skilled local suppliers and freelance contractors who can add specific skills to projects that the firms cannot economically justify having in house – almost 80 percent of the firms in the sample worked with freelancers between 2010 and 2011. Hence, an important strength of the local cluster relates to its ability to update and improve a widely distributed body of knowledge. This in turn benefits from the diversity and depth of the local sector, which allows knowledge and experience to be reused across projects. The firms in this cluster can, despite the positive development of the cluster, be considered "precarious" project-based firms according to Whitley's (2006) classification.

As mentioned earlier, PNWs may overlap with the other two archetypes. PBOs and traditional organizations with project orientations (PSOs) may be parts of clusters as well as networks, that is, those clusters or networks in which project-based organizing dominates. More importantly, when the project is finished, the system may go back into a less active state, sometimes even to a state similar to hibernating characterized by at least partially latent relationships. The actors in the project return to the organizations in which they are employed or for the many self-employed involved in PNWs (e.g. in the creative industries) enter either a new project or bridge idle time by some training program. The network or the cluster can therefore be seen as an arena where the formation (and deformation) of a project may take place. The strength of the ties in a network, including the degree of multiplex relationships, may vary considerably. These range from a common brand or locality name for marketing to long-lasting research teams constituted across organizations. PNWs sometimes activate firms, researchers, and public actors within and across clusters and are therefore critical for action.

In line with the previous discussion of overlaps, there is no such thing as a context-free form of either the archetypes or of projects per se. Each of these archetypes, even allegedly stand-alone projects, is in fact embedded in various field and time contexts, that is, industries and/or regions with their unique properties and practices and how they develop over time (cf. Engwall 2003; Manning 2005). Given that, organizations as well as networks are always on the move within the fields. The various archetypes are parts of and interact with contextual fields, which means that they move and develop as a result of unforeseen events as well as intended action. The result is that it is difficult to control development and forecast implications from development and projectification. The outcomes become manifested in an increasing relevance of the three archetypes of temporary organizations, reflected not only in the physical world but also in our way of thinking and talking (Packendorff and Lindgren 2014). The traditional way of looking at economic activity becomes increasingly obsolete when the shift toward Project Society takes place. The main reasons why project thinking and project talk have developed so quickly and spread so widely into different business and life ventures have been described by Ekstedt et al. (1999). One reason is probably that PBOs as well as PNWs have been efficient and effective when it comes to delivering results. The physical evidence, be it a building or a TV program, is there to prove that the project way of organizing works. On the other hand, projects may also be less successful, as is amply demonstrated by the new Willy Brandt Airport on the outskirts of Berlin that should have been opened years ago. Also, another indicator of the acceptance of project thinking, for better or for worse, is that the vocabulary of projects has been absorbed into everyday language, not just management contexts, to a previously unheard-of extent. While there are instances where the word "project" is used in a demeaning way, most of the time, for the majority of people, it is connected with positive accomplishments.

## 2.1.   PROJECTIFICATION VIA PROJECT-BASED ORGANIZATIONS

Projects play the most critical role in PBOs because the organization's income comes from projects delivered to various external customers. This characteristic is what dominates the PBO archetype. Each specific delivery project is less important, since the survival of the PBO is typically not dependent on one single project but rather on how efficient the organization is in handling an entire portfolio of projects to provide for its present and future profitability. The exception to this general characteristic of PBOs is an organization that is established for carrying out a single specific project; examples of this rare species can be found in the U.S. movie industry.

Remember that in the preindustrial era, economic endeavors usually took the form of isolated or stand-alone projects. These endeavors were not generally treated like projects as we know them today, but they could still be thought of and labeled as projects. The development of PBOs as we describe them here came later and essentially in connection with industrialization or inspired by industrialization efforts. The present account outlines the paths to the creation and development of PBOs. This archetype is of course also related to specific institutions – societal, interorganizational as well as organizational – that we discuss and develop in the coming chapters.

## Historical accounts of projects and PBOs

Many activities in preindustrial societies can be seen as important precursors to the more formalized project organizations of today. Even if few artifacts and stories are left from early hunter-gatherer periods of our history, it is still possible to learn from them. In these times, each hunting expedition could be thought of as a recurrent project (Diamond 1999). Agrarian Societies, on the other hand, have left astonishing artifacts such as the pyramids, the Great Wall, and the Coliseum, as the end result of huge endeavors on an organized basis lasting for long periods. Similarly, the roots of what we now call projects can be seen in the medieval handicraft and guild systems where craftsmen would work on a temporary basis for a specific client to produce a one-off job (a project). Many of our history books that take the predominating Euro-American perspective have actually focused on projects taking place in farming societies. They are also full of stories about successive military expeditions conquering vast areas of land, such as the ones led by Alexander the Great, Julius Caesar, Genghis Khan, or the founders of the British Empire. Project thinking is also found in the descriptions of specific expeditions such as when Pizarro cheated the chief of the Incas to take over a mighty nation or when the Ottomans conquered Constantinople. Project thinking has also been present, but not overtly acknowledged or described as such, in many trade and discovery adventures throughout history. The sometimes-violent trade expeditions undertaken by Vikings along the rivers of Eastern Europe all the way to Constantinople and via Greenland to the American East Coast could be viewed as visionary projects (Sawyer 1997; Diamond 2011). The Vikings' recurrent trade in commodities and humans in markets in Ireland and England on the basis of the need to acquire revenues and, they hoped, profit from each trip can be thought of as present-day PBOs. Other well-known and imaginative endeavors that could be thought of as projects include the fantastic stories told of the Venetian tradesman Marco Polo, who followed the Silk Road all the way to China; the Genovese adventurer Cristoforo Colombo, who succeeded in obtaining funding for an expedition to find a shorter way to India; and the Moroccan Ibn Batuta, who on his pilgrim trip to Mecca also visited and thereafter spread information about life in Africa, India, and China.

The eastbound trading expeditions to China were more modern efforts that eventually ended up as PBOs. The expeditions were made to trade European goods for spices from China and elsewhere in the Far East. Originally, such expeditions were handled as isolated projects whereby each expedition voyage could be evaluated after the return of the ship(s) to their port of embarkation and after the liquidation of the traded goods. Eventually, these expeditions were handled by specific companies (mostly the East India Company in European countries), which were in fact PBOs, as they were making money on handling expeditions of this type and their *raison d'être* was dependent on their ability to handle the expeditions to avoid all threats (e.g. piracy, mutiny, malnutrition of the seamen crews, and diseases) facing them in those early days. The East India Company played an important role in planning the ventures, financing the expeditions, and taking most of the monetary risks involved (Muller 2003).

The important point about the development of the East India Company is that it had its origin in fairly isolated and mostly privately financed ventures. In other words, the projects came first and the companies – as permanent organizations – were formed around expectations of future projects and expected profits connected with these projects. Furthermore, these organizations became carriers of knowledge related to ventures of this type by learning from their repetitive character, and this knowledge increased their chances of realizing future ventures (Muller 2003). The East India Company was also an important part of the fertile environment that developed into commercial capitalism in harbor cities such as Antwerp, Amsterdam, or Hamburg. Many business institutions of today were actually born in this context (North 1981).

It is also interesting to note some early historical examples of combinations of service and product offered on temporary concessions. For example, in fifteenth-century Italy, *condottieri* ("contractors") were given the responsibility of raising, arming, provisioning, and leading mercenary armies with specific expertise (Sturgess 2011). Such arrangements have become increasingly popular in the twentieth and twenty-first centuries as ways of developing and managing public infrastructure.

The development that a limited venture in practice led to the formation of a company as a "home" for future ventures is possibly to be found in the construction of buildings. Initially, the construction of a house was often a once-in-a-lifetime experience for many, especially in remote and isolated areas. A farmer complemented the buildings on his farm by adding a new barn, for instance. He might have made use of artisans, such as carpenters, for the more difficult parts of the construction work, but it is likely that he did the work himself with the help of the entire farm family. So for the farmer, this was a one-shot deal, in a similar way to the founding of a start-up company for most entrepreneurs today (see Chapter 6).

The same is also true for most major construction efforts. For example, the Pantheon in Rome was not only technically complicated – it is said to be the first stone construction with an arch – but the number of people working on the site was quite high compared with the those involved in the construction of less prominent buildings of that time. The mere size of the construction effort made it a development ground for expertise in construction work and combined with the technical complexity made the Pantheon effort a base for artisan and crafts trades. A more recent effort, which involved several thousands of workmen, was the erection of the Versailles Palace during which the architect had to work with a number of engineers to make sure the lavish designs could be built. The same is true for many of the world's churches, which took decades to complete (in some cases up to hundreds of years) mostly because the financing of the construction work was not at hand when the construction work was initiated. Handling complexities in construction and making use of a huge workforce opened up the need for special expertise in the field and with that came the development of the guild system.

### Construction projects in the more recent past and at present

The development of the construction sector differs between countries because of the ways in which the professions emerged. This was an important factor in the fragmentation of the industry in the UK. Historically, many constructions were designed and built by master builders. Later, the roles of design and construction were separated as architects sought professional status. In turn, as Morris (1994) points out, the structures of UK and U.S. building and civil engineering industries discouraged strong owner-driven project management. Generally, building and civil engineering work was carried out by contractors who bid for work once a design was developed, and costing was carried out by someone else – cost engineers in the United States and quantity surveyors in the UK. The contractors bid against drawings, specifications, and other documents such as schedule of rates (in the United States) or bills of quantities (in the UK). This structural separation of design and construction meant that knowledge of construction was not included in the design phase and only entered the picture once the design was fixed. As a result, many designs were suboptimal from an engineering perspective. It also meant that the construction team – the contractors and subcontractors – were viewed as outside the project/management team: "In short, there was next to no project integration, either structurally or behaviorally" (Morris 1994: 108).

In the United States during the mid-to-late 1960s, professional construction management began to be used on complex projects, building on the systems approach (Johnson 1963). This was similar to the systems engineering approach to weapons systems development promoted by the U.S. Department of Defense and the Apollo moonshot program by NASA. In the UK, the approach was subtly

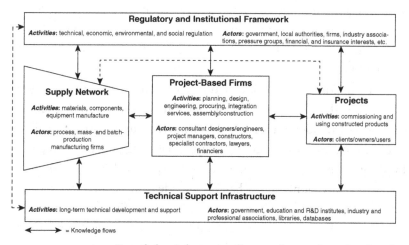

FIGURE 2.2. Knowledge, information flows, and actors in project-based processes. (Source: Gann and Salter 2000: 959.)

different. In the United States, the construction manager was essentially a consultant – a member of the professional design team. In the UK, the management contractor acted as a professional member of the design team in the early stages but crucially was also still present later in the project to deal with the allocation and management of work to subcontractors.

In line with this, Gann and Salter (2000) view construction as a process rather than an industry. The process includes the design, maintenance, and adaptation of the built environment, which involves organizations from a range of sectors, temporarily cooperating on projects, as illustrated in Figure 2.2. These projects bring together functional activities such as planning and design, engineering, supply and integration, construction per se, and installation of a diverse range of materials, components, and increasingly complex technologies. PBOs have to manage networks with complex interfaces, and collaboration is crucial to the extent that performance depends on the efficient operation of the whole network rather than on single firms. The main characteristics that describe PBOs in construction are that their design and production processes are organized around projects; they usually produce one-off, or at least highly customized, products and services; and they operate in diffuse coalitions of companies along the supplier–customer chain (Gann and Salter 2000).

To continue with the construction example, one might argue that with the industrialization and urbanization, construction work was also industrialized. An illustrative example is the so-called million program in Sweden (meaning a national target to complete 1 million apartments in 10 years; see Apleberger et al. 2007). Although the roots of division of labor had been evident in the need for special expertise in construction work, industrialization further transformed the work at the same time as societal trends led to a high demand for new dwellings and factory buildings. The same is true for general infrastructure for transportation. It is probably fair to say that this era also witnessed a kind of industrialization of construction work with more specialized people working in construction as well, at the same time as mass production of goods made its victorious triumph in some parts of the world, including England.

Pinney (2001: 15) argues that the construction business is an early promoter of project-based organizing on the more general level. Like in the East India Company example described earlier, it is likely that each construction site initially was considered to be an isolated venture under the auspices of the builder. But when production en masse with a series of construction endeavors reached the building activities, the basis for project-based organizing with an efficiency focus was formed. The expansion of construction work to the point of being able to form a project portfolio and make a living out of delivering buildings was also the basis for project management to be handled by a professional construction company. The PBO was born.

Seemingly, the notion of a project portfolio adds a problematic twist to construction in the sense that handling a set of projects – the portfolio – is difficult seen from both the side of the individual projects and that of the aggregation of projects and the management of the construction company as a permanent organization. However, it also represents a profitability opportunity as similarities might be exploited for efficiency, not the least by adding a mass production ingredient to construction work. Obviously, these opportunities outweigh the awkwardness in handling the portfolio since the original piecemeal construction approach does not reappear.

It goes without saying that buildings are constructed for different purposes, but one thing they have in common is that the technical opportunities have expanded and been made part of the expectations that owners of buildings have for the function of their buildings. Establishing special standards to be included in the blueprints for the building to be constructed is among the most important tasks for a new building today. This goes far beyond the need for efficient ventilation and heating. The concept of "smart buildings" emerged a couple of decades ago to denote the new opportunities provided by adding computerized controls to features provided in modern buildings, including various safety measures, early warning systems, gardening, and so on. These new systems were not part of the previous most extravagant buildings, but nowadays, they make construction even more diversified, not least in terms of projects.

It has already been claimed that complexity in construction work changes the character of construction per se. This complexity involves among other things, including additional professions in the construction work; for example, when smart buildings are wanted and delivered as "turnkey projects," even more outsourcing becomes common. Services provided for those customers or clients have developed over time and come in three major forms:

(1) "Total contract by tender" essentially implies that the client hands over all responsibilities to the builder once there is a general agreement.
(2) The "general contract by tender" means that the client specifies most of the new building, but the builder takes on the responsibilities for the construction work.

(3) "Divided contract by tender" is a form in which the client takes full responsibilities for coordination of various subcontractors. Under this scheme, the builder is merely one subcontractor among several to deliver to the client according to contract specifications.

However, these traditional forms have been subject to developments. For instance, the architects handling the blueprints in fact specify many subcontractors. In the early days of construction, the network of firms, which was useful for recruiting specialists and thus for erecting a building, was to be found in a geographically small area around the building site. The form of the network was simply based on interpersonal relationships or networks. Mass production of construction material, for the façade as well as for the interior, created a need for a wider range of subcontractors. Potential subcontractors made themselves known to the architects by visiting and by sending samples and catalogues to the architects in charge. These practices have now changed with the extended use of the Internet, substantially changing the nature of how subcontractors and suppliers are contacted. Trust developed through previous cooperation efforts and as a result of successful interaction, but more or less instant trust was needed initially for temporary activities such as projects (Meyerson et al. 1996). That is also true now when architects and builders use the Internet in their planning of the work to be done with new contacts. The net has taken over much of the face-to-face contact in the construction sector; trust-building processes, hence, are mediated by IT.

In summarizing the case of construction, one might conclude that no matter the form of tender and with due consideration paid to the developments of the cyber world, the following holds:

- Construction companies are project based in the sense that their income comes only from various forms of construction projects run for clients.
- As PBOs, they rely to an increasing extent on subcontractors or outside service providers with whom they sustain a broad network of business relations.

- Economies of scale in some activities dominate over disadvantages from coordinating a variety of projects inside and across organizational boundaries, implying that the company itself is manifested in a "permanent" form aiming to handle temporary construction sites.
- Since construction activities are bound by the state of the market and the market is volatile, outsourcing has meant that entrepreneurs can free themselves of personnel responsibilities and thus avoid the cost of direct labor during downturns and push the risk down into the supply chain.
- New "smart functions" in construction have also added to the reliance on subcontractors and suppliers.
- Ability to plan and coordinate construction activities is more important now as compared to previous eras of construction work; new forms of expertise have entered the industry.
- The opportunity involved in evaluating each project is valuable for the acquisition of future projects; the impetus for instant follow-up is strong.

Hence, it is not by chance that the construction industry not only continues to be an important field for studying temporary organizations (e.g. Bryman et al. 1987; Bresnen et al. 2004) but can be considered as the nursery of the PBO archetype.

## PBOs elsewhere – in particular IT, services, and TV production

PBOs have developed in many other industries – consulting, advertising, special events, architecture, law, and public relations and also in IT services and TV production, following the outsourcing of these activities. In some cases, outsourcing, more often than not followed by insourcing some time later, may well be a matter of fashion trends rather than well-considered strategic changes of the organizations (Abrahamson 1991); however, for many companies, services are now bought from the outside rather than produced internally for interior use. This development is described in terms of organizations having to concentrate on "core" activities and consequently outsourcing work that is "not core" (Pralahad and Hamel 1990). Many of the activities previously considered to be activities or services provided within are being outsourced to specialized companies.

The way these outsourcing processes have been taking place is similar to the way outsourcing occurred in construction. Outsourcing of IT services, for instance, originated from a company's wish to concentrate on its major line of business. By forming a special company for IT services (inside a corporate group, for instance), the door was also opened for revenues and profits by making effective use of the IT specialists at hand. The outsourced companies eventually attracted more customers. When this market was formed, freestanding competitors appeared with IT solutions that could be adapted to a variety of clients. Because of the project-based character of the IT business, these companies resemble PBOs, no matter whether they are still part of the corporate group or external organizations that maintain either rather fragile and market-like or more long-term network-type relationships with the organization that originally outsourced the service and now is only one of the service provider's customers.

IT consulting is one of the fastest-growing sectors in Western economies, and consulting firms are strongly rooted in the PBO structure. Their revenues are generally strictly based on projects sold to more traditional organizations including PSOs. There are also permanent structures within these IT consultants, but projects form their main offering and therefore also define their strategic position within their industry or field. Moreover, management and strategy consultants have developed into PBOs through a similar route, although they started out much earlier.

Outsourcing of services led to a similar dominance of PBOs in the TV production industry. In the Nordic countries, Germany, and, up to the 1950s, the UK, TV production was dominated by publicly owned broadcasters (Saundry 1998; Windeler and Sydow 2001; Lundin 2008). The production projects were essentially in-house. Thus, before TV privatization and advertising were let free, the programs broadcast were essentially produced in the studios of the public broadcaster if they were not bought from abroad. When the ban was lifted on TV advertising – in Germany and Sweden in 1984 and 1988, respectively – a number of free and independent or semi-independent TV production companies were established to meet the demand for the production of TV programs to be broadcast by the commercial channels. Even the publicly owned television eventually became one of the customers of these TV producers.

These TV producers make and sell TV programs to the broadcasters according to specifications and previously agreed-on terms. The TV programs produced are usually on well-established formats that follow the copyright form for TV programs. The rights to produce the programs are bought from the owner of the format, and the program can then be produced according to the specifications accompanying the format. The connections between the TV producers and the broadcaster, which turned into PBOs and PSOs respectively in the course of this organizational change process, is tight and of a business-to-business character. The producers keep track of the various broadcasters and are ready to suggest new items to the broadcasters' repertoire when there seems to be a need for that. TV producers are in other words active vis-à-vis the broadcasters. One basis for that active stance is that viewer statistics are essentially known the day after each program has been broadcast.

TV production companies are generally small – in extreme cases only one or two individuals – even though as many as 100 people might be involved in the production phase. The use of subcontractors, including many self-employed people, for the shooting of programs is extensive. The production phase is extremely efficient – TV production companies appear to be expert at coordinating the various activities during a short period of time. They have essentially learned the lesson that there is no such thing as a black screen on the day when the program is to be broadcast. Furthermore, to continuously produce content that has appeal to the broadcaster to fulfill its program mandate or its commercial interests (or any combination of the two), the producers, providers of artistic or technical services, or any other subcontractors, themselves PBOs, coordinate their activities in PNWs (see further discussions of PNWs in Section 2.3).

Delivering programs to customers is to construction activities where the problem is similar to deliver buildings on the agreed on day. In this case, though, coordination is about having a filming team ready to shoot the program, actors to appear on the program, personnel responsible for the lights, people associated with the manuscript in case rewriting is needed, and the like. However, TV producers do one thing that does not have a direct counterpart in construction; many TV producers dream of establishing a new TV program format to be delivered to several broadcasters. This is when real creativity comes into play for the TV producer whose business is otherwise dominated by creativity channeled by established formats (Manning and Sydow 2007). Establishing an innovative format can be profitable. Even though it is difficult to come up with good ideas for new formats and very few succeed in doing so, success in establishing a new format is worth a lot depending on the global market. The format known as *Survivor* on U.S. TV and *Robinson* in the Swedish version was the result of the inventiveness of a Swedish TV producer; *The Farm* and *The Bar* are other examples of successful formats developed in Sweden, but only a handful of Swedish efforts have resulted in really profitable world-conquering formats. Even so, this organizational development has enabled internationalization of TV production to an extent that previously was not possible.

## 2.2. PROJECTIFICATION VIA PROJECT-SUPPORTED ORGANIZATIONS

The second archetype is the increased use of projects inside traditional organizations and is driven by two related trends: the growth of innovation-based competition and the rise of service strategies in traditional manufacturing companies. This archetype is also related to specific institutions – societal and interorganizational as well as organizational – that we develop in the following chapters.

*From organizing for efficiency and productivity*
*to organizing for innovation*
Many economists as well as strategy management authors have,
after Schumpeter (1947), emphasized innovation as the key factor
in capitalist development. After the post–World War II mass production period, an economy of variety emphasizing mass customization
(Pine 1993) and the dynamic flexibility needed for putting it into
practice developed in the 1980s and 1990s as the dominant competitive regime for industry. The growth of product diversity and the
speed of product obsolescence are among the key indicators of such a
competitive context. This is also complemented by an increased
level of individualization and modularization of products and
services (Henderson and Clark 1990). Manufacturing firms, which
were dominant in the previous mass production regime, developed
various strategies to cope with the new context.

Authors such as Benghozi et al. (2000) and Le Masson et al.
(2010) propose the notion of "intensive innovation-based competition" to describe the more recent competitive context, wherein the
dynamic capabilities of organizations (Teece et al. 1997; Eisenhardt
and Martin 2000), that is, their ability to dynamically reconfigure
resources with the help of certain routines, are the source of sustainable competitive advantages. In such a context, enhancing the new
product development capacity while reducing the cost and lead time
of product and service developments appear as key competitive
advantages.

The 1980s and 1990s saw deep strategic as well as organizational
renewals to build up and enhance such dynamic capabilities. The
number of projects within organizations has been on the rise
(Figure 2.3). Platform management, for example (Cusumano and
Nobeoka 1998; Fourcade and Midler 2004), has at the same time
been a key concept to enlarge diversity in product range while keeping
standardization cost efficiency – just as required by the concept of
mass customization. Reengineering the design activities (R&D,

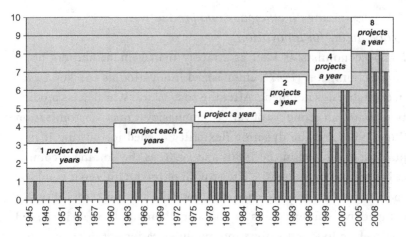

FIGURE 2.3.   Evolution of a European car manufacturer's new product development capability. (Source: Midler et al. 2012: 2.)

marketing, style, engineering design) and processes through the projectification concept was a dominant trend in the 1980s and 1990s (Giard and Midler 1993; Midler 1995); without its supporting role, the transformation from a purely productive to a productive and creative organization would not have been possible.

### From product manufacturing to service offering

The rise of projects within organizations is also reflected in an increase of service content in these companies' offerings, that is, the trend toward combinations of products and services (Normann 2001; Baines et al. 2009). There is therefore a significant change in the relation between PSOs and their customers in the direction that the importance of physical products for customer satisfaction decreases while the importance of more intangible services increases. This shift in the balance between products and services does not render the physical products obsolete, however. Products continue to be crucial and often function as a qualifier for sales even if the resulting customer evaluation of a business relation is more directly related to the service content.

The transformation of traditional manufacturing companies into PSOs is also linked to an expanding international division of labor, often referred to as globalization. Labor-intensive work is outsourced (or offshored) to companies with production units in low-cost areas of the world at the same time as service- and knowledge-dense activities, such as R&D, are retained and still organized by the original company. Projects play an important role here for identifying functions to be outsourced and/or offshored, and for implementing the respective strategy. However, the increased service orientation that goes along with these organizational trends and the accelerated dynamics of the organizational change itself are also likely to drive traditional organizations toward PSOs.

Manufacturing firms have become increasingly service and project based. These firms that traditionally were rooted in permanent line structures are changing into organizations whose offerings contain greater service content (Normann 2001; Baines et al. 2009), and the project has become an important organizing principle (Midler 1995; Whittington et al. 1999; Hobday 2000). The successful definition and execution of such projects should be driven by the need to solve each customer's business or operational problems. This involves a major strategic shift for many companies, especially those that have been driven from a strong technological product base. Early examples of this shift in focus can be seen when IBM and General Electric transformed from being internally focused, functionally driven, product-centric organizations into organizations that drove their activities backward from the customer as they moved to customer-centric solutions business models (see Gerstner 2002 and Welch 2001 for personal accounts of these strategic transformations). Suppliers of complex capital goods and services in all types of industries – such as Accenture, LogicaCMG, Rolls Royce, Ericsson, C&W, Alstom, and WS Atkins – have followed IBM and GE in adopting integrated solutions delivery business models (Davies 2003, 2004; Davies et al. 2006; Davies et al. 2007) by occupying new strategic positions in the value stream centered on systems integration. To do this, they had to develop new service capabilities (systems integration, operational services, and finance and consulting skills) and create customer-oriented organizations.

IBM's turnaround after the debacle with mainframe computers in the early 1980s and the consequent change of its industrial business model illustrate the tendency toward PSOs and PBOs (Dittrich et al. 2007). In the early 1980s, only about 16 percent of IBM's global revenues came from services; the share rose to 27 percent in 1993 and 48 percent in 2004. Sales increased more than 50 percent between 1992 and 2004, according to a 2006 article in a major Swedish newspaper, SvD. Since then, IBM has developed into a service and consultancy company (Dittrich and Duysters 2007). The Swedish firm Ericsson has undergone a similar change process. Projectification and servicification (or servitization) seem to go hand in hand and manifest important organizational trends among manufacturing firms in the Western world.

The shift into high-value, customer-centric, service- and project-based solutions has three wider implications. First, because of the strategic importance and high value of such projects, super-heavyweight bid and project managers are needed to drive sales negotiations involving senior managers up to and including CEOs if the involvement of top echelons helps close the deal. Traditional forms of project management based on hierarchical control, vertical lines of communication, and functional specialists are being replaced by flatter, horizontally managed, and commercially focused team-based structures that are organized to respond flexibly and rapidly to each customer's needs at the highest level. The need to organize integrated solutions projects around individual customers' requirements thus elevates the role and status of the bid and project managers within the managerial hierarchy of the firm. Second, the traditional triple constraints model of project success (within cost, on schedule, and to exacting technical specifications) has now been extended to include a new measure: customer satisfaction. The growth of integrated solutions means that a project is now regarded as successful only if it solves an individual customer's immediate and longer-term business problems. To satisfy a customer's needs, a solutions provider not only has to respond to detailed contractul specifications but also has to be able to respond flexibly – even during late stages in the life of a project – to changes in a customer's needs and priorities. This means solutions providers must work closely with their customers to identify, create, and share in the value addition generated by each project. Third, demand for integrated solutions means that the traditional project life cycle now extends over many years or even decades. The solutions life cycle model includes four main phases: engaging with the customer in high-level strategic negotiations, often before an invitation to tender has been issued; working closely with the customer to develop a value proposition during a bid or offer phase; project managing the systems integration process; and operating the product or system during a specified contractual period. Suppliers and customers need to establish long-term strategic partnerships and create co-located organizations to foster the kind of close cooperation and innovative environment required to ensure that a customer's problems are solved. To avoid being held accountable to established bureaucratic procedures, project businesses that can operate independently from their parent companies are needed so that they can come up with creative solutions to a specific business problem or market opportunity.

### Historic accounts of PSOs

Nevertheless, as characteristic of a PSO, the project organization developed only as a complementary structure in organizations that have traditionally been dominated by more permanent structures in the form of functional hierarchies, divisions, and/or matrix structures. The business environment during the 1950s was stable with an abundant demand in the post–World War II era, which implied that organizations' prime concerns were focused on creating internal efficiency. The conclusions from Taylor's scientific principles and Fayol's bureaucratic structures were taken to the heart of these organizations, and their organizational structures became distinctly hierarchic, mainly bureaucratic, and well adapted to a stable business environment.

However, as market and business environments, more broadly, changed during the 1970s, there was a need for more flexible organizational structures. Firms were seeking new solutions and the use of matrix structures and the adoption of some kind of project organization started to emerge. A typical evolutionary process started from a basic functional hierarchy based on key organizational units such as, for instance, purchasing, production, R&D, logistics, sales and marketing, and after-sales service. When the business environment launched new challenges and calls for adaptability, the organizations often adopted projects as a temporary structure on top of the functional hierarchy. It was still the hierarchy that controlled resources and made important decisions, whereas the projects were aimed at enabling the organization to learn how to act in a changing environment.

In the following phase, this temporary overlay was made permanent, but it was still regarded as a secondary feature. Two separate and parallel structures lived side by side. In a later phase, the two structures – the functional hierarchy and the project overlay – were considered equally important and neither was a priori dominating the other. The firm's organizations had developed into a mature matrix wherein a balance of authority between the two structures was maintained (Larson and Gobeli 1987). It is these types of organizational setups that we call project-supported organizations or PSOs.

Another step in this evolutionary path appeared when projects reached a certain level of significance within the mature matrix and organizations saw a need to coordinate different projects and their sub-projects. In such cases, there might paradoxically be efforts constituting a new permanent function with the responsibility to oversee the temporary projects, that is, project management offices (PMOs). These PMOs are set up to handle project portfolios with large budgets and a multitude of sub-projects as well as complex connections to the permanent functions in the matrix and often grow as a result of external turbulence and internal evolution (Hobbs et al. 2008).

Our discussion thus far has focused on the organizational structures in PSOs, but these structures are interesting only if we also add the dimension on how they drive action and decision making in organizations. If we believe that managerial decision making is far from perfectly rational but rather driven by a will to solve the most important and imminent problems as and when they appear (Simon 1947; March and Simon 1958; Cyert and March 1963; Brunsson 1989), it is likely that management in the actual organizational structures often decides which problems do appear. The structures therefore define problems and drive managerial action. A matrix structure will bring problems; for instance, how the functional responsibilities are related and harmonized with geographical markets, and so on. As the project structures become more important, the need will increase for managerial decision making and action related to how projects are to be harmonized with permanent structures. Our focus on structure therefore does not exclude the importance of organizational processes but rather emphasizes the importance of structures, which have to be reproduced or transformed with the help of social practices (Giddens 1984).

*The conceptual characteristics and variations of PSOs*
The PSO is a result of a long-term evolutionary process that is driven by internal ambitions to compete successfully as external conditions demand organizational change. Accordingly, one definition of a PSO can be an organization that has "cross-functional overlays that create multiple lines of authority and that place people in teams to work on tasks for finite periods of time" (Ford and Randolph 1992: 272). Hence, the PSO is a permanent organization in which projects – as a form of temporary organizing – are institutionalized.

Clark and colleagues (Clark and Fujimoto 1991; Clark and Wheelwright 1992) characterize three degrees of empowerment of project structures in relation to the permanent structure: from the "lightweight project manager" to "heavyweight" and "tiger team" structure. The lightweight team structure is represented by a liaison from the functional departments, usually managed by a middle- or junior-level person, who has little influence, status, and/or power. The project manager of a heavyweight team has direct access to top management, has experience from the project domains, and is empowered for the work by everybody involved in the project. The core members of the project team are dedicated to the project. In the tiger teams structure, project managers are empowered to create their own policies and procedures. These teams take full responsibility for a project's failure or success. They have no established boundaries and usually provide unique solutions as a result.

Many authors analyze the contingent context in which such different project forms take place as the consequence of decision making. For example, Giard and Midler (1993) propose that few key projects (as, for example, in the auto or aeronautic industry) will favor heavyweight project structures, while portfolios with large number of small and risky projects (as in pharmaceutical research) will coexist with rather lightweight structures.

We believe that PSOs develop not only in these two directions. In addition, some may develop inside an M-form organizational structure, while others adopt what has been called the N-form. In both cases, we might find lightweight or heavyweight project management. The M-form – or multidivisional form (Chandler 1991) – emphasizes the permanent functions and is more strongly based on the functional hierarchy within the PSO. It is therefore more ideally structured for situations in which economies of scale and scope as well as diversification are critical success factors. This type of organization can easily add or subtract new business areas – or divisions – to achieve adaptability in relation to the external environment. It is not, however, well equipped to create internal flexibility and creative restructuring of existing capabilities. Here, the alternative N-form – or internal network form – (Hedlund 1994) is superior. This type of organization relies on action driven by temporary constellations of people and units whereby lateral communication and dialogue are key characteristics. Top management's role is primarily seen as that of a catalyst and architect of the communications infrastructure as well as a guardian of knowledge investments. The organization is "heterarchic" (Hedlund 1986, 1993) as opposed to hierarchic, although all decentralization (also of decision making) takes place in the shadow of hierarchy and can be reversed by fiat. The strengths of the N-form are the internal ability to combine and recombine capabilities and resources swiftly and creatively as external turbulence grows and the need for radical innovation increases. Söderlund and Tell (2009), by building on the N-form, have advanced this thinking further in their discussions of the P-form organization. Their study of ABB's evolution over a 40-year period uncovered what they called "project epochs," during which the nature of the output of its delivery projects and the organizational arrangements associated with these deliveries developed over time and new capabilities to plan and execute projects were created. In the first epoch, projects were embedded within the organization and involved ABB personnel in collaboration with a few selected partners. The second epoch involved ABB acting as a key subsystem supplier to large international clients that had their own in-house capabilities for delivering major investment projects. The third epoch extended ABB's capabilities to new markets for turnkey projects for which they took responsibility for many of the activities that clients previously managed. The current epoch includes further extension of its capabilities into the area of finance for turnkey projects. Today, we may thus see different forms of PSOs where one is more heavily leaning on the functional hierarchy and permanent structure while the other is better at using projects and the temporary structures inside an organization.

Even if the discussion here focuses on recurring projects within an organization, both these types of organizational structures also involve nonrecurring projects, that is, projects that are more or less one-off solutions to organizational problems. These may, for instance, involve changes in administrative systems such as the IT or accounting system or – as mentioned before – aim at the outsourcing or offshoring of activities. These types of change projects are seldom directly focused on the core business processes but rather on support functions and we therefore focus our discussion on recurring projects.

### Current organizational trends among PSOs

This evolutionary process took a leap forward in the 1980s, when companies strongly dependent on R&D investments increasingly used projects to organize these efforts. As budgets for R&D projects increased, companies saw the need to formalize project management and structures as well as to create better links between the traditional permanent structures and these more temporary structures. Companies in the pharmaceutical industry were among the first to more formally adopt projects as a complement to the traditional hierarchies, but firms in other industries soon learned from these pioneers. In Sweden, the pharmaceutical company Astra – now AstraZeneca – was one of the first to launch the path of projectification and is seen as a pioneer and PSO role model for other Swedish companies. Today, companies such as Ericsson and Sandvik are heavily influenced by their project structures, even if the permanent functions are still important.

Driven by the rapid change and evolution in the IT/telecom sector, Ericsson has made projects critical for its business development and moved in a direction where the need for innovation and change is high (Räisänen and Linde 2004). Here, the traditional matrix structure was complemented with an additional project structure, thereby creating a new, semipermanent organizational entity that aimed to integrate all projects whose results would affect product releases during a specific year.

This was called a *program* and aimed to coordinate all work done in the projects that had bearing on the program's objectives (cf. Artto et al. 2009). The aims were to avoid sub-optimization of individual projects, which could harm the overall objective of the

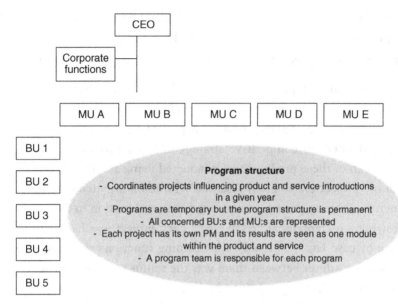

FIGURE 2.4. Schematic picture of the organizational structure. (Source: inspired by Arvidsson 2009.)

program; manage conflicts between projects as well as between projects and the permanent organization; and ensure that the final project results were well integrated into the permanent organizational entity that would have the responsibility for activities affected by the project delivery.

Sandvik, on the other hand, is active in a more stable competitive environment and was using projects less aggressively than Ericsson. Sandvik is in this sense more traditional and puts greater importance on the permanent structures than does Ericsson. Figure 2.4 illustrates how project- and program-related structures complement a matrix structure, which in this case combines business units (BU) and market units (MU).

To sum up, both Ericsson and Sandvik are PSOs; however, Ericsson's structure is more similar to Hedlund's N-form, while Sandvik's organizational setup is more like the traditional M-form or divisional structure.

*From functional organization to PSO in the auto industry*
To further illustrate the emergence of the PSO, we trace the evolution
of project management in the auto industry through a set of stages:

1. From the postwar period to the 1970s, there was no differentiation
between the product strategies of car manufacturers in North America
and Europe. Disciplined management of projects was seen neither as a
core component of competitive strategy nor as a core competence.
The design of these products was conducted using an organizational
form of "project craft" in an essentially function-oriented corporate
structure. Projects passed in sequence from one function to the next,
following a metaphorical "relay race." Each project was handled on
a case-by-case basis. The only actor joining functions together and
acting as an arbiter between them was the senior management team
and often the CEO.

2. During the 1970s and 1980s, the gradual saturation of markets
changed the competitive environment radically. Japanese manufacturers
succeeded in breaking into the North American market using novel
product proliferation strategies, especially for vehicles, and the direct
consequence of this business model was an explosive increase in the
number of projects to be managed. Project management for new vehicles
now assumed strategic importance. It is at this point that we see the
beginnings of a professionalization of project management: the first
project functions were created in the early 1970s, along with periodic
review systems involving corporate management. The careful guidance
of projects to completion was gradually put in place, along with formalization of development timetables and the deployment of economic
reporting tools integrating all the variables in the projects concerned.

Other than this centralization of control, there was no change in
the relationship between strategies for the building of technical skills
occurring in engineering design offices and central process-planning
departments, on the one hand, and development policies, on the other.
Project teams had neither the political weight nor the expertise to
defend their own logic against the strategies of technical departments.

This period can be characterized as one of the lightweight project manager (Hayes et al. 1988).

3. In the late 1980s and early 1990s, manufacturers radically reorganized their approach to the management of projects for developing new products more quickly and producing a greater number of products of increasingly higher quality at lower cost. Managing projects for new vehicles was now at the heart of corporate strategy. The most visible sign of this break with the past was the creation of project directors who were destined to become genuine entrepreneurs in automotive development. The time had come for the heavyweight project manager (Hayes et al. 1988).

These structural changes (to be treated further in Chapter 3) went on to drive profound modifications in project communication and decision processes. These changes occurred inside the organization with parallel developments of the type now denominated concurrent engineering. The new project actors laid down new rules for the coordination of project contributors. Changes were seen at three levels. First, they related to the timing of the contributions by the various specialists: traditional sequential processes gave way to a planning logic aimed at maximum anticipation of problems through the early involvement of the trades involved in production; plants were involved in the manufacture of prototypes to validate process feasibility; and future products were tested with the sales networks. Second, communication between functions changed: previously, intertrade dialogue had occurred largely at the top of the management hierarchy. Project management departments now began to promote such dialogue at the bottom in decentralized workgroups responsible for all aspects of the development of a given part of the vehicle (seats, dashboard, etc.). And third, there were changes related to the spatial organization of work, with systematic use of co-location of participants in project office suites and development of tools to accelerate intertrade communications.

These changes also affected relations with other organizations, with a move from clear-cut subcontracting to ambitious co-development with suppliers. Automotive projects usually unfold in a space much wider than that of single organization. Today, the proportion of production cost relating to parts bought in from suppliers is generally more than 70 percent. The new project actors have come to play a major role in the development of new co-development or co-creation relationships with suppliers (Prahalad and Ramaswamy 2004; Grönroos 2011). Calls for bids from and subsequent selection of suppliers operate from the outset of a project on the basis of agreement on core project objectives. The chosen supplier is then associated closely with the engineering study process: co-location in the project office suite, participation in project progress meetings, and so on. Compared with the conventional template for competition between suppliers based on detailed project specifications, this new template for the collaborative relationship involves modifying organizational and contractual frameworks (Garel et al. 1997; Kesseler 1998; Dyer and Nobeoka 2000; Wilhelm 2011).

4. Such reorganizations have had a dramatic effect on project performance in terms of reducing the lead time, quality, and cost of developments. But by the late 1990s and the first decade of twenty-first century, new challenges emerged. Market globalization as a necessity to introduce more breakthrough innovation initiated a new wave of reorganization along three different axes (Midler et al. 2012):

- Project to program management, to cope with the business dimensions of what are now completely internationalized projects (Maylor et al. 2006).
- Development project to exploration projects, to scout out technologies and prepare new generations of vehicles, adapted to the constraint regulations and ecological trends of the market (Maniak et al. 2014).
- Entrepreneurial "vanguard" projects (Brady and Davies 2004), exploring breakthrough products such as new hybrid technologies such as the Prius project by Toyota (Itasaki 1999), the low-cost Logan (Midler 2013), or the full electric cars (Midler and Beaume 2009).

*Projectification of a French chemical group*
The case of the French chemical group Rhodia (formally Rhône Poulenc) is interesting because it is quite different from auto firms.

First, the chemical industry is a science-based industry with a strong tradition of corporate research centers, which differs significantly from the engineering-driven development in the mechanical industry of the auto type. Second, chemical groups are "upstream suppliers" (Lenfle and Midler 2001) involved in business-to-business markets, as opposed to business-to-consumer car manufacturers. In spite of such differences, we can see a similar trend of projectification over the past 40 years even if longitudinal research (Charue-Duboc 2006; Gastaldi and Midler 2010) shows a rather different frame of organizing the project function in the structure of the firm. This is based on the science and research focus push sequential model of innovation, whereby the firm evolves into an empowered project-driven PSO with two categories of projects: market-driven projects with the clear leadership of business units as product managers, and exploratory projects having research-oriented project managers. The development of the chemical group went through a number of stages:

1. In the 1960s and early 1970s, Rhône Poulenc (RP) was positioned in basic chemistry markets, focusing on major intermediate chemicals such as phenol, aspirin, and certain direct hydrocarbon derivatives. These were low-value-added commodity products sold to other manufacturers located further downstream in the chemical field. RP focused on a volume-based strategy, with economies of scale allowing the company to dominate in terms of costs (Porter 1980, 1985). At that time, RP adopted a functional organization, with heavy and centralized research laboratories ruled in a "science-push" way.

2. From 1975 to 1995, critical changes in the economic and competitive landscape, alongside a major repositioning with regard to competition, led to a rethinking of the original research and strategy link model. Now, industrial and sales issues started to play a greater role in driving research projects. RP bore the full brunt of the 1973 oil crisis. The hike in raw material prices and sharp drop in volumes on highly cyclical commodities markets significantly eroded the company's financial situation as well as its ability to compete. Chemical

business management became more rigorous and industrial processes were streamlined. The early 1990s also saw a gradual decline in the competitive advantages historically enjoyed by the company across several of its markets, as a resut in particular of the emergence of new competitors benefiting from lower production costs.

This was a time for dramatic changes in strategy. RP shifted from manufacturing molecules to developing more sophisticated, innovative products such as polymers, silicones, surfactants, various additives, and mineral nanoparticles, which offer useful features for industrial clients and beyond (including consumers). As a specialty chemical company, RP therefore had to build knowledge of the end user and determine the functional performance factors these users might value. When selling polymers to a detergent manufacturer, for example, the company had to ask itself what the end user was looking for and consider such factors as softness, cleanliness, and a pleasant scent. It was now the function provided by the polymer in relation to these client-perceived factors that created its value and no longer its chemical characteristics alone. This strategic turn is a typical example of how a former product company added services.

This strategic turn led to deep renewals in the organizational structure of the firm. First, a company-wide decentralization process rolled out from 1975 to 1995. At the close of this process, RP had become a company structured into business units, each with a high level of autonomy vis-à-vis the corporate division, which experienced a significant decrease in its personnel and prerogatives. The business units were organized as profit centers, equipped with their own strategy and responsible for handling all of their own business activities. Each unit covered a strategic business area and centralized all of the operational and functional activities it required, including factories, business services, marketing, and purchasing. Then, a new project organization was implemented, matching the Anglo-Saxon client-contractor model on the business unit–research center structure that included project managers in the business unit and financing of the projects headed by R&D project managers. Portfolio management was implemented to monitor the multiple new project opportunities in line with the business strategy. This created a market pull context for research that generated genuine renewal of corporate laboratories. The limits of such a short-term market orientation rapidly appeared as big client firms such as L'Oreal and Procter & Gamble looked for partners whose capabilities surpassed their own competencies and aimed toward breakthrough innovation more than incremental solutions to their problems.

3. In a reaction to the limitations of this model, in 1995 the scientific division initiated a set of proactive reforms that involved a third form of research and strategy linkage that can be called "concurrent exploration" (Gastaldi and Midler 2010), to make the analogy of the concurrent engineering model that in the 1990s spread through engineering departments. The formal contractual asymmetric model between the business and research units gave way to a more procedural team-oriented project regulation, similar to that experienced in the auto industry. Exploratory projects were recognized as a specific category that needed a specific approach and tools to be monitored. At the same time, the research department underwent a deep reorganization as it adapted to this more strategic and proactive role.

These cases show, on the one hand, that the projectification of organizations and their transformation into PSOs is a quite general trend throughout various sectors and countries. They also show the importance of mimetic learning effects through Industrial Society. Project organization patterns are copied and hybridized from one situation, sector, tradition, country to another and often vice versa. The importance of mediators in this diffusion process, such as professional associations, consulting firms, media, and last but not least scholars, to handle mechanisms of the managerial fads type (Midler 1986; Abrahamson 1991) and organizational learning inside the firms must be pointed out.

## 2.3. PROJECTIFICATION VIA PROJECT NETWORKS

A third focus is the frequent and increasing use of interorganizational projects or project networks. The move of broadcasters to outsource production is an example of this trend. But it is also manifested in other industries including IT, music and events, and specialized forms of consulting. These industries seem in part to have already been dominated by PNWs from the perspective of the move from the single organizations (i.e. PBOs) to the level of whole networks (Provan et al. 2007).

PNWs describe a setting in which different parties, typically organizations but also the self-employed or "entreployees" (Pongratz and Voß 2003), are either loosely or more tightly connected in a system that could be referred to as an interorganizational network. PNWs can be either strategically led by a "hub firm" (Jarillo 1988), such as a production company in the case of producing content for TV, or governed on more equal terms, also described as "participant-governed network" (Provan and Kenis 2008). While PNWs with this shared form of governance tend to be found in certain regions or clusters, PNWs governed by lead organizations may be more likely to stretch well beyond regional boundaries.

Of course, some interorganizational projects only occur a single time, but repetitive cooperation embedded in social systems or networks of relations that transcend organizations and that provide at least some "permanence" is of a more general interest. The idea is that members of the system or network can be activated for a certain task that in turn can be transformed into a project. When the project is accomplished, the system may revert to a less active state, sometimes even to a state of hibernation. The actors in the project return to other activities demanded by the organization that employs them. Examples of this kind of projectification that transcends single organizations have been detected, for instance, in the British and German television industries and are called "latent organizations" (Starkey et al. 2000) and project networks (Sydow and Windeler 1999), respectively. The idea behind both concepts is that projects are created and, after termination of a particular project, recreated from latent relationships. The running of projects in turn impacts the quality of relationships. In effect, many studies in this field show that there is a strong tendency to form "repeated ties," even though the projects often require different actors (e.g. Sydow and Windeler 1999; Starkey et al. 2000; Delmestri et al. 2005; Sorenson and Waguespack 2006; Manning and Sydow 2011). In some cases – and we believe in an increasing number – the field, a region, or an industry, in consequence of this very process, may turn into a lively "project ecology" (Grabher 2004) in which individual and organizational actors form projects and then dissolve into at least latent relational structures after the project has been completed (or discontinued for other reasons) before reforming around another project. Such project ecologies, as cases of biomedical innovation show (Newell et al. 2008), tend to be in a region, but transnational firms or strategic networks may connect them via global projects they initiate or are tied to.

The strength of the ties in such a system may vary quite a lot. It could range from a common brand name or a name of a district not involving much interorganizational interaction to a long-lasting network of lead organizations, subcontractors, and service providers engaging in project business (such as the Berlin television cluster). See also the later historical section on Third Italy. The initiative to start projects could come from different actors in the system, most frequently from major companies that are interested in commissioning R&D or reorganizing the provision of services. But it is also common for public authorities such as local governments, universities, or EU agencies to take an active part in forming interorganizational projects in a wide range of areas, from huge construction endeavors to cultural events. Whoever takes the initiative, small and medium-sized enterprises are quite likely to be part of it. In the case of TV production, small firms – often in close collaboration with broadcasters – may even lead project networks or latent organizations (Sydow and Windeler 1999; Manning and Sydow 2011) and, in consequence, actively transform systems or fields into project ecologies.

The following sections provide a short background of how the traditional industrial organization is challenged by such networked project-based systems. In addition, with the help of detailed examples, we show how systems like clusters or networks are related to projects, not least in the form of PNWs. To illustrate these relations, we use examples from our own research, particularly, though not exclusively, from the Swedish construction and the German television industries. As with PBOs and PSOs, the PNW cases are presented in this chapter and then used in the following chapters when discussing the characteristics of management, work, and related institutions in an interorganizational setting.

## Historic accounts of PNWs

Piore and Sabel (1984) analyze in some depth what they call "the second industrial divide." The first divide is the transfer from manual production to mass production, which took place around the turn of the previous century in the United States and somewhat later in Europe. Taylor (1911) and Fayol (1949) have come to be associated with this dramatic transformation. Later, a second divide was identified: the inability of the traditional Fordist mass production to adapt to the increasingly more complicated variations of what people and other companies demand becomes apparent. Piore and Sabel (1984) refer to the Third Italy's model for "flexible specialization," in particular to be found in the Emilia Romagna, as a system for dealing with this. The well-organized cooperation between companies (the Italian industrial districts are formally sanctioned by the government) allows small and medium-sized companies to keep up with the competition in important and demanding market segments. In many cases, advanced design and rapid adaptation to customer demands can beat high-tech mass production. When looking closer at this – at its heart – the interorganizational model, one actually finds a frequent use of projects, even if that concept is hardly explicitly used in this context. The leading agents of the textile industry in Prato, the "impanatores," work like project managers, transforming the demand of international customers to production units. Temporary constellations of several small companies form a project team with the task to respond to a specific demand. When Manuel Castells (1996) approximately a decade later tried to describe the organization of the production system in what he calls "the network society," Piore and Sabel (1984) was still the main source.

The importance of the institutional context for the development of the Third Italy has gained a lot of attention. Djelic (1998) has shown that the U.S. management ideal of organizing large industrial companies did not get a foothold in Italy in the same way as, for example, it did in Germany and France. Porter (1990) is one of several who had the Italian districts in mind when arguing for the importance of cluster formation for economic development. Also, Putnam (1992) started from this point when discussing trust and the importance of social capital for, among other things, economic development. He contrasts this with the development in the United States, where in a later book he describes seeing a shrinking social capital in a society full of lonely people. Whatever the future may have to offer in this respect, it has been well established by empirical research, not least in the television industry, that "institutional thickness" (Amin and Thrift 1994), at least up to a certain point, is conducive to the development of a regional cluster or industrial district or other types of PNWs (Lutz et al. 2003) – and, in consequence, to projectification.

*Projects in a relational context: regional clusters and strategic networks*
In the spirit of Porter's (1990) thinking, several scholars have pointed to the importance of the surrounding system for the development of economic activities in general and of companies in particular (e.g. Malerba 2002; Geels 2004; Grabher 2004). Specific attention has been paid to the relationship between companies, research organizations, and local authorities (the so-called Triple Helix; see Etzkowitz and Leydesdorff 2000). Cluster maps have been drawn and different forms of support to existing clusters (including "wishful thinking" clusters without too much potential) have been developed (Ketels et al. 2006). For the sake of simplicity,

two ways of looking at the phenomena of clusters and districts can be noted.

According to one broad view, a considerable proportion of industrial companies belong to some kind of cluster, which could be anything from local density of a certain industry to genuine cooperation between companies and other organizations. The political system and the authorities can create opportunities for cooperation and dynamic development. Government agents can work as facilitators.

According to a second and more proactive as well as more specific perspective, there are possibilities to directly contribute to the growth of regional clusters. Consultants, authorities, and researchers actively seek to build a cluster dynamics. Government agents work as drivers in the process. Whether or not this leads to success is heavily discussed (e.g. Enright 2003; Andriani et al. 2005). Most research seems to show that regional clusters that have grown organically have been more successful than those that have been initiated by political authorities. It has also been pointed out that this policy has a tendency to cement certain patterns, for example, by contributing to traditional activities whereby old patterns are locked in (Grabher 1993; Isaksen 2003), although project ecologies, already mentioned, are currently assumed to constitute an environment that is less likely to be locked in (Grabher 2005).

Of all the different concepts related to this approach, regional clusters are no doubt the one that has had the greatest impact on researchers and even more on authorities and politicians. But to differentiate regional clusters from the other system phenomena is actually rather difficult and the definition of clusters in itself seems to be vague (Martin and Sunley 2003). In his famous book *The Competitive Advantage of Nations*, Michael Porter (1990) regarded clusters as an agglomeration of firms stemming from "functionally related industries." However, as time has passed, he seems to be emphasizing the location aspect more and more, and in a later publication the definition is as follows: "a cluster is a geographically proximate group of interconnected companies and associated institutions in a particular field, linked by commonalities and complementarities" (Porter 2000: 16). This slide in the definition of clusters appears to be unfortunate as other research (Malmberg and Power 2006) has shown that organizations in the local setting are less interrelated than suggested by Porter and policy makers. One problem is that regional clusters have reached the status of an ideal type and as such a persuasive theoretical construct badly suited for empirical tests and policy formulations. Malmberg and Power conclude by arguing for a greater degree of conceptual flexibility, although the cluster notion may be more appropriate the more the system is characterized not by an agglomeration of firms in functionally related industries but by actual interorganizational interaction.

Even economic geographers have started to question the spatial aspect of interaction between organizations. It seems that most interorganizational interactions do take place outside the borders of geographical clusters (Maskell et al. 2006). Companies, not least in the face of the Internet development, seem to establish trans-local relationships, and strategic networks tend to span different regions. Bathelt et al. (2004) used the concept of "global pipelines" to characterize these kinds of linkages that, often by necessity, complement the "local buzz" that is characteristic of clusters. The flexibility aspect of this mode is especially important when it comes to knowledge formation with the help of projects. To reduce the search costs in this process, it is common that professions and industries organize gatherings such as fairs, conventions, and similar "temporary clusters" (Maskell et al. 2006). The opening up of the cluster thinking is actually much in line with the ideas of networks. While network thinking is quite old, structural network analysis of interorganizational arrangements began three decades ago in the field of public administration in the United States (e.g. Provan 1983). And the Uppsala School on international business (Johanson and Vahlne 1977, 1990) started to publish articles on the subject close to 40 years ago. Researchers of business administration showed that many actors in a company had much deeper relations with suppliers and customers than with the top management of the company they formally represented (Axelsson and Easton 1992). Sometimes the deep relations between members of the network promote learning processes with implications for the future.

The strength of cluster and network thinking in general is that the "mysterious" entity of the company or the organization more generally is placed in a wider *relational* context; it is considered as linked to other organizational actors. It is, however, difficult to know whether there is a tendency toward more clusters or networks, or whether it is just another perspective of how to understand organization of economic activity (Grabher and Powell 2004). The answer to the quantitative aspect of this question depends entirely on how the different concepts are defined. It seems as if policy makers have a tendency to promote the rather broad definition resulting in an abundance of regional clusters. In Sweden, state agencies such as VINNOVA promote cluster relations and cluster thinking in an active way. The same is true for Germany, where both the federal and almost all regional state governments are actively engaged in fostering the development of regional clusters in a variety of industries, starting with the BioRegio contest in the mid 1990s in which several regions applied for funding from the federal government to support cluster development initiatives (Dohse 2000).

Network thinking makes the border between what organizations are and what markets are unclear; it is not least for this reason that economists consider interorganizational networks as a hybrid form mixing market and hierarchy (Williamson 1991; Ménard 2004), while most sociologists consider it an organizational form "beyond market and hierarchy" (Powell 1990). The companies in interorganizational networks are considered as more or less intimate collaborators although not freed from competitive elements (Sydow and Windeler 1998; Wolvén and Ekstedt 2004; Huxham and Vangen 2005). Such collaboration/competition relationships are also referred to as "coopetition" (Nalebuff and Brandenburger 1996; Bengtsson and Kock 2000). An increasing number of the companies seem to collaborate to compete in what are sometimes called not only strategic networks but also "constellations" (Gomes-Casseres 1996) or "alliance blocks" (Vanhaverbeke and Nooderhaven 2001). However, the way of looking at companies in these networks, constellations, or blocks is rather traditional. For instance, it is taken for granted that the company is a leading separate unit related to other entities, such as universities or research organizations in the field of biotechnology (Padgett and Powell 2012). Network thinking sometimes goes beyond this as it actually questions the hegemony of the firm as an organizational entity. Though actors in a firm may actually have stronger economic and social ties to other actors (individuals and organizations) outside the firm, this does not lead to dissolution but only to an opening up or blurring of organizational boundaries. Interorganizational projects may be considered on the one hand as an important means and outcome of this process – they help to cross organizational boundaries; and on the other, they are easier to initiate and implement if an organization is well embedded in a web of interorganizational relationships.

Even though clusters and networks and projects are related to each other, they are also different. Projects are generally formed to accomplish a certain task. The project is in general dissolved when the task is fulfilled; it is a temporary organization. In discussions about clusters and networks, it is often hard to find out if task-oriented action actually takes place, as the setting, the precondition for, and the outcome of interaction seem to be in focus. Sometimes it is difficult to know whether a description of a cluster actually is just a description of how to form a cluster. As stated earlier, some researchers have therefore tried to separate real clusters from cluster initiatives (Malmberg 2001), which seem to be what many authorities actually deal with. One way to test if a described cluster consists of more than empty rhetoric could be to find out if there are any ongoing projects among the cluster members. In consequence, these systems would be described as consisting of "networks in clusters" (Sydow and Lerch 2007), where projects are created from interorganizational relations and reproduce or transform these very relations.

Time is a crucial aspect of projects. Most projects can be described in terms of a life cycle with a specific time for starting and a specific time for finishing. More or less binding contracts concern time as well as the participants in a project. When it comes to clusters and networks, time and other parts of the relations remain quite open (Powell 1990). Periods of hibernation may be interrupted by periods of activity. It may be difficult to find out what part of a cluster or network is active and what the activity really consists of. In any case, regional clusters, industrial districts, innovation systems, and other kinds of networks, if compared to projects as temporary systems, should be seen as being more than temporary systems (Sydow and Windeler 1999). This is why – given a perspective that takes time seriously – fluid projects are likely to be embedded in more stable contexts with comparatively permanent structures.

Many interorganizational projects are formed in the context of a relational system, more precisely in networks or clusters. Combining the social context embedded in a system with the well-organized action performed by projects has advantages. Social relationships and common identities offered by clusters or networks in an industry or a local area are likely to lead to lower search costs for many transactions. In addition, they may help stabilize relationships, that is, foster the occurrence repeated ties. In some industries and in some regions, ties are getting so strong that one could talk about a network culture, such as that in the construction sector or those in particular areas such as Gnosjö (which is a well-known network example in a prosperous area in southern Sweden). The project and its members are working in a context of strong, but often informal, institutions. Its members are guided on how to act in specific situations by clear expectations and mutual obligations. The formal or informal rules and roles (i.e. of professional) make interaction smooth and predictable. This kind of strong social capital facilitates efficiency, but it could sometimes also hamper renewal and development. Project networks are illustrated in the next section and also in Chapter 4.

*A project network in the Germany television industry*
Sectors in which PNWs dominate are organized in a variety of ways. Production networks in the television industry tend be quite diverse, depending not only on the content to be produced. While the production of news is generally still an in-house affair (especially in the world of public channels), documentaries and TV movies are produced by smaller and larger networks of independent companies, including the providers of artistic and technical services (e.g. post-production, studio facilities, catering). These latter networks are often strategically led by a production company, mostly in close collaboration with a representative of the television channel that commissions the program. While the production of these latter types of content clearly resembles PNWs, the production of soap operas – like news – is significantly more integrated. One reason is that the division of work is even more extreme. More important, the production of soap operas, at least in the German television industry, is still a profitable business with significantly less economic risks than the production of documentaries and TV movies. Major production firms, often a part of large media groups such as Bertelsmann, tend to keep the production of soaps in-house. Nevertheless, these production firms also cooperate with some external providers of artistic and technical services, so that the label of a PNW may still be appropriate. While the managerial challenges and the implications of this organizational form for work and institutions are discussed later, it should be mentioned here that this form of value creation relies heavily on an institutional context that allows the outsourcing of many activities into a network of partners with whom the production firm collaborates on a project-to-project basis.

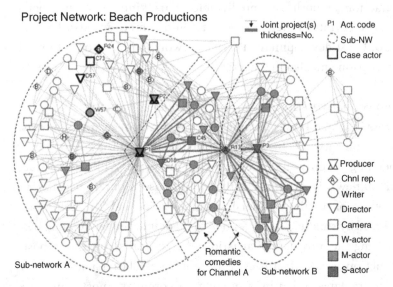

FIGURE 2.5. The project network of Beach Production. (Source: Sydow and Manning 2004.)

Beach Production (pseudonym), one of the largest film and tele-vision production firms in Germany, leads one important PNW. Taking into account only the ties to channel editors, directors, writers, camera operators, and main actors (not to the many providers of artistic and technical services), Figure 2.5 illustrates the complex network of relationships this firm or, more exactly, three producers of this firm have developed over a period of six years – and are orches-trating today.

Beach Production, without doubt a PBO itself, organizes the production of TV movies in close collaboration with major television channels (in this case, public channels, which still have a significant share of the German TV market) in PNWs. These networks are as much the outcome as the means of organizing projects (Sydow and Windeler 1999). As indicated, PNWs in this industry or field heavily rely on resources provided by the institutional environment in the region. What may be called a "media region" (Lutz et al. 2003) is composed of numerous institutions including universities and media schools (for the supply of qualified labor), professional associations (for lobbying), state agencies (for providing finance), fairs, festivals, and other temporary settings (for exchange of project ideas and information about employment opportunities).

## 2.4. CHANGES WITHIN AND BETWEEN TEMPORARY FORMS OF ORGANIZATION

By providing insights into the historical development of project-based forms of organizing in general and the emergences of PBOs, PSOs, and PWNs in particular, we have already touched on the question of organizational change: not only from permanent organizations to PSOs but also from PBOs to PNWs – if we switch from considering the development of a single organization to that of a whole network.

The study by Söderlund and Tell (2009) is of particular interest in this context since it depicts projectification processes within an organization – ASEA/ABB – over a long period of time, including changes from one archetype to another. The study outlines that not only does projectification create tension in our societies, it also creates challenges within organizations. In short, the study shows how the company developed from a PSO in a form that the authors call the epoch of embedded projects to a different kind of PSO as it entered an internationalization effort (or epoch), to a PBO, which they refer to as the epoch of complex turnkey projects, and finally an epoch of complex and financed turnkey projects. This change of business models is important for several reasons. It demonstrates that an organization is not stuck forever in a particular form of temporary organizing – which we call archetypes – and that the evolutionary aspects of projectification create challenges and tensions in relation to the society or the field in which organizations operate. In a sense, the results indicate that ABB never gets locked in to a business model but instead adapts to changes in market and technical complexities. Part of that adaptation involves what has been called "project competence" by the authors. The study also contributes to one of the messages of this book, which is that Project Society will most likely not be an end point but in fact an era in which future transformations will appear.

## 2.5.   PROJECTIFICATION OF INDUSTRIES AND FIELDS

PBOs, PSOs, and PNWs are organizational archetypes that are expressions as well as drivers of the ongoing projectification process in society. In consequence of this process, entire industries (e.g. construction and consulting) or regions (e.g. media regions) and more generally "organizational fields" (DiMaggio and Powell 1983) become projectified. At the same time, as argued earlier, a broad range of complementary and more permanent institutions makes it possible that a firm, an industry, or a region can survive even when dominated by temporary forms of organizing.

Organizational fields, sometimes also referred to as inter-organizational or institutional fields, consist of organizations that "in the aggregate, constitute a recognized area of institutional life: key suppliers, resource and product consumers, regulatory agencies, and other organizations that produce similar services or products" (DiMaggio and Powell 1983: 148). Although similar to the concept of industry, this term emphasizes the importance of cultural norms, subjective perceptions, and institutionalized practices rather than the relevance of the number of competitors and customers, the height of entry/exit barriers, or other aspects of market structure (cf. Porter 1980). In addition, the field concept highlights the role of regulatory agencies, trade and professional associations, and other organizations that are likely to contribute to the institutionalization of the field. What is particularly important, the concept is rather open and can thus be applied to any industry or region or combination thereof, allowing us to contextualize projects beyond PBOs, PSOs, and PNWs as organizational archetypes of project-based organizing.

In the course of projectification processes, temporary forms of organizing – including our three archetypes – become dominant in certain fields, as in the media regions mentioned earlier. With good reason, such fields are then characterized as either "project ecologies"

(Grabher 2004) or "project arenas" (Overtrup 2006). While these two concepts emphasize the relatedness of projects in time and space, they do not specify exactly how project *activities* are governed. Our three archetypes, by contrast, go one step further and specify in the cases of PBOs and PSOs the organizational or in the case of PNWs the network form of governance. While a governance perspective is quite informative, it has to be acknowledged that the study of particular formal governance structures is not sufficient to explain what is actually going on in projects as temporary systems. For this reason, we argue (in Chapter 6) that a process or practice perspective should supplement the analysis of governance structures.

This chapter has shown how projectification has not only been increasing during the past decades and how it continues to increase but also the forms projectification takes and how the character of projectification is changing. We have also touched on several aspects of how this is changing our markets and our companies or other types of organizations, the way work is done, and ultimately the institutions governing our societies. In the coming chapters, we analyze more deeply how management and work are reshaped in the era of projectification. Chapter 3 on management points to the specific challenges and benefits that projectification implies for managerial responsibilities, while Chapter 4 on work takes the perspective of what happens with employees and their work environment when projectification increases.

# 3 Managing in Project Society

Projectification has deeply transformed management practices in firms and in other types of organizations. The contexts have been changing and so have the ways managers today think about managing and the contexts for management. Project Society evolution has transformed the traditional institutions for managerial work. These traditional institutions are by no means homogenous; however, the transformations in the making are shaping new traditions and new ways of thinking. These transformations combine two separate but related trends:

(1) *An evolution of managerial practices and managerial models within projects.* First was the rationalization from an informal managerial art (see e.g. Lenfle and Loch 2010 and Lenfle 2011 on the Manhattan project) to the implementation of the operations management toolbox in the 1950s and 1960s, then a second transition since the 1980s to a more organizational- and strategic-oriented perspective. The first trend was clearly supported by the engineering professional communities. The more recent trends were clearly driven by the academic community's influence on organizations, introducing, for instance, cultural perspectives on management (Jönsson and Lundin 1977), and on projects as a means for management, which has been called management by projects (Gareis 1990), strategic project management (Morris and Jamieson 2004; Shenhar 2004; Artto et al. 2008), Patanakul and Shenhar 2011), or stakeholder management (Newcombe 2003; Littau et al. 2010). Eventually, this evolution led by the academic community shaped the International Research Network on Organizing by Projects (IRNOP) begun by a group of researchers in Umeå, Sweden.

The network was initiated by Rolf A. Lundin and colleagues in 1994 and has grown since then.

(2) *An evolution of the embodiment of project management in the management of organizations and other social systems, as the transition from managing a single project to management of projects* (Morris 2013). Peter Morris's (1994) book and "Pilotage de projets et entreprises" (Giard and Midler 1993) in France and an article from Lundin and Söderholm (1995) constitute landmarks in this domain. Such a perspective enlarges the inside project perspective to the project definition phase, in interaction with the firm strategy and business (Morris 1994; Artto et al. 2008; Söderlund and Tell 2009, 2011). It focuses on characterizing organizational capabilities to handle a multiproject perspective within an organization: developments regarding portfolio management (Cooper et al. 1999; Petit 2012) to allocate resources within projects, the spread of program management (Maylor et al. 2006) for better multiproject coordination, a focus on organizational learning within and through projects (Lundin and Midler 1998; Brady and Davies 2004; Schüßler et al. 2012; Midler 2013), and the implementation of project management offices (Hobbs et al. 2008).

This chapter addresses these two levels of analysis. We first focus on the management practices within the projects, although, in the real world, projects are contextually embedded in so-called permanent organizations or more complex organizational arrangements. We then address this contextual embeddedness by separate discussions on the project-based organization (PBO) context with its rather loose ties to permanent organizations, the project-supported organization (PSO) context with its intriguing mixture of permanent and project organizations, and the project network (PNW) context with its temporary vitalization of all kinds of organizations and/or individuals in a specific effort. For each form or context, we focus on the managerial dilemmas that have to be addressed and illustrate those dilemmas with case studies.

### 3.1.   PROJECT MANAGEMENT FROM THE INSIDE: AN ARCHETYPAL CHARACTERIZATION

In the beginning, a project is often just an idea, a target, a slogan. The project management mission is to transform this uncertain, tenuous, and fuzzy initial identity into a clear tangible reality. It is defined with more or less detail as the responsibility for conducting all operations necessary for the study, development, and implementation from this initial point occurs. We characterize the project management role by two key components: the development and embodiment of the identity of the project and the management of its convergence toward the target. Then we discuss the role of management in the different phases of the development of a project as well as project management competence.

### *The project organization: a social incarnation of the project*

The originality of project management is that it embodies the identity of the project, the entire project, and nothing but the project. It is created with the explicit statement of the target; it evolves with the development of formal and informal rules; it ends with its completion or abandonment. Stopping a project before completion is not to be seen as a failure of project management but as a result of the analysis of the feasibility of the initial idea that is opening up a possible redefinition of the initial target.

Projects can involve a small or a large number of actors. The contributions of these actors are required to fulfill specific tasks and generally occur at a given phase. The project management mission however, is not the success of a fraction of the project, but the result of all interventions and the integration of the overall contribution to build up the identity of the project in accordance with the initial goal. Failure in a part of the project is a failure for the entire project and for project management, but a success of only a portion of the project is not a success for project management. As has been frequently noted, successful projects have a lot of parents, but unsuccessful ones are blamed only on project management.

So, management's mission has an extensively large scope, compared to the responsibility of the other contributors in the projects. However, it is at the same time narrower because it limits its perspective to the project. Project management's goal is to create focus and identification as well as a priority for the project's specific goal and end, whereas every contributor legitimately pursues other perspectives such as developing his or her own expertise, building assets that will be exploited later, and implementing a long-term strategy for a firm.

*Managing the project convergence*

From its early days, academic literature on projects emphasized the temporal framing of the project creation process, from the fuzzy and uncertain target to a precise reality. In their paper about decision making in complex development programs, which has been ignored by mainstream project management research until recently (see Brady et al. 2012 for a fuller analysis), Klein and Meckling (1958) contrast the optimization view of an ideal type, Mr. Optimizer, who at the start of the project examines all possible paths and solutions and decides on a single one, with that of another ideal type, Mr. Skeptic, who says that not enough is yet known to make a sensible choice about which path will lead to the right solution. Klein and Meckling argue that in the early phase of the development program, there have to be experiments on a trial-and-error basis, enabling learning to take place to create knowledge that can lead to better-informed decision making about which paths to follow and which to abandon in pursuit of the project goals.

In a similar way, Midler (1993, 1995) proposes defining project convergence as a dual process of learning about and deciding on the project. These two processes are intertwined: decisions need to be based on knowledge to be relevant; on the other hand, learning depends on decisions (choosing a scenario to be explored, spending budget, time spent in prototyping, market studies, etc). Figure 3.1 depicts this understanding of a project. The dotted line represents

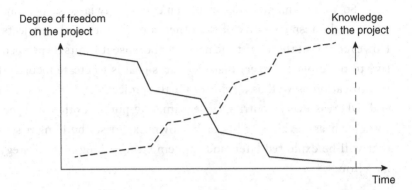

FIGURE 3.1. The progression of projects as a dual learning and decision diachronic process. (Source: Midler 1993:18, 1995.)

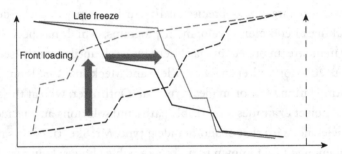

FIGURE 3.2. The concurrent project strategy. (Source: Midler 1993: 101, 1995.)

knowledge accumulated during the progression of the project. With the solid line, the decision curve represents the remaining degrees of freedom available to decide on the project. They diminish as the freeze of the project variables leads to irreversibility. Managing the project convergence appears as simultaneously increasing the knowledge on the project (the dotted line) while progressively freezing the project options.

On this understanding, Mr. Skeptic's strategy appears as a learn early–freeze late choice (Figure 3.2), what was later systematized as a concurrent exploration/concurrent engineering development strategy (Midler 1993; Lenfle 2011).

Such a strategy creates a project that splits its dynamics into three contrasting phases: the upstream phase, the project-freezing phase, and the implementation phase.

In the *upstream phase*, the problem is to explore the possible scenarios and enhance the quality of these studies (in particular by involving downstream actors) and to "bump" up the curve of knowledge about the project and improve the relevance of the freezing decision. A no-go decision should happen at the end of this phase.

During the second phase, the *project-freezing phase*, creativity and optimality are no longer the issue; realism is needed to secure the implementation of the project. Ideally, such a freeze should come as late as possible: it is better to delay these commitments, for both purely financial capital reasons and the ability to react to unforeseen events. The weakest link in a project is the overall performance: if a single detail starts to diverge, it is useless to have effectively frozen the rest of the project design. Hence, the importance at this level is the completeness of control on all the parts of the project.

The last phase is the *implementation phase*. Delay becomes the structuring variable. As a result of the financial pressure on the project, when the project budget is almost spent, the end is expected to be reached as soon as possible to get the value from the completed project. An additional factor is the obsolescence phenomenon if there are severe time-to-market constraints on the project (Bower and Hout 1988; Brown and Eisenhardt 1998): new product obsolescence does not begin at the commercial launching, but at the freezing phase, as soon as the product specifications are defined and the technology choices are set. The different imperatives driving the project through its life cycle mean that the project management approach varies greatly across the different project phases.

### Managing the project in the upstream phase

Five key issues structure project management in the upstream phase: formulating the project strategy, setting the managerial specification of the project, recruiting and involving participants, stimulating creativity, frontloading potential problems, and identifying risks.

In the first instrumental view of project management, projects are supposed to implement a clear initial target, formulated by the project's client. The project role is to "do the project right." This naïve vision has been strongly and deeply challenged by many academics who emphasize the importance of the upstream phase to define the project strategy and provide key momentum for the project. Projects are target oriented, but these targets generally have to be settled in the upstream phase. The problem is not only to do the project right but also to define the right project (Cooke-Davis 2004). Project literature has emphasized this strategic dimension of projects (Morris and Jamieson 2004; Shenhar 2004; Artto et al. 2008; Morris 2013) and the importance of the strategic vision formulation in the upstream phase (Kim and Wilemon 2002), project meaning (Verganti 2009), or sense-making (Weick 1995) of the upstream project management activity (Keller 1992).

The reason behind the importance of this strategy formulation is that the traditional single "project client" category is an over-simplistic representation of the real actors identified by the project definition. The social context of the project is complex and unstable, at least in our contemporary world. The formal economic client or "owner" of the project is far from being the only social force to be involved and therefore to evaluate and react to project planning and implementation, as we learn from the changes in project field in practice over the years (cf. Engwall 1995). This is particularly true for megaprojects, which involve a variety of public authorities (local, national, or international) as well as many private contributors (Flyvbjerg et al. 2003b; Flyvbjerg 2014). This has led to the development of ongoing research domains on project stakeholder involvement management (Newcombe 2003; Bourne and Walker 2005; Littau et al. 2010; Eskerod and Jepsen 2013) and project governance definition (Miller and Hobbs 2005; Crawford et al. 2008; Müller 2011).

The second act of project management is usually the definition of methods that will govern its implementation, the project managerial specifications, in line with the project strategy. Projects generally gather people from different professions, firms, statuses, or nationalities to contribute to a collective original achievement. Defining the governance structure and the relationships between the various actors is therefore a preliminary condition to settle the project's organizational identity.

The third mission is recruitment and mobilization of the project. Project managers initially act as "recruiting sergeants" for the project, ensuring that the various businesses allocate to it sufficient and relevant personnel in a timely manner. This role is even more important now that modern approaches involve an enrichment of a project's upstream phases, while companies naturally tend to mobilize all resources on downstream phases, where problems are more concrete and critical.

One of the fundamental roles of project managers is to stimulate exploration (Lenfle 2011, 2014) and creativity (Amabile et al. 1996; Mumford et al. 2002; Ordanini et al. 2008), thereby transcending existing solutions (thinking "out of the box") to enhance the performance of the project or even the organization. If the early phase does not leave a place to explore new ambitions, there will certainly not be space for such thinking afterward. During the upstream phase of projects, the role of project management is to encourage and guide creative ways depending on the specific program for which it is responsible. As a manager of an automotive project stated, "Our role is to create challenged overruns" (Midler 1993).

Risk anticipation and problem frontloading (Clark and Fujimoto 1991) make up the necessary hard side of creativity and voluntarism. It is important to identify any issues early in the project life cycle so that they can be resolved as soon as possible rather than hiding beneath the surface until the implementation phase, when they become critical problems even if not crises (Ericksen and Dyer 2004). Many authors have emphasized the importance of project leadership to create a social context that encourages transparent relations between project team members to address problems (Barzac et al. 1989; Lindgren and Packendorff 2009; Tyssen et al. 2013).

London's Heathrow Airport Terminal 5 (T5) project provides an interesting example of an attempt to create an atmosphere within the project that encourages this early surfacing of problems with the aim of solving them collectively. The T5 project was one of Europe's largest and most complex projects. In a world where megaprojects (Flyvbjerg et al. 2003a) – such as Wembley Stadium, the Millennium Dome, the Channel Tunnel, and major airport developments such as Denver International, Berlin's Willy Brandt, and Paris's Charles de Gaulle – are usually delivered very late and over budget, T5 stands out as a major success story as it was completed within budget and on schedule. The leadership of Sir John Egan, the CEO of BAA (formerly the British Airports Authority) during most of the 1990s, was a significant factor. Egan recognized that by learning from the experiences of other industries and applying these ideas, practices, and technologies, BAA could improve its own project processes. He oversaw the development of a strong internal capability in the management of projects and programs in the buildup to T5, which had twin aims – for BAA to become the best client to the construction industry and to develop an approach that would enable it to successfully complete T5.

One of BAA's main roles in the T5 project was to create an environment within which members of integrated project teams were able to create innovative solutions by working with the client as a partner. The development of an innovative kind of contract embodied in artifacts such as the "T5 Handbook" and the "T5 Agreement" created the processes required to deliver the T5 project. However, it became clear during implementation that effective integrated teamwork depended on fostering new types of behavior to enable suppliers to work together with the client to solve problems and to create innovative solutions. BAA made continuous efforts to break with traditional practices by reinforcing and rewarding team-based behaviors and fostering a culture of learning among suppliers

(Davies et al. 2009; Brady and Davies 2011). These behaviors were based on "soft" skills such as trust and cooperation required to work constructively on the project, rather than the "hard" skills of traditional contracting based on the commercial estimation of risks and making legal claims when problems arise. Toward this end, BAA put in place not only a project governance structure but also a change program with specialist change consultants and introduced a T5 newspaper, poster campaigns, and other measures to continually reinvigorate and reinforce the learning culture and create a sense of identity for the T5 project that transcended individual firm allegiance (for a critical account of the popular distinction between hard and soft skills, see Gustavsson and Hallin 2014).

Addressing all such issues simultaneously appears as the difficult challenge of upstream project management: they are in many ways contradictory. How can you mobilize people when uncertainty is high? How can you call for new ambitions and deal with risk anticipation? The upstream phase "must bear the chaos, and even create one" (project manager of a large process unit). In such a context, project management leadership appears contradictory to the traditional analytical and instrumental project approach. Many studies (e.g. Amabile et al. 2004; Mumford et al. 2002; Thamhain 2004; Slevin and Pinto 2007) suggest that in this phase both task-oriented and relationship-oriented actions are needed. We emphasize the following three components as key managerial capabilities for the upstream project phase:

(1) *The mobilization of networks.* The project network is a central concept in project management (Obstfeld 2005). Major projects are open systems, which transcend organizational as well as professional frontiers and can be affected by various events or actors who are well outside the scope of the formal procedures of the organization. This network capability can be analyzed as an important component of the project management "weight" (Clark and Wheelwright 1992), alongside the formal position and governance structure.

(2) *The symbolic management of projects.* Analytical management is almost irrelevant in this upstream phase. The vision and strategy have to be settled, while the processes to achieve them are still uncertain (Barckzak and Wilemon 1989; Midler 1993; Kotter 2001). Project managers are often talented communicators, wielding the formula or image to print messages and organizing conventions to convince and mobilize the project team. What may appear for technically oriented project management to be a communication gadget is actually the acknowledgment of the ownership of and buy-in to the project-by-project stakeholders – a capability that has been proven extremely effective in professional worlds such as advertising and design (Verganti 2009).

The art of using communication symbols can also apply not only to characterize the content of the project but also to disseminate the principles of management that are desired for its realization. Jolivet and Navarre (1993) and Jolivet (2003) formalized meta-rules as high-level rules to produce rules in large and complex projects. Such meta-rules substitute for overly detailed control and empower decentralized coordination that fits with the uncertainty and evolutionary nature of such projects. Renault's Logan project is a good example of how such meta-rules management can frame a fast-growing development of a global project. Six meta-rules were enforced by the heavyweight program management team: continuous exploration of new market opportunities; identification of specific values to be highlighted in the new market; permanent cost reduction priority; speed of execution; fast and flexible industrial investments to test new market robustness; and opportunistic, ex post facto use of the program's successes to take advantage of the often unforeseen circumstances characterizing the global markets (Midler 2013).

(3) *The material dimension of project management: managing project space and physical artefacts.* In the early 1990s, in the automotive as well as in the aerospace industries, project co-location was a powerful management strategy implemented by heavyweight project managers to enforce the project-specific identity among the various professional involved in the project (Midler 1995; Garel 1996).

Previously, the geography of the organization was dictated by the functional departments: product engineering building, process engineering, purchase and marketing offices, plant, and so on. The physical separation matched with the formal hierarchical organization to control cross-department relations. The project processes then had to find the difficult way through the various institutional and physical frontiers. Project colocation reinforced the social identity of the project and helped the deep communication on tacit knowledge (Nonaka 1994) of the shared understanding of the project vision and the transparency of relations. It weakened the hierarchical control of the departments on the different professionals involved in the project and encouraged faster decision making.

Physical proximity by itself is not sufficient to induce an effective dialogue between various professionals involved in a creative process. "Boundary objects" (Star and Griesemer 1989) more often than not enable the interactions between different social worlds or thought worlds (Leonard-Barton 1995; Dougherty 1992; Carlile 2002), represented in, for instance, a multidisciplinary design team. Such objects are often a key vector to communicate with other members of the organization or even across the organization's boundaries with users, customers, or suppliers. They allow an extensive dialogue between the specialists involved by helping in the clarification of the differences and the dependencies across the specific disciplines.

Therefore, mockups, demonstrators, prototypes, simulation tools, or more generally "intermediary objects" (Jeantet 1996) are important project management tools to help innovative ideas emerge (Junginger 2008; Mahmoud-Jouini et al. 2014) and to frontload problem and risk detection (Thomke 1998).

### Managing the project in the freezing phase

While the role of project management in the first phase is to open debates and call for out of the box creativity, it changes radically into a freezing role in the second phase. Project management's duty is then to "close debates." Modern principles such as concurrent engineering and agile development aim at ensuring convergence by "progressive focusing," while the traditional approach is to set up in a sequential fashion the different variables (functional specification first followed by technical product and process specification, then industrialization and marketing). Modern project principles integrate these variables at each step, but obviously with gradually more precise and certain scope. Progression through successive iterations stabilizes assumption frames within which detailed studies can be conducted.

This period is a socially difficult one for project management. Hard trade-offs are often mandatory to secure project feasibility. On the one hand, these trade-offs can contradict the prior objectives that were put forward to create mobilization as out of the box explorations from the team. Such denial can undermine the project manager's credibility. On the other hand, project managers more often than not have conflicts in steering committees with more senior levels, which, because they are aware of strategic opportunities or changes in the project environment, suggest new avenues to explore or challenge some options. The existence of a strong project actor to provide the continuity of involvement of project stakeholders in governance processes is then essential to rebut the perceived destabilizing effects of such deviations on the project's progress.

Once the project is stabilized, the project team must typically provide memory and continuity for the development process. It is here when, with the help of support services, the successive stages are based on contractual commitments and tracking devices. The use of the traditional project management toolbox (planning, milestones, budgets, risks) is an important way to decentralize and secure responsibilities. A project bureaucracy seems to be unavoidable, in particular in contracting, although in some settings (such as some parts of the television industry) formal contracts are signed after project delivery.

**The project bureaucracy.** This is the traditional core role of project management – maintaining methodologies and processes for reporting and decision making on the project. Here, the role of project management is not to intervene directly but to establish and maintain the process that directs the decision-making processes of the participants, within the project team as well as with the project stakeholders. Methodology, together with the contracting, is the main lever for locking phase of projects.

**Formal contracting.** Neither the registry of project bureaucracy nor the direct action of project management is sufficient. Literature on project leadership emphasizes the importance of empowering people on their contribution to the project (Pinto et al. 1998). "I need to rely on my project actors, not consulted people" says a heavyweight project manager in the auto industry (Midler 1993: 39).This emphasis on responsibility coming first is the essence of the role of project managers, which is to leverage the global constraint of objective quality-cost-delivery of the project to all people who contribute. From this point of view, all analytical methods, devices, and transversal dialogues are in themselves no guarantee. They may even have inflationary effects such as resulting in a list of problems getting longer instead of diminishing. Or they may even result in disempowerment effects, whereby respecting the procedures to the letter becomes the target instead of meeting the actual project target.

Contracting is obviously also essential to stabilize the compromises that have been determined; however, it also proves fruitful in the upstream phase to enrich the quality of investigations. As one project manager remarked, "When personally involved upstream, an individual pays attention to all the terms of this contract and has the opportunity to discover problems that might otherwise be missed at this level" (Midler 1993: 103).

*Managing the project in the implementation phase*
In the implementation phase, project management is once again deeply transformed. This phase fits the general description of what project managers are supposed to do on a daily basis. This is where the manager starts managing by giving orders and handling disturbances. The project manager now acts as a firefighter. During this phase, "the

devil is in the detail." The project team is no longer to contribute to hypothetical gains that could further improve the equation of the project. Rather, it mobilizes the countless seemingly trivial reasons that could yet result in significant losses. Its role is thus to maximize the speed loop responsiveness, to be an efficient troubleshooting structure. In this context, commando-style management often becomes an imperative. People-oriented management gives way to task-oriented management; quick decision-making capacity becomes paramount, even if an excessive hands-on style can risk disempowering people involved in project.

The issue here is that what a project manager has to do to successfully manage a project is over and above what is included in the typical, rather technical approaches to project management that appear in guidebooks and manuals. The concepts of necessary and sufficient conditions illustrate this: whereas it might be necessary to have a process that is followed and actions that are certified, these are not sufficient to ensure success. It is what is *not* written down in these methods and procedures that a project manager has learned through experience that can make the difference between success and failure of a project – factors such as judgment about when to let things drift and when to clamp down, and so on. The skill to handle such exceptions to the methods and procedures becomes one of the critical skills of project management (see Snickare 2012).

### Project management competence: from professional expertise to collective capability

We conclude this analysis by addressing the question of the project management competence. For years, we saw the development of the methodological corpus of project management and a significant effort from professional associations such as the Project Management Institute (PMI) and the International Project Management Association (IPMA) to professionalize project management and integrate the knowledge of these methods in their certification processes. The corpus first focused on rational control of the iron triangle (costs, time, and quality of the project delivery); then, in the past two decades, it has progressively incorporated soft skills such as leadership capacity, strategic analysis, and stakeholder management. The academic community has played an important role in this change. The "instrumental approach" was still heavily supported by the professional academic business and engineering communities involved in the project field in the late 1980s and 1990s. The creation of the IRNOP network in 1994, in line with the emergence of "temporary organization" (Lundin and Packendorff 1994) as a concept, is surely an important landmark in this enlargement of project management as a professional and scholarly field that has integrated insights from management and organization research (Kreiner 1995; Davies and Brady 2000; Turner and Müller 2003; Sydow et al. 2004; Davies and Hobday 2005; Schüßler et al. 2012; Lundin and Hällgren 2014).

The previous section clearly demonstrates that such competencies have their role in project management. At the same time, however, this development shows how project capability is larger than project manager professional expertise, for two main reasons.

First, we saw in the previous section how a project manager's competence evolves during the life cycle of the project, from being an initially creative and proactive strategist who transforms into a realistic and careful manager, then into a firefighter as problems arise. Such adaptability is rare in the same professional; nevertheless, changing project managers along the way to specialize them on the specific leadership style is not an effective answer. The convergence of a project depends on the effectiveness of cumulative learning resulting from consistency in engagements within an organization. Therefore, turnover in project teams generally creates discontinuity, subsequently leading to drifts in project results (Fizel and D'Itry 1997). It is generally accepted that a variety of management styles within the team composition is a better answer to cover the different registers of its mission.

The second specificity is the context of project management competence. Several characteristics of project management capacity appear as highly contextual to the project domain: the strategic vision formulation is highly dependent on deep contextual knowledge of the project field. An excellent project manager for construction would probably be a disastrous one for an aerospace or pharmaceutical project, and vice versa. Project management needs to be hands-on with respect to the technical aspects of the project, and the relative importance of institutional contexts has to be taken into account in project organizing (e.g. is detailed reporting a useless time- and resource-consuming burden or a key success factor of the project?).

Project management in consequence appears more as an *organizational capability* than an individual competence (Davies and Brady 2000). The classical metaphor of an orchestra can be put forward in this perspective. The conductor is surely useful to help an orchestra achieve good music, but no conductor could succeed with a group of expert musicians who has not already constituted an orchestra, which means that each expert musician has already learned to play together with others. And a good conductor for romantic music is not always appropriate for baroque music.

Again, the academic community had an important role in the 1990s to develop this larger perspective. Concepts such as the management of projects rather than project management (Morris 1994), projectification (Midler 1995), CoPS (Miller et al. 1995; Hobday 1998), project business (Artto and Wikström 2005; Davies and Hobday 2005), and project networks (Jones 1996; Windeler and Sydow 2001; Manning 2010) are academic landmarks in this growing research field, all having implications for what managing projects as an organizational or collective capability is supposed to mean.

Defining project management as a collective capability implies analyzing how project management is embedded and distributed in the project context. To clarify the diverse challenges for project management and, in particular, to implement this organizational capability approach, we need first to characterize the context of the project. We schematize the variety of possible contexts through three types that should be well known by now: PBOs, PSOs, and PNWs. Then, we analyze how project and context are articulated in each archetype. The notion of "projectification" (Midler 1995) does not only mean that firms or other types of organizations perform projects (which they always do) but also mean that the processes, structures, or systems of the so-called permanent organization have been transformed to better embed and sustain the collective project capability. This means that on the one side we analyze how projects are managed in each context. On the other side, we outline how context is managed because of the intrusiveness of the project problematic. We focus this analysis on three variables: the business model, the governance, and the management of human resources. Such analysis reveals projectification dilemmas that are specific to each context.

### 3.2. MANAGING PROJECTS IN A PBO CONTEXT

The PBO is a natural organizational context in which projectification has been deeply intrusive, affecting basically all important managerial issues. The failure in projects must thus be analyzed as a consequence of such projectified organization settings. Winch (2013) analyzes the escalation in budgets within major projects and finds that whereas the engineering management perspective has focused on technical failings, more relevant and efficient explications to project performance are to be looked for in organizational processes and strategy formulation. This is what we do.

### The contextualized project management in PBOs

*At the business model level*, projects are central. Projects (or rather the results of project work) are sold to clients (owners) and hence generate the turnover of the (contractor) organization on a market. The construction sector and industries producing complex products and systems (CoPS) are typical of such a situation. But the project market is quite different from product markets because actors' commitment can only be founded on expectations or promises; in product markets, the customer can more easily appreciate the product before buying it. Three additional features are important.

First, the contractual arrangement takes the lead over more procedural settings for project management. Team building, solidarity within the group of project participants, "teamwork quality" (Hoegl and Gemuenden 2001), and so forth are more of an inside organization notion than a commercial relation between the client and the supplier of the project. The prospect of a juridical conflict at the end of the project for perceived gaps between promises and deliveries is rather common (in big international construction projects, the provision for legal actions is often about 30 percent of the contract).

During the long process of preparing for T5, BAA, the owner and client, recognized that existing construction industry practices and project management could not cope with the complexity, scale, and risk associated with the project. A radically new approach was required to manage the T5 project. In its preparation for T5, BAA carried out systematic case study research between 2000 and 2002 of every major UK construction project costing more than £1bn undertaken during the previous 10 years and every international airport opened during the previous 15 years. This benchmarking analysis found that no UK construction project had successfully delivered on time, within budget, and to the quality standards originally determined in the contract. Few projects had good safety records. Based on its study of 12 major airport program, BAA concluded that without a radically different approach, the T5 project would cost an additional £1bn more than was affordable, would be two years late, and would result in at least six fatalities.

The BAA study specifically identified two areas that contributed to the poor performance of megaprojects: the lack of collaboration among project partners and the client's reluctance to assume responsibility for project risk (Davies et al. 2009; Brady and Davies 2011). The study found that transferring the risk onto the contractor offered no real protection for the client, because the client is always ultimately accountable for cost, time, quality, and safety. BAA recognized that the only way it could achieve the desired outcome on a major project such as T5 was to change the rules of the game by establishing a new type of partnership based on the T5 Agreement mentioned earlier. BAA created a breakthrough in project management by recombining a variety of business techniques and management practices already found in other industries (Hargadon 1998, 2003). Those responsible for implementing the new approach faced the challenge of overcoming the construction industry's traditional resistance to change and reluctance to embrace new ideas from other industries.

BAA's main role in the T5 project was to create an environment within which members of integrated project teams were able to create innovative solutions by working with the client as a partner. BAA had to make continuous efforts to break with traditional practices by reinforcing and rewarding team-based behaviors and fostering a culture of learning among suppliers. These behaviors were based on trust and cooperation and required working constructively on the project. Although the T5 Handbook and T5 Agreement created the useful processes for delivering T5, it soon became clear during project execution that the effective implementation of the T5 approach could not be accomplished without radical changes in the behavior and mind-sets of suppliers to the project. BAA had to embark on a network-oriented change program of almost an industry-wide scale to overcome traditional construction practices and behaviors that had been in place for many decades.

Second, this context emphasizes the importance of accountability in project decisions. The issue of justification is of major importance in contractual relations, taking into account the possibility of legal actions. This creates acceptance for project bureaucracy, not because of its efficiency in relation to management performance but because of its importance in case of legal conflicts – just as a marriage contract is not created to make a happy marriage but to help conciliation in case of divorce. This is particularly the case when the client of the project is a public authority and needs to prove that it did not make unethical decisions that violated the economic pure competition norms. However, it should be noted that most of the empirical research on PBOs is based on the private sector and concerned with paying customers; the general ideas also apply to the public sector, however. To put it simply, setups in public offices are very similar to those in the private sector. Essentially, what PBOs do is deliver project results, whether their clients are in the private or public sector. That is their one and only *raison d'être*.

Third, the initial contract creates a key stable point for commitments. It is a useful tool for project management to motivate all participants; however, it sets irreversible limits when the knowledge about the project is minimal. Such an anticipated freeze is particularly problematic when the project has a significant exploratory dimension: all changes from the initial (uncertain) plan will be analyzed not as necessary learning but as uncontrolled project management drifts.

Such a situation leads to risk-averse behavior from both the client and the contractor, which limits innovation possibilities. Construction is characterized as a relatively uninnovative sector, which is often analyzed in literature as the "renewal paradox" (Ekstedt et al. 1999: 7): whereas projects are supposed to be able to take into account the singularities of unique situations in uncertain contexts, the PBO projects typical in construction usually do not take such adaptation opportunities into account, which leads to a rather repetitive type of project. One consequence of such repetitiveness is that project evaluation is easier with a stress on efficiency in operations, using routines for examples. Since project managers are evaluated on how well their projects have been running in terms of time, money, and results, they have to stress efficiency. Similarly, project managers in PBOs have little time to devote to tactical or strategic thinking since project delivery on time and at low cost is imperative.

In the past decade, literature on project business (Artto et al. 2011) experimented with new project business relation approaches to address these problems. The general trend is to agree to relations between clients and contractors that enable changes to take place over the life of the project and encourage innovation and problem solving within integrated teams.

In the UK, the success of T5 and, more recently, the 2012 London Olympics construction program does provide examples of how to deliver complex one-off projects. Both of these cases illustrate a different approach to projects and project management. Interestingly, it is the client that led the successful approaches rather than the suppliers. Indeed, one of the contractors on T5 found that the role of the client was to create an environment in which it was possible to succeed. This concept – the project environment – extends the notion of context a little bit further beyond factors such as size to include other dimensions such as sociopolitical complexity and technological or economic uncertainty. The key issue here is that complexity and uncertainty are only important to the extent that they make it difficult to manage the project. Geraldi et al. (2011) make this point, reinforcing the context issue: if an organization is constantly delivering complex projects, then it is more likely to be able to harness its knowledge for future complex projects, whereas an organization that is used to delivering straightforward projects will find it much more difficult when faced with a more complex one.

At the governance level, the PBO is characterized by a high empowerment and autonomy of the project management in general and the individual project leaders in particular. The consequence is a decentralized, rather polycentric or heterarchic organization that is supported by overarching project functions such as corporate strategy, managerial accounting, and human resource management. As mentioned before, a classic example of a PBO is a construction company for which several construction sites are operated partly in parallel. The role of the single project managers is to run the different construction sites in a responsible way, report back to top management of the PBO, and be ready to solve problems instantly at the site. Project managers in the construction business, as well as in the CoPS industries more generally, are well known for their ability to be instant problem solvers. The prevalence of unforeseen events is quite high in that industry because of the amount of coordination needed between the various individual and collective actors involved and the frequent changes of the circumstances under which the project is carried out. The evaluation of the work of a project manager is done exclusively on a project basis. Also, the evaluation is based on two factors, economics on delivery and then customer satisfaction (which probably is less formal and more haphazard than the economic evaluation).

However, the context of PBO drives the project manager's mission to specificities. As indicated previously, a PBO is an organization making money from selling a project promise to an existing customer and by delivering project results at the end. The initial phase of contracting on the project target between the owner and the contractor is of major importance on following project management practices.

The typical setup of a PBO involves a small core of top central officers handling the coordination of the various projects that the organization is working on currently. Top-level management usually also includes marketing on a macro level for projects to be run in the future and to control the project portfolio development. Other overall tasks are to organize for learning across projects, to develop human resources, and to handle financial matters.

Since the number of projects in the portfolio usually changes over time as a result of business conditions, the task of keeping a smooth development of the portfolio is often stressed as an important one (Archer and Ghasemzadeh 1999; Petit 2012). One implication of attending to this problem is how to stabilize quantity in terms of labor needed (some countries, for example, Sweden or Germany, have quite stringent rules as to how the labor force can be decreased during business fluctuations) and counterbalance the downs, possibly by lowering prices or by being more proactive in marketing efforts.

Thus, top management controls the project portfolio and financial matters, but there is also a need to keep in close contact with the different project managers to determine when projects are not running smoothly and to assist in solving local problems with overall approaches. In contrast, the responsibilities of the project managers are restricted to the project or the projects (if there are parallel tasks) they are involved in. In many, not to say most cases, project managers may be responsible for several projects concurrently, which means that their work situation might have some similarities with that facing management at the top PBO level.

The project management office (PMO) has been developed in the past decades to perform various roles in multiproject contexts: supporting the projects, controlling the projects, and partnering between various projects (Hobbs and Aubry 2010). Most PMOs function to standardize how projects are set up and used in the specific PBO. The main rationale is to make it possible for project managers to "cut corners" and save time by keeping potential and active project managers informed about how to set up and run projects.

*At the human resource management level,* an important decision is how PBOs allocate project managers and other personnel to different projects. This means that the project managers have to devote some of their time to enhancing their reputation among the top-level managers. Project managers, well known for doing a good job, usually get rewarded by being allocated to the projects they prefer. Conflicts between project managers do occur, especially when the project work is starting and the project managers want to recruit the best people to their projects (Arvidsson 2009). According to Eskerod (1997), who investigates how human resources are allocated to projects, project managers tend to fight for the best personnel. The project manager views his or her responsibility as being to the project rather than to the PBO as a whole. So it is an important part of the central level of the PBO to sort those situations out and to stress the importance of the total company rather than the project level. In particular, the top management of the PBO has to be aware of the needs single project managers confront, including the need for managing their personal reputation.

As a result of external constraints of reputation and institutionalization of project markets, the prevalence of certification and efforts to make project managing a profession are probably of most importance in PBOs (see Chapter 5). When many similarities between various projects exist, the apparent appropriate behaviors become prescribed and taught as the way to solve recurrent problems in the industry in question. In fact, certification of project managers has become an industry in itself and thereby also a tool to assist the overall PBO level. Of all project management certification schemes, the one promoted by the Project Management Institute is most successful in terms of numbers of certifications provided over the years. Outside North America, the International Project Management Association certification scheme is the most successful. Whereas the PMI certifies knowledge, the IPMA certifies competence. One drawback with certifying actions is that actions rather than results (in terms of project product delivery) are stressed. If a project manager adheres to the prescribed recipe, he or she cannot be blamed, at least not as harshly as if there were no recipes.

One difference between the work done by a top manager of a PBO and a project manager is that the project manager is, with few exceptions, held responsible for his or her project(s) only. Comparatively, the work of a top manager of a PBO is related more to general management even though many managers of PBOs may have a past career as project managers in the same industry. The pattern is similar to that in other organizations. There is a career ladder. Data from a study of the careers of a set of 20 or so top business leaders in Sweden showed that they all had one thing in common: early in their careers, they had been responsible for at least one major project that they labeled as a success (Jönsson 1995).

In some PBOs, the project manager has solid experiences from doing all the nitty-gritty and detailed work pertaining to the project level. In TV production companies (which are essentially PBOs), newcomers usually start working as unpaid production assistants when TV programs are prepared and shot. If they are perceived as competent, they might climb the career ladder.

A project manager related to a PBO might be responsible for several projects at the same time because there is a certain degree of repetitiveness involved in running projects in such a context. This does not mean that projects are repeated sequentially, but that the projects run are so similar that "standard operating procedures" (Cyert and March 1963) usually have been developed. For that reason, the presence of the project manager is not needed at all times at a specific project work site; he or she can be free to take on other tasks as well. Another reason is that the responsibilities voluntarily taken on by project participants might fill in for the manager when needed, although this appears to differ between countries. The differences need to be taken into account since the popular saying is that in some countries and cultures, the manager is the manager is the manager, which essentially means that no one but the manager takes on the task of solving problems as they occur and project members are less active in solving immediate problems. In other countries, the members of a project group consider themselves as a group of equals and leave another type of role for project managers.

Whereas the project manager gets evaluated almost instantly on the completion of a project, the managers at the PBO level get evaluated on an overall basis, with the projects run by the organization just one part. And the dimensions chosen for such an evaluation (if it ever gets done) are not given, as are the most important ones for the project manager. The line between success and failure is completely different for the general manager, so these two categories simply play entirely different roles, even though they share a similar context.

Human resource (HR) management in PBOs is also more affected by societal changes (Garel et al. 2003; Söderlund and Bredin 2005; Bredin and Söderlund 2011). For instance, the recruitment of project managers as well as workers puts new demands on the HR department, which most PBOs continue to have. Moreover, this department has to manage, or at least support, the often frequent change of personnel between projects and the integration of employees from external service providers, including temporary work agencies. However, most human resource management tasks, in particular those of strategic importance for the project, will be coordinated between the human resource department, the line management, the project management, and the project workers. Given the corporate demographics whereby the younger generation tends to favor projects over working in the line organization, we may also hypothesize that project structures are likely to become even more influential to the detriment of line structures in PBOs in the future.

### Key management dilemmas in PBOs

Out of the many dilemmas management may envisage within PBOs, we focus on three key ones.

**Organizational identity versus project identity?** In many ways, the importance of projects in the PBO creates difficulties in enhancing the global identity of the organization. Know-how is embedded more in individuals than in a collective asset; professional norms, especially for project management, make it possible to change easily from one firm to another. In PBOs, it requires an extra effort from management to build an organizational identity that embraces each project and helps coordinate the portfolio of projects beyond a technocratic static approach to portfolio management (Archer and Ghasemzadeh 1999; Petit and Hobbs 2010). This is a demanding task as project managers are at the same time eager to build a distinct project identity, which was illustrated in the Manhattan Project, where the different project teams competed in parallel (Lenfle 2011). In consequence, managing a PBO requires a balancing act between the individual project identities and the portfolio of projects that – only in the case of a PBO – contributes to the identity of the organization.

**Organize cross-project learning.** Systematic efforts to learn and to store knowledge are difficult in PBOs in spite of the fact that projects are fairly similar and a PMO might have been erected. Project members, and not least project managers, are learning by doing their work, but the learning is primarily personal. At best, it is shared with the other project participants and with the project manager. But a major problem with PBOs in general is that of knowledge storage and retrieval. There is not much incentive to formalize and share new knowledge beyond specific projects, as Nonaka (1994) demonstrates in his widely discussed organizational learning model. This cross-project learning difficulty has been identified as a key dilemma, which is at the origin of the renewal paradox – Exchange project mentioned earlier; that is, PBOs have often been reproducing traditional standardized solutions, whereas projects are supposed to be temporary organizations that are adapted to innovative and singular missions. Hence, it comes as no surprise that learning in and across projects has attracted a lot of scholarly interest, as demonstrated in special issues of *Organization Studies* (Sydow et al. 2004) and *Long Range Planning* (Lampel et al. 2008).

Efforts are usually made to document projects if possible so that knowledge can be made available beyond the personal level, but real success stories in this field are rare (the T5 megaproject constitutes an exception with learning at the organizational level). Architectural firms store blueprints after the project result has been delivered. The main use of what is stored seems to be that in designing solutions to new architectural problems, inspiration might be found by going through old solutions to similar problems. The attempts of consultancies, another type of PBO, are similar (Hansen et al. 1999). Sometimes, the caretaking of organizational learning is a task for the upper PBO level. Follow-up meetings are arranged in a formal way, but there is still the problem of how to distill and store what has been learned in such a way that retrieval is possible. A systematic problem that has prevented much of this knowledge management from becoming a success is the difficulty – if not impossibility – of extracting and codifying what Polanyi (1967) calls "tacit knowledge," which seems of utmost importance when managing projects and about which Nonaka (1994) is quite optimistic.

**Anticipate from the customers' demand to develop innovation push strategies.** In the more rapidly developing sectors, firms' strategies resemble innovation push. This means that firms do not wait for a demand from a client to develop a new product or service but rather initiate projects themselves to satisfy emerging customer demands. Examples such as the Walkman by Sony or the iPhone by Apple demonstrate a capacity to transcend the customer preference for sustaining innovations (Bower and Christensen 1995) and a capacity to deliver disruptive ones that, ex post, become financial jackpots. The strategic culture of most PBOs is nevertheless more reactive than proactive to market demand. PBOs generally do not have powerful research or advanced engineering departments that could prepare innovations without a client paying for them. Innovation in a client-driven project is an outcome of a client lead-user initiative (Von Hippel 1998) or generally only of an incremental nature. The T5 case shows the importance of the client in driving the innovative process through the construction industry supply chain (Davies et al. 2009; Brady and Davies 2011). And when cross-project learning happens (which has been found to be difficult), it is often an imitation practice rather than an experimental capitalization process: the incentive for one project to take risks that will be fruitful for the following ones is zero.

### 3.3.   MANAGING PROJECTS IN A PSO CONTEXT
In contrast to PBOs as a prototypical example of project-based organizing, the backbone of the PSO remains the permanent organization. Projects are only added to the more conventional ways of organizing work in functional departments or product divisions. As in the case of PBOs, we discuss the challenges of managing in PSOs with reference to our three variables (business model, governance, and human resource management).

*The contextualized project management in PSO*
*At the business model level,* PSOs are like most organizations characterized by a business originating in a customer mass standardized production history. Since the 1980s, such a tradition has been changing, however, because of two convergent trends. The first is the deployment of innovation-based competition, where product life cycles are shortened, and differentiation strategies call for more frequent, diverse, and radical renewals of existing products or services. New exploratory and development projects are the organizational

form that has been deployed to handle such renewals. The second is the transition from pure product offers to integrated solutions composed of product and services, allowing organizations to enhance value in use for customers. Such enlargement of scope calls for a more complex and diversified supply system, the project notion appearing as a relevant concept to manage the needed supply chain coordination. In Chapter 2, we devoted space to how Ericsson transformed itself from a manufacturing-focused business to one in which service offerings now account for more than 40 percent of its turnover, which can serve as an illustration.

These two transitions have important consequences on firms' practices for performance evaluation. Until the 1980s, operational excellence or exploitation performance was the key indicator that impacted the firms' value. More and more, financial analysts try to base their evaluation on increasingly prospective and dynamic perspectives, as the performance of ongoing exploitation usually declines fast and will rapidly become obsolete because of competitors' innovation efforts. Therefore, project performance appears as the key efficiency indicator to certify firms' business sustainability. The pharmaceutical sector is emblematic of such a trend. The R&D project portfolio evaluation is central in the value evaluation of Big Pharma. This business orientation also requires a significant change in terms of relevant performance indicators for the firm. The cost of product and margins was the traditional alpha and omega concept for profitability. In a more service-oriented perspective, economic flows are significantly more complex. A relevant evaluation of projects' economic performance needs to have a clearer formulation of the project strategy (Artto et al. 2008) and more sophisticated economic instruments and reasoning than the classical net present value calculus.

At the governance level, PSOs have a tradition of being organized as functional or divisional bureaucracies with a strong manufacturing focus but are now facing a transition toward becoming more project organized. The contextual environments in which projects in

PSOs operate are imprinted by these structures, although they strongly call for a deep renewal of this organizational tradition, affecting both projects and their members (Grabher 2004). Management in PSOs therefore focuses on handling the intersections or boundaries between permanent and temporary structures and processes. In other words, management has to handle the collision between strong institutions of the traditional industrial organization model and the more or less tacit, but also strong, institutions of project organizations (Midler 1993, 1995; Ekstedt et al. 1999; Sahlin-Andersson and Söderholm 2002; Arvidsson and Ekstedt 2006).

These boundaries are, as emphasized before, constituted in four particular dimensions – time, team, task, and transition – in which the permanent and temporary structures and processes differ (Lundin and Söderholm 1995). The different relations to these four dimensions also lead to tensions within PSOs and therefore make them critical factors for managers. More particularly, sources of tensions in PSOs are primarily created by the coexistence of fundamentally different organizing principles, the way employees identify themselves with either the line function or with projects, and by competition between line functions and projects for limited organizational resources (Arvidsson 2009). Debourse et al. (1983) sum up potential causes of tension between project-oriented activity and functionally oriented activity via six characteristics or dimensions (see Figure 3.3).

A key question for project management in the PSO then becomes the participants' capacity to adopt the project orientation vision when project participants are embedded in functional institutions. The specific formal matrix structure is important to this articulation issue between permanent and temporary organization. Saying that a firm has a project-oriented form of organization does not mean much if the status and profile of project managers relative to functional departments are not specified for the PSO. As we saw in Chapter 2, Hayes and coauthors (1988) identify three project matrix structures in PSOs, considering the formal power of a project:

| Characteristics of project activity | Characteristics of functionally oriented activity |
|---|---|
| Goal-oriented activity, dedicated resources and methodologies are a consequence | Activity defined as performing existing procedures and skills, extrapolated from experience |
| A singular situation to take into account | Repetitive and standardized situations |
| Success depends on the good integration of a mix of variables and discipline | Excellence based on task division and specialization |
| A very uncertain and open-ended situation | Low uncertainty |
| Irreversible and historically (diachronic) dynamic process | Synchronic and stabilized processes that can be handled with the help of statistics |
| Open systems, highly environmentally dependent | Rather closed systems, protected from outside influence by institutional boundaries |

FIGURE 3.3. Characteristics of project and functional activities. (Source: Adapted from Declerck et al. 1983.)

(1) The "project coordinator" (lightweight project manager) is in charge of coordinating participants but has no decision capacity on the functional experts involved in the project. Reporting to hierarchical steering committees is his or her essential leverage on the project orientation.

(2) The "project director" (heavyweight project manager) has a formal responsibility and decision capacity on the project, because of a larger delegation of responsibility from the high executives and a profile of experience. This delegation recognizes the arbitration authority of the project director in case of dispute, negotiation of resources allocated to the project, when the project actor is not responsible for the budget. Its hierarchical status is the same as functional department managers. Commando and contracting management are possible leverage for this institutional setting.

(3) Actors in the "tiger team organization" working on the project are physically and institutionally out of their functional structures and transferred to be under the authority of the project manager for the duration of the intervention. After project completion, they either return to their original profession or move on to another project.

Another important issue for PSOs is the activation of actors outside of the organization. The scope of a specific project generally transcends the organization's frontiers: the network of suppliers or customers could be a key ally in achieving project success. External contributions might be more profitable than inside propositions for a specific project. The project manager is then in the position of challenging his or her own organization (Midler 1993, 2013). Involving these actors in the project as inside contributors can be difficult, however, because of organizational boundary keepers, purchase departments, and other organizational routines. In the auto industry, the empowered project manager played an important role in the 1990s in promoting new co-development and co-innovation practices with suppliers, in particular with so-called first-tier or system suppliers. Stakeholder management, which includes these constituencies, is a growing field of interest in the academic as well as practitioner fields of project management (Karlsen 2002; Littau et al. 2010).

*At the human resource management level*, the project-driven environment of organizations implies that employees must become attractive in internal markets for project employment and therefore adopt a different career risk exposure as compared to employees who build their careers in a more traditional hierarchical promotion process. Project workers in this sense are continuously facing internal competition for assignment to particularly attractive and challenging projects. They take on a different type of employment risk compared to line workers – even if both groups are employed in the same organization. The two ideals, with their institutional base in the difference between project and permanent organizations respectively, may lead to problems for employees about how to prepare for a career in a PSO. Project leadership is likewise more results oriented and less people oriented compared to traditional line management.

### Key management dilemmas in PSOs

Three management issues appear particularly challenging in a PSO context: managing the tensions between projects and functional units; maintaining the economies of scale that are a competitive advantage of mass production firms in spite of the project proliferation; and developing the radical innovation impulse while rationalizing development projects in a cost, risk, and lead time reduction perspective.

**Managing the tensions between projects autonomy and functional departments.** Tensions between functional departments and ongoing projects appear as a key issue in managing PSOs. The projectification of organizations has gradually given power and autonomy to projects, undermining the formerly dominant logic of functional departments. But excellence in functional skills remains a key capability for PSOs.

There are indications that the boundaries between permanent and temporary structures in PSOs are not systematically managed (Arvidsson and Ekstedt 2006). Issues are primarily solved by individuals on an ad hoc basis. Managerial attention consequently needs to focus on structures and processes that would provide systematic solutions to these sorts of problems.

The issue of maintaining solidarity between these two complementary logics ("complementary" is often a euphemism for "conflicts") is of major importance within PSOs. This includes efforts to develop a more long-term view on leadership in and by projects, whereby not only the immediate results of the ongoing project are in focus. Attention could focus on, first, creating clear relations between the business model and the organizational processes and, second, creating a better fit between employees' identities and values in relation to the organizational processes in which they work. Building different career paths for line people and project people often seems in order. Another answer, which had been implemented in automotive and aeronautic firms, was to alternate the functional and project missions in career management (Garel et al. 2003). With such career management, people could take back to their functional department what was learned in the project. Project people typically know that they will soon be on the line if they want to progress in the hierarchic ladder. Last, managers could develop principles on how to allocate resources between permanent and temporary structures, on the one hand, and between different projects, on the other.

Another important managerial implication from this discussion about tensions between line functions and projects in PSOs is that managers must aim to see such tension in a conscious or reflexive manner; that is, they must act as "reflective practitioners" (Schön 1983). Managers should make stronger efforts to develop leadership styles that are more prone to acknowledge the positive effects from tensions. Perhaps they should even stimulate tensions in certain cases.

**Controlling the project proliferation and maintaining the scale-effect performance.** Project organizing means focusing on an ex ante specific target. But as projectification develops, dissemination of projects in organizations in general and PSOs in particular creates a dilution of involvements, for people cannot usually be dedicated to a single project. At the same time, as each project is driven by its own singularity, project proliferation creates the risk of thwarting the scale effect, which has always been one of the key competitive advantages of this type of firm. To cope with this divergence problem, at least four multi-project approaches emerged in the 1990s and 2000s:

(1) *Project management portfolio,* accompanied by stage-gate processes (Cooper et al. 1999; Teller et al. 2014), introduced competition between projects for access to key resources. Pharmaceutical, chemical, and IT firms had largely developed these sophisticated systems in the 1990s. The purpose is to move from a single project performance reviewing process to a more global view of the demography of the projects of the firm, key criteria being good alignment with the firm strategy and relevant risk/attractiveness balance of the portfolio.

(2) *Programmification* (Maylor et al. 2006) had emerged in the mid 2000s to organize coherences between projects that contribute to a shared strategic target. Here, coordination and communication between projects are the organizational efficiency/effectiveness drivers, though interproject competition is underlying the portfolio approach. Figure 3.4 differentiates projectification and programmification in terms of a number of different factors, including structure and governance.

Projectification and programmification

| Issue | Implication of projectification | Implication of programmification |
|---|---|---|
| Unit of analysis | Individual projects | Multiple projects, programmes and portfolios of programmes, alongside 'business as usual' work |
| 1. Structure | Increasing use of project structures | Application of semi-permanent structures |
| 2. Governance | Move of power away from line managers to project managers/directors | Move of power to those controlling the programmes or portfolios of programmes |
| 3. Relative status between different functions, and the erosion of functional demarcation | Projects granted official status and legitimacy by the organisation; functional demarcations eroded; in heavier-weight project organisations, project managers have direct authority over resources | Functions less of an issue than relative status between projects and programmes |
| 4. Communication | Predominant mode in project team will shift from vertical to horizontal, between people at lower levels in the organisation | Horizontal (within the team and between projects) and vertical (reporting to programme control) |
| 5. Level of enterprise | Expected to be enhanced by reduced bureaucracy and functional; 'controllability and adventure' | Expected to be enhanced by mature processes |
| 6. Importance of project processes/methodologies | Importance increased – often codified in bodies of knowledge and represented in artefacts (e.g. project manuals, standardised process models) | Established processes, possibly accompanied by reduced standardisation |
| 7. Process of learning | Intended to move from little learning due to dispersed knowledge, to single loop | Across projects, potential for double loop learning |
| 8. The output or outcome – the level of benefits | Level of benefits needs to be assessed for each project. Level of benefits expected to rise following projectification | Delivery of a package of benefits; 'value creation' |
| 9. Career management and permanent structures: professionalisation | Project managers will develop a permanent 'functional' home – the project office; they will gain legitimacy by professionalizing their role | Hierarchy (project – programme manager – director) emergence evident in contrast to flat organisational structures in use elsewhere |
| 10. Supply networks and buyer–supplier relationships | Cheapest supplier to best partner in the project | Uncertain the effect – area for further research |
| 11. The number of projects that are/can be managed | The number of projects and the relative proportion of organisational resources that they consume, will increase | Managed, potentially reducing |
| 12. Competencies required | planning, resourcing and executing projects | Managing across projects and programmes| |

FIGURE 3.4. Projectification versus Programmification. (Source: Maylor et al. 2006: 671. Reproduced with permission from Elsevier.)

(3) *Platform management* (Cusumano and Neoboka 1998) pursues the same objective with a specific logic. As is typical in the automotive industry, platform management imposes ex ante standardization constraints on new product projects: they have to share the same component and be manufactured with the same industrial processes. In this perspective, convergence of projects' choices is ensured through such ex ante constraints. In organizational terms, this leads to a two-level project management structure, with platform (or program) managers who are hierarchically dominating product project managers who share the technical and industrial assets of the platform.

(4) Last but not least, *lineage management* is a multiproject perspective that focuses on the cross-learning efficiency (Midler 2013; Maniak and Midler 2014). In this perspective, the program manager is superior to product project managers. He or she has the key role to organize the project-to-project learning within the sequence of different projects. This could also be one of the roles of program management office supervision.

**Maintaining the innovative impulse and learning in PSOs.** Beyond the tension surrounding the cooperation between project and competence-based functional departments is the issue of maintaining learning capacities within specific trades. Projectification within PSOs has focused on the quality/cost/delay performance of product development processes. One result is that the innovation efforts, which generally are associated with costs and risks, are more and more decoupled from new product development (Beaume et al. 2013). Here again we see a manifestation of the renewal paradox by which PSO projectification leads to development of me-too products but also creates new obstacles to significant innovation thrusts. But innovation is still a strategic necessity to stimulate demand and escape from price war competition on non-differentiated products.

In their research on an aeronautic firm, Lefebvre and coauthors (2010) demonstrate how the projectification of the firm led to a weakening of a core competence of the firm on compressor mechanics. The authors analyze how this crisis led to renewal of the competence-based department with the creation of a new role, that of knowledge field manager, and formalization of diversified carrier trajectories to maintain in the long term the complementary objectives of implementation performance on projects and dynamics of technical knowledge on key competences of the firm.

Another solution developed in the auto industry in the late 1990s and early 2000s was to develop upstream advanced engineering departments, whose role was to explore and improve "on the shelf" the maturity level of new technologies and features that, when proved in term of feasibility and value for customer, could be incorporated in new products (Midler et al. 2012). However, such "featuring capability" (Maniak and Midler 2014) rapidly revealed its limits to more radical systemic innovation (such as electric vehicles or semiconductor manufacturing technologies). Disruptive projects as the Toyota Prius, the Logan low-cost car or the zero emission vehicle by Renault, exemplify the return of breakthrough innovative product development as pilot concept projects that have to initiate new lineage on innovative options (Midler 2013; Maniak et al. 2014).

This leads to the development of a new kind of exploratory project (Lenfle 2008) having a different perspective than typical new product development projects. Historical projects such as the Manhattan Project leading to the atom bomb (Lenfle 2011) or the Sidewinder Project about the development of a missile (Lenfle 2014) in the defense context are emblematic cases for such exploratory projects. They explore extreme uncertain contexts ("unknown unknowns"), where both the value perspectives and the solutions to be implemented are to be explicated. Exploratory projects are more concept or domain oriented than precise goal-oriented ones (Maniak et al. 2014). Combining parallel with sequential learning strategies and managing flexibility in their orientation based on low-cost and short-term experiments create a specific managerial context, far away from the traditional development project practices and tools.

3.4.   MANAGING PROJECTS IN A PNW CONTEXT

Not unlike in PBOs, management attention in PNWs is typically focused on the projects and their relationships to one another. Organizations continue to matter in this organizational form only insofar as they are linked by network projects. However, it is not rare that self-employed project entrepreneurs (Manning and Sydow 2011) or "entreployees" (Pongratz and Voβ 2003) rather than organizations are involved in PNWs. This is actually particularly common in the media industry. Schwab and Miner (2008) find this to be the case even in the early Hollywood studio system with its still deeply integrated organization of production. As several actors and directors preferred to be engaged in film projects as self-employed participants, Schwab and Miner speak of "project-hybrid systems." The entrepreneurial element of filmmaking has been in a sense projectified because filmmaking in the past was dominated by PBOs but now has changed character and is mostly found in PNWs (Storper and Christopherson 1987). This industry swing is affecting managerial tasks of the old PBOs as well as in newly developing PNWs.

Before we examine a few key management dilemmas that characterize the PNW context, we discuss the particular context this organizational form provides with respect to the business model, governance, and human resources.

*The contextualized project management in PNWs*

One important trend of the past decade is the emergence of networks as a key form to manage projects (see Bakker 2010 for a review). While the notion of a network is often used in a rather loose and metaphorical way, also in the context of projects and projectification, two different but more precise understandings of project networks have been developed. The first understanding refers to organizations (or entreployees) that collaborate at a certain point in time on a particular project, typically requiring a diverse set of complementary capabilities and skills not available in a focal organization (Hellgren and Stjernberg 1995; Jones 1996). By contrast to such "inter-organizational projects" (Jones and Liechtenstein 2008) that are either confined to a one-time collaboration or unspecific about their future and past, the second notion of project networks pays attention to the issue of time and the mechanisms that make coordination across organizations feasible: the recurrent collaboration of actors in projects, enabled as well as constrained by experience (the shadow of the past) and expectations (the shadow of the future) (Sydow and Windeler 1999; Manning 2010; Manning and Sydow 2011). The connections between the past and the future are illustrated in how patterns of top-performing films develop and how networks are stabilized in the film industry in Japan (Wakabayashi et al. 2009). Successful networks that work with repeated collaboration projects nevertheless allow for some variation. And repeated collaboration offers management the opportunity to develop formal rules (as well as to stimulate the development of informal rules) that are not all too different from those in intraorganizational settings, although, as to be expected, a cooperative mode dominates hierarchial fiat (Dischner et al. 2013).

With regard to dynamics, project networks in this latter sense are not always interesting but may consist of a rather limited or extensive series of collaborations over a shorter or longer period of time; take, for example, the production of a television series of long or short duration (Manning and Sydow 2011). With regard to geographical space, project networks may be of local or regional but also of global reach. More often than not, both local and global spaces will be covered as in the case of the optics cluster in the metropolitan area of Berlin, which, because of its character as a science-based industry with a strong emphasis on research and development, is marked by numerous project networks within this regional cluster (Sydow and Lerch 2007) as well as by global linkages. Such linkages are established either by global players in this industry or with the help of a "network of clusters" (Schüßler et al. 2013) in which the Berlin cluster is a member. In addition, management of (as well as working in) project networks is supported by IT. With this virtual dimension of project networks, the value of geographical nearness is increasingly questioned and the relative importance of social over physical distance emphasized (Ganesan et al. 2005).

*At the business model level*, network as well as cluster contexts create new opportunities for projects and project management, opportunities that never could emerge in a PBO or PSO context. By stimulating cross-organizational communication, by lowering the risk level through investment mutualization, by organizing fluent and deep connections between the organizations (as well as the entreployees), networks as well as clusters and in particular "networks in clusters" (Sydow and Lerch 2007) create an arena for innovative ideas through open innovation processes (Chesbrough 2003). Above all, however, the management of PNWs is enabled and constrained by the fact that collaboration in the network is of more or less relevance to the organizations collaborating, depending on the business and the business model applied. It depends, more specifically, on the "scope of the alliance" (Khanna 1998) and its relative importance for the business of the network members. High-tech start-ups, characteristic of clusters in science-based industries, are nothing other than firm projects; in many ways, their management is much the same as with a typical project trajectory (Midler and Silberzahn 2008): an ex ante initial target (the "pitch" and business case), the building of a new organization dedicated to implementing deliverables that are scrutinized in reviews that are similar to project classic stage-gate processes. During the start-up phase, project governance dominates organizational governance (see also Chapter 6). More importantly, the network for this very reason may exhibit a distinct business model, explaining in part the diversity of business models in project business (Wikström et al. 2010).

*At the governance level*, interorganizational networks as well as regional clusters typically provide a relatively stable context for projects as temporary systems, in the same way as do PBO and PSO contexts. Hence, PNW management, as management in organizations, has to be concerned with the temporary–permanent dilemma (Sahlin-Andersson and Söderholm 2002), although research on this organizational form is still quite silent on this particular issue.

Nevertheless, managing projects in networks or clusters is radically different from managing PSOs and PBOs because of the distinct governance mode of networks/clusters. While even extremely decentralized organizations, projectified or not, can when in doubt rely on hierarchical fiat (Williamson 1985), networks and clusters work quite differently. At the very least, there is consensus in the literature on these organizational forms – and in consequence on networks in clusters – that the hierarchical mode of governance systematically fails in these new forms. But what coordinative mechanism exactly substitutes for fiat is debated in the literature, although hardly in practice where actors – like some researchers – tend to argue for the role of trust or reciprocity. Since the management of temporary systems – that is, projects – in "more than temporary systems" (Sydow and Windeler 1999) – that is, project networks – depends on the understanding of the coordinative mechanism, we enter this debate before discussing networks and clusters further as particular contexts for project-based organizing.

For quite some time, the issue of network governance has been debated in the literature. While some researchers conceive networks as hybrids (Williamson 1991) combining market as well as hierarchical modes of governance, others see networks as an organizational form "beyond market and hierarchy" (Powell 1990). Without going into this debate in extreme depth, it is important to note that networks and clusters are indeed special: even if they intelligently combine market and hierarchical elements, the network mode of governance is quite distinct from both. This is expressed well by considering networks and clusters as an organizational form wherein the market is domesticated because of intensive interaction and coordination but nevertheless the "market test" (MacMillan and Farmer 1979) remains intact. That is to say, for instance, in-suppliers may well be turned into out-suppliers when the quality and/or the price of their products or services cease to be competitive. Despite this fundamental competitiveness, networks and clusters are usually characterized by more or less intensive interorganizational cooperation based on reciprocity and trust (Powell 1990). Hence, the management of these organizational forms remains concerned with organizing for both cooperation and competition. This is obvious in the project networks of television production referred to earlier, which are, at least in Germany, embedded in media regions (Lutz et al. 2003) or respective industry clusters.

Even short-term projects are often embedded in long-term relationships that allow for reciprocity and enhance trust even though the project and network members are selected in a somewhat competitive mode. Examples for such media regions that are characterized by many project networks and, hence, project ecologies are Cologne, with its emphasis on television production, and Berlin (including Potsdam-Babelsberg) and Munich, where many feature films are also produced. Another good example for the subtle but more often than not reflexively designed interplay between cooperation and competition in interorganizational networks is the strategy of "dual sourcing," which is well known from the automotive industry wherein a second supplier stays in the game and the total supply is divided between these two suppliers according to certain performance criteria. Moreover, these two in-suppliers remain, despite their long-term contracts and their tightly coupled relationships with their customer, exposed to the competition by out-suppliers. Although no evidence was found for this practice in a study of television production in Germany (Manning and Sydow 2011), it is quite likely to be adapted in the near future when other fields start imitating practices in the automotive industry.

This is similar to the situation found in CoPS sectors, where the number of customers and suppliers tends to be limited right from the beginning. For example, in the defense market, firms can play different roles in major projects/programs. In some cases, a firm will win the bid to become the prime contractor, whereas in other tenders it will not win the overall bid but may still participate in the final project as a supplier of specific elements of the project. So even if the firm does not win overall control of the project/program, it will still have work on the project, which helps maintain its level of competence for future bids. Sometimes the client (holds for most national ministries of defense) will insist on sharing the work post tender depending on the bids that have been made.

The prime contractors usually take on the role of systems integrator, which is similar to that of network manager or cluster entrepreneur. Whatever the solution, competitive forces remain at work in the dominantly collaborative network form whose external legitimacy varies from field to field but often is based on the level of legitimacy achieved internally (Human and Provan 2000; Larson and Wikström 2007).

Managing projects in networks and clusters requires a fair knowledge of advanced project management techniques. However, it is interesting to note that the German film and television industry does not seem to use such techniques to a large extent. Rather, project management here is only supported by basic tools such as a database and a time planner. Nevertheless, project managers do need a practical understanding of projects as temporary systems with their particular goals and resources and their limited capacity for storing project-relevant knowledge or for interproject learning (Prencipe and Tell 2001). This capacity is actually likely to be even more limited than that of PBOs and PSOs. In addition, project managers require an understanding of the governance of the organizational and/or interorganizational context in which they manage the project, including the temporary/permanent interface. In the case of project networks, it is essential for project managers to acknowledge that they can never really rely on the hierarchical authority that characterizes organizations (including PBOs and PSOs) when it comes to coordinating activities across the boundaries of single organizations. Instead, they have to expect that negotiating and renegotiating the social order of a focal PNW (e.g. producing content for a public broadcaster) is decisive. Moreover, project managers working in these contexts should acknowledge that PNWs allow for an additional form of social control: "network control" (Sydow and Windeler 2003). This form of control relies, to a significant extent, on the presence of others and acts less as a substitute for direct control than as a potential source of trust springing from information that is "overdrawn" (Luhmann 1995). It shows, incidentally, that managing projects in networks and clusters is not simply more or less demanding than managing projects in organizations but also different.

*At the human relation management level*, project networks have been studied as specific social spaces concerning professional development. Individuals are potentially more attached not only to the project, exhibiting perhaps what has been called "project citizenship behaviour" (Braun et al. 2012), but also to the network or cluster rather than to a specific organization. This may require an approach to human resource management that allows balancing identification and commitment between projects, networks/clusters, and organizations. The reputation that results from previous project achievements is an important asset in this open market of talents. Studying the video game milieu in Montreal, Cohendet and Simon (2007) explained how an urban concentration of heterogeneous organizations can provide opportunities for fruitful trajectories for creative ideas and for creative people's careers. They stimulate connections between the creative and experimental underground milieu and established innovative firms by providing an original middle ground where projects as well as professionals can be evaluated, matured, and socialized.

### Key management dilemmas in PNWs

A superficial but common view is that networks and clusters are positive places for projects: new opportunities, motivated and dedicated people, involvement for fun or passion, and fewer rules or barriers to cross than in a PBO or PSO context. Nevertheless, such networked contexts also create specific challenges for management.

**Making things happen in project networks.** The subtle interplay of cooperation and competition in networks and clusters poses new challenges to managers, not only to network managers or cluster entrepreneurs. Rather, all managers in organizations who work at the boundaries of these systems and are thus involved in networking across organizational and sometimes network and cluster boundaries are affected. First of all, they are exactly the ones who cannot rely on hierarchical fiat when trying to make things happen (Huxham and Vangen 2000) but have to use alternative, more collaborative, and trust-based modes of communication and coordination. In addition, they have to take on new managerial tasks: selecting network partners, developing cluster rules, allocating network resources, and evaluating what network members contribute to and receive from the network or cluster respectively (Sydow 2005). That is to say, managers are confronted with at least one *additional* level of managerial action above the level of the project as well as the level of the portfolio or organization: the network and/or cluster level. These individuals may well be supported by specialized network or cluster managers or even by a "network administrative organization" (Human and Provan 2000). Nevertheless, they are confronted with all the particularities of network and/or cluster management, not least the tensions and contractions arising from the simultaneity of cooperation and competition in these systems.

Another example of this can be seen in the mobile telecommunications sector, where operators have outsourced various aspects to telecommunications suppliers. Ericsson, for example, won a contract to manage the network for 3UK; within this contract, it also bid for specific project or program work to supply equipment to upgrade and maintain the telecoms networks. In one such bid for supplying equipment, Ericsson was in competition with other suppliers such as Nokia-Siemens, which eventually won the contract. Ericsson then had to manage the upgrade program with one of its competitors as a main supplier. The relationship between the two was rather tricky to begin with; however, later in the program, they worked well together because both parties had a good incentive to collaborate to ensure a successful outcome of the program. As stated earlier, this tension between cooperation and competition is characteristic of interorganizational networks and hence project networks and must not be overlooked when trying to make things happen.

**Project networks – flexible or path dependent?** Arguably, at least at first sight, no organizational form is more flexible and dynamic than that of PNWs. Thus, early on they were referred to as "dynamic networks" (Snow et al. 1992). However, these networks, based on past experience and in the face of future expectation, enable as much as constrain coordination of work across organizational boundaries, and they may well become somewhat persistent or rigid. With regard to interorganizational networks in general, Kim et al. (2006) therefore ask for considering "network inertia" when researching and managing network change. Sometimes, PNWs, like networks and clusters more generally, may become not only inert but even locked in (David 1985; Grabher 1994). In a study of the German television industry, Manning and Sydow (2011) were able to show, at least in the field of series production, that because of recurrent collaboration of some core organizations and individuals, PNWs are quite likely to develop interorganizational path dependencies that allow routinized collaboration and identification with the network or cluster but at the same time limit the strategic adaptability of this organizational form. Like other forms of project-based organizing (see Hodgson 2004), PNWs are by no means exempt from tendencies toward bureaucratization. This does not come as a surprise as even projects are subject to cognitive inertia such as group think (Janis 1972; Hällgren 2010). Cantarelli et al. (2010) find similar effects for megaprojects such as the Betuweroute and the HSL-South projects, where a lock-in emerged from escalating commitment of managers to an ineffective course of action – not only in the early phases of the decision-making process about the two large-scale infrastructure projects in the Netherlands but also later in the projects, that is, after the formal decisions to build. In consequence, project management should at the very least become sensitive to the ambivalent character of commitment, routinization, and repeated transactions in this organizational form.

**Talent management in project networks.** Attracting and keeping talent in such an open and fluid social space is an important but difficult challenge both for projects and for permanent organizations. Networks, including PNWs, allow for easy exchange of information, not least about job opportunities. At the outset of network research, Granovetter (1979) demonstrates the relevance of, in particular, weak ties in labor markets for those who search for jobs. The same is likely to be true for those who offer jobs or even poach for talent. PNWs, like most interorganizational networks, are likely to be characterized by a mixture of weak and strong ties. Their combination not only explains the – more often than not – superior performance of this organizational form (Uzzi 1997) but also the relevance of networks for talent management. The example of the Japanese film-making industry demonstrates that there are strong ties in those networks where past successes in the market strengthen the ties beyond the experience of working together (Wakabayashi et al. 2009). Potential additions to the talents needed are evaluated by the existing network with the market potential as a background.

## 3.5. MANAGING IN PROJECT SOCIETY – SOME CONCLUSIONS

The general challenges for managerial action that rise as an effect of projectification can be seen and understood at several layers of organizing. First, there are important challenges at the project management level even though we see that these challenges have been given a lot of attention both by researchers and by practitioners. The main challenge at the project level (especially megaprojects) may be to enable better connectivity between projects and context without losing the efficiency of traditional project management, and we pointed to the importance of understanding a project's three phases: upstream definition, freezing, and implementation.

The second layer and challenge concerns the immediate organizational context in which projects are run and the ambition to improve cross-project learning and synergies. This is where our main discussion rests in this chapter. Significantly different managerial challenges depend on whether the dominating context in which a project is run is a PBO, a PSO, or a PNW. The management dilemmas in a PBO focus on managing two important actors, namely project workers and customers. Project workers must be made to identify with projects if they are to provide value primarily to the project. However, in most cases they should continue to identify with the permanent organization, in particular if their main role lies in creating value across projects. The challenge related to customers lies in engaging in dialogue and co-creation to receive input to and push innovation but also to enable effective management of a project's three phases. The management dilemmas in a PSO focus on two types of issues: managing tensions between the temporary and the permanent, and in particular creating an organizational set-up that stimulates cross-project learning and synergies. The management dilemmas in a PNW focus on three types of issues, which have a different character than the challenges in PBOs and PSOs. Here, the challenges are, first, to initiate and realize projects by attracting interest and resources from external actors. The project has to be "sold" to critical actors in the relevant networks. Given this multitude of actor, the second challenge relates to whether the project should be tightly knit around the initial ideas or whether various unique interests should be given room to influence the project evolution. The management of the project in a PNW is likely to be more complex in this respect. The final challenge relates to balancing the tension between cooperation and competition that is characteristic of most types of interorganizational networks, not only PNWs.

One particular aspect of management, HRM, should also be mentioned briefly, since management tasks differ among the three archetypes. However, such a detour would be too heavy a task to be treated here. However, HRM concerns also work regimes and is relevant for the next chapter. Similarly, in the literature on burnout, little is to be found on how project work situations and burnout are related in the three archetypes focused on here.

An overall conclusion of this chapter is that managerial challenges become complex and must be adapted not only to the context in which a project is run – PBO, PSO, or PNW – but also to the phase of each project's life. The next chapter illustrates how work organizations and employment regimes develop at the emergence of Project Society. The changes in the use of time and space for work open up the borders between work, training, and leisure. Institutions related to the work organization such as the regulations of working time and the workplaces as points of reference are challenged.

# 4 Work and employment regimes in Project Society

Work is naturally an important activity in most organizations. However, it has a specific character in project or temporary forms of organizing. Project-organized activities, such as those in the consultancy or construction sector, can be labor intensive, and well-established work routines are often present in these more "mature" project-based industries. Here, practical experiences from different work situations are inherited from one project to another and from one generation of professionals to the next. Some individuals may experience project work as liberating, while others may feel imprisoned by projects that discipline time, space, and intellect (Lindgren and Packendorff 2006a). Many management activities in project settings are actually devoted to ways to implement models of how to work and how to change ingrained work habits of temporary as well as permanent organizations (Ekstedt et al.1999). Working as well as managing work in Project Society needs to be better understood.

However, work has been much neglected in modern management and organizational research. Barley and Kunda (2001) therefore ask for "bringing work back in." One needs to study how actual work is organized to be able to build theories about the organizations of today. While some studies include aspects of work, such as learning, work practices themselves are not the focus. Bäckström (1999), Ackroyd et al. (2004), and others argue that since the 1970s, management and organizational research has moved from studies of work to studies of group dynamics, learning, discourses, talk, and rhetoric. Above all, the dimensions of conflicts are often absent in research on project work. In sharp contrast to organization studies more generally (Cyert and March 1963; Brunsson 1989), simple and rational decision making is still supposed to be the norm in project contexts. Textbooks contain simplified advice and solutions and lack information on problematic contexts; consequently, they have a low bearing on real-life situations (Czarniawska 2005). However, there are good early examples of empirical studies on work content (e.g. Carlsson 1951; Mintzberg 1976) on what top managers actually do, and by Wirdenius (1958) on what supervisors do. The studies by Tengblad (2006), comparing Mintzberg's findings with the later findings, provide updated information in this tradition. However, few explicit studies focus on work practices in project activities. The limited knowledge of the nature of modern project-based work practices in and among organizations makes it difficult to form adequate institutions for the working life of today. The existing ones are more or less a reflection of the past.

Despite some recent theorizing about work in organizations responding to Barley and Kunda's call to "bring work back in" (see also Okhuysen et al. 2013), when discussing how work is organized, one is generally leaning on a stereotypical model originating from the traditional industrial organization. This model has spread to most parts of society and is characterized by flow-process operations often supported by heavy investments in machinery and equipment driven by economies of scale. Work is characterized by specialization and an extensive division of labor. A managerial bureaucracy has been developed to run such large and complex organizations, whether it is a factory or a hospital. Employment regimes and professional codes are the most influential institutions in forming work conditions and logistics (see Chapter 5). Conceptions of how the industrial workplace looks – or should look – become an important framework when these rules and roles are developed into practice, and these conceptions are not in line with actual work in Project Society. Unions still represent the rough division between blue- and white-collar workers of traditional industry in many countries, although in Norway this division between blue and white collar has been abandoned. Also there is often an intimate interaction between the social partners – trade unions and employer confederations – and the representatives of the political and legal systems based on the principles of the Industrial Society in many countries. This is manifested in salaries, wages, working time, calendar thinking, work content, workplace, knowledge or educational demand, training programs, traditions, and other working conditions that are reflected in formal as well as in informal employment contracts between the employer and the employee.

Some persons or work situations are hardly influenced by formal contracts. Those involved in agriculture and small businesses often work for themselves with a seemingly limited need of employment relations. The same seems to be true for much volunteer work. The growing category of self-employed persons in official labor force statistics in many European countries may become an important challenge to existing employment regimes. According to the European Forum for Independent Professionals (self-employed iPros [independent professionals]), between 2004 and 2013 the number of persons working with these kind of arrangements increased from 6.2 million to 8.9 millions in the EU; estimates also show a fast-growing category of independent workers reaching almost 18 million persons in the United States in 2013 (Leighton and Brown 2013). These categories, sometimes also referred to as freelancers and supertemps, seem to have grown quickly during the past decade, which has been dominated by economic crises and unemployment. The definition of independent workers is wider than that of independent professionals (MBO partners 2013). The work of independent professionals is taking place in entertainment, journalism, design, and consultancy often related to IT; independent workers include all kinds of activity. These persons work by themselves with rather weak ties to employers. However, the work is often performed in a project with well-defined tasks, no matter whether the project is carried out within the context of a PBO, a PSO, or a PNW. Sometimes this kind of weak employment contract is balanced with ingrained traditions or stable working codes.

Additionally, some well-populated Asian countries, where a substantial fraction of the labor force still works in agriculture, use sharecropping as an indirect way to regulate work relations. A fixed share of what the farmer produces belongs to the landowner.

Historically, it was common in traditional agricultural societies that farmers put in a certain number of working days on the owner's land; farmhands and servants had other kinds of contracts, which as a rule were renewed once a year. (Similar arrangements exist for some professional soccer players and other athletes today.) The room for negotiations for farmhands and household servants was even more limited in feudal societies such as those of Russia, Germany, and Denmark some centuries ago. Servitude relations were characterized by unbreakable bonds to the estate where one was born. The rules and roles were fixed. The remains of a feudal or colonial order can be traced in the way low-paid work in, for example, the textile industry is organized in some parts of the world even today.

Employment relations and conditions in modern society – as least in the Western world – are in most cases still based on formal rules, such as the contractual agreements between the social partners and labor laws. In some sectors and professions, employment agreements and work routines are also influenced by professional education, codes, and ethics, sometimes confirmed by legitimating agencies and authorities. The social partners of the labor market – the political and legislative systems – are involved in forming the rules and roles as a reflection of their understanding of working practice, which is not necessarily up to date. The collective bargaining system often comes into focus when discussing employment relations; however, there are considerable differences between countries and industries. We may talk about a Nordic or Rhineland model or an Anglo-Saxon or southern European model (Moreau et al. 2009; Sandberg 2013), mirroring the categories of coordinated and liberal market economies respectively (see Chapter 5). More specifically, the social partners engage in wage bargaining in Sweden at the collective level; in France and Germany, minimum wages are legally established. Nevertheless, the characteristics of industrial relations also follow industries and thus cross national borders (Elvander and Elvander-Seim 1995). Project organizing is one of these dividers, which becomes evident when international consultancy companies, a popular branch of PBOs, try to use the same organizational model wherever they are active (Martinsson 2010).

In line with Barley and Kunda (2001) and Okhuysen and coauthors (2013), we argue that to be able to understand and build theories of modern organizations one has to study how actual work is organized. As work in projects plays an increasingly important role, it is consequently of major interest to find out what work and employment look like in project-dense contexts, such as PBOs, PSOs, and PNWs. Despite limited direct empirical research, several researchers discuss the character of work in projects and the implications for human resources (e.g. Lundin and Söderholm 1995; Hobday 1998, 2000; Ekstedt et al. 1999; Lindkvist 2001, 2004; Söderlund 2005; Midler et al. 2010; Bredin and Söderlund 2011; Borg 2014).

It is said that work in projects is task and action oriented, as well as perceived as stimulating by workers because of its problem-solving character. Work in projects often includes direct dialogue with customers and members of other organizations; that is, it is, to some extent at least, interorganizational in its character. Work in projects, which promises to be interesting, could simultaneously cause stress from time limits and responsibilities laid on the individuals concerning both business results in the specific projects and the need to constantly perform to ensure their own future employability. Most importantly, project work is more likely to be associated with the "nonstandard employment relations" (Kalleberg 2000), which are on the rise not only in the United States but almost everywhere (Kalleberg 2011; Capelli and Keller 2013) and described earlier, although working in projects does not always share the characteristics of part-time work, temporary agency and contract company employment, short-term and contingency work, or independent contracting. Nevertheless, these characteristics open up questions about work and employment conditions in projects.

The action orientation of projects is also related to the nature of work, as work in projects is directly goal and results oriented. Indeed, the phenomenon of projects is closely related to how work is organized. A case in point is the suggestion by Okhuysen and coauthors (2013) to focus future work research more on products or projects as the "engine of collaboration" (rather than on job definitions and team compositions in more permanent settings). Our definition of projects consisting of specific conceptions of time, task, and team underlines this further; all three relate to how work is actually organized (Lundin and Söderholm 1995). They are related to what work consists of (i.e. considering knowledge formation), when and where it takes place (i.e. considering the proximity to customers), and how formal and informal work contracts are designed (i.e. affecting empowerment and health of individuals). However, problems occur when an attempt is made to be more specific about how temporary organizations look in these respects, as studies on practical work in project settings are quite rare. Even more problematic, project work is extremely varied, depending among other factors on the degree of routinization and the degree to which the individual's work situation is tied to the temporary and/or the permanent parts of the larger organization (Packendorff 2002; Lindgren and Packendorff 2006b).

## 4.1. USE OF THE WORKING TIME AND SPACE

Aspects of *time* are crucial in all work organizations (Bengtsson et al. 2009), and the importance of temporal structuring in organizations is increasingly recognized by researchers (Orlikowski and Yates 2002). Length of engagement, including the duration of the working day or of employment contracts, is often discussed. In the case of projects, it is the duration of the activity itself that is in focus. Some authors argue that control and supervision of working time becomes of minor interest in task-oriented organizations with many projects (e.g. Isidorsson 2001). During the past decades, the length of employment arrangements has been discussed, as there seems to be evidence of a general reduction (Wikman 2002; Labour Force Survey 2013). Employment forms such as temporary, project, and contingency work are now used more often and for longer periods at the same time as the dominance of permanent employment diminishes. It is important to distinguish between the use of the term "project work" to refer to the duration of employment contract and to refer to the concept of working in project organization. The latter refers to the form of organization where the cognitive or physical work is performed, while the former is referring to one institutional setting, namely the employment duration.

There are of course situations wherein the increased use of project work (defined as short-time assignments) may be positively correlated with the use of project forms of organization as suggested by Söderlund (2005), although there are reasons to believe that this is not always the case. Whether work in itself is permanent or temporary in such organizations is actually an open empirical question. Most consultants are employed on permanent terms, but their work contracts and conditions are nevertheless generally very different from those of persons working in traditional industrial organizations. Social and psychological aspects of the emerging forms of time-limited work contracts have also been investigated (e.g. Allvin et al. 2011). Diffuse work demands, complex social relations, extremely vague contracts, and insecure working conditions have been emphasized as being particular to these work situations. Studies have also paid attention to the frequent use of employment agencies (e.g. Olofsson 2013), and how the relation between permanent employees and persons hired from an agency at the same workplace affects work (Olofsdotter 2008). Most importantly, working for an agency, like other forms of co-employment and joint employer arrangements, constitutes a triangular employment relationship in which not only the employer (the agency) and the employee but also the customer of the agency participate, not least with respect to time and space of the actual work arrangement (Kalleberg 2000).

Some research has focused on the length of working days and weeks and how it influences work practices. The introduction of the 48-hour week in combination with the diffusion of Frederick Taylor's principles (e.g. time studies of work) in the first part of the previous century seems to have enhanced the pace of work (Johansson 1977;

Rosengren 2009). Similar tendencies have also been observed during the past decades. The efforts to reduce costs in organizations by applying different organizational models, such as the "just-in-time" production model, are likely to have consequences for work intensity and time arrangements. Business approaches such as "process reengineering" and other ideas dealing with the phenomenon of cost reduction – sometimes referred to as "low road" by trade unions – have led some observers to talk about an emergence of a "neo-Tayloristic" era. The low road implies a routinized and hectic work regime; the "high road," in contrast, is supposed to lead to versatile and innovative activity (Streeck 1992).

The predominant approach to regulating employment relations (via collective agreements) was formed in the interplay between the social partners of the traditional industrial organizations and during the past decades has been challenged not only by a reduction in the number of union members but also by the increased use of employment agencies and of short-term and part-time employment. These versions of temporary work must be attended to before we discuss our main theme, namely, how work and employment regimes are challenged by the use of project organizational solutions.

Employment or temporary agencies are more and more frequently used in many sectors of the economy. A liberalized approach to the use of agencies took place in Austria, Denmark, Finland, France, Germany, Great Britain, Greece, Italy, the Netherlands, Portugal, Spain, and Sweden during the 1990s; nevertheless, some EU countries still have restrictions (Johansson 2010). The relative number of workers employed by these agencies and then hired by customers in relation to the total number of employees (the penetration rate) varies between countries, industries, and not least during business cycles. By country, it is still quite low with an average of 2 percent in Europe with the highest level in Great Britain of almost 5 percent (Ciett 2013). The share could naturally be much higher in some types of industries.

The working conditions in employment agencies used to vary substantially between countries. This was supposed to have changed when an EU directive from 2008 established a nondiscrimination principle for persons hired in employment agencies. Wages and other working conditions should be the same for those working for the employment agencies as for those employed by the customer company for the same kind of work. The incorporation of the temporary agencies into the traditional system has been institutionalized in Sweden, where the formal employment conditions are actually about the same as in other companies, including the relevance of institutions such as collective bargaining agreements and permanent employment (Johansson 2010).

The shutdown of a (former Ericsson) Flextronics factory for telecom production in northern Sweden in 2010 illustrates the temporary as well as the permanent character of work in temporary agencies. An extensive use of personnel from a local agency meant that a substantial part of the employer's responsibilities was moved to another company while the supervision of work still remained in the industrial organization. The number of persons hired from the agency could easily be changed and adapted to the fluctuations of business cycles, which was one reason behind the change. The insecurity for these persons sometimes referred to as project workers was obvious and there were also signs of tension when persons hired by the agency worked side by side with persons employed by the industrial company (Olofsdotter 2008; Banerjee et al. 2012). At the time of the closedown, white-collar workers, blue-collar workers, and persons working for an employment agency each accounted for around one-third of those employed. From a job security point of view, at the closedown of the factory, those who were employed by the agency were actually somewhat better off than those who worked for Flextronics, as the work for the agency was permanent. They could look to the agency to find them subsequent employment, while the others faced a higher risk of becoming unemployed (Ekstedt 2013).

The flexibility of the labor market is affected by another tendency, namely, the use of short-term and part-time assignments, and this phenomenon is confusingly sometimes referred to project work.

This is common for people working in hotels and restaurants, in trade and shops, as well as in health care. The privatization of the health sector during the past decades has led to the establishment of many new suppliers. In health care, organizations of different sizes provide an increasing number of personal assistants to older and disabled persons (Ekstedt and Sundin 2006). This work is characterized by irregular working hours, part-time contracts, and short notice about changes of work sites and tasks. In Sweden, the formal employment security and working conditions are less beneficial for those having short-term and part-time contracts than for those with permanent contracts. The demand for full-time employment has therefore developed into a political issue not only in Sweden but also in many other countries (Ekstedt and Sundin 2006).

There is a much-cited misconception that projects automatically lead to short-term engagements and work. Organizational planning in permanent organizations today is often based on quarterly, semiannual, and annual reports. This results in planning horizons that do not usually extend beyond a year, and it is in fact heavily controlled by the calendar year. In project-organized activity, however, the nature of the project determines the planning horizon, which can range anywhere from a few days, as for a news or science magazine in television production, to 25 years as in the case of a new space program or the construction of a nuclear power plant. Compared with a calendar-based planning cycle, the time frame for projects and employment can be shorter or longer. What is indisputable is that the project model leads to a planning horizon that is directly business and task oriented and thus reflects the nature of the business well. This is not always the case in calendar-based planning, which is mainly based on bureaucratic considerations. The calendar is in turn the framework for many formal institutions, including taxation and vacations. It is of interest to find out if such differences are reflected in the way work is organized and institutionalized in the two kinds of organizations. The business and task orientation, for example, is likely to loosen the borders between work and leisure time.

To sum up, one may say that short and part-time assignments (including work for employment agencies) are not very different from work in traditional industrial organizations, which is unsurprising as most of it is performed in industrial factories, in the service and health care sectors, and in trade. The use of employment agencies means that the size of the workforce is flexible. The model is therefore useful in activities with short-work introduction; in other cases, long-term relationships are built not only with particular agencies but even with specific employees working for these agencies (Olofsson 2013). The same is true for advanced work when the individuals have personal and professional responsibilities, like those of physicians. While the content of work itself is much the same as in permanent organizations, the major difference is that the work often takes place at the premises of another employer and that the other employer – or customer – can even supervise the work. This implies that more organizations are involved in designing work as well as in taking on responsibilities for work situations.

The more extensive use of loose and short-term employment undertakings may affect the power balance between employer and employee, but it seems to leave the traditional institutions of work more or less intact. It is easy to understand, however, that representatives of unions become frustrated by this development, as do young people facing insecurity when searching for permanent employment, especially when youth unemployment is extremely high in many Western countries. However, short-term employment, including agency work, is often less useful in work that focuses on problem solving – areas where project organization dominates. It is more likely that the projectification trend, whereby the time of activity is related to the nature of the task and business, will challenge the dominating institutions of work organization in a more profound way (see Chapter 5). It is also likely that the challenges include questions of where work will take place, which we now discuss in greater depth.

Where does work in projects take place in *spatial* terms? Much of it is performed in close cooperation with customers in the sphere of their organizations or in networks or clusters of interrelated organizations. The physical presence at a specific workplace becomes less important in project-based forms of organizing, even if the activity, as characteristic of a PSO, may take place in close connection to more permanent parts of an organization. But the R&D projects of a PSO may have connections with organizations all over the world. The omnibus character of project-based organizing is facilitated by the fact that more and more work is transformed and connected through rapid IT, in particular the Internet. This is very different from work in employment agencies where the challenge is to move from one specified workplace to another and quickly start to participate in the daily activities of each workplace. The spread of modern information and communication technology and work in projects seem to go hand in hand though, allowing people to work in virtual teams spread across not only nations but continents. Changes in the use of space will no doubt challenge the institution of the workplace, which in turn will have a profound impact on other working conditions.

In permanent organizations, the workplace is a premier point of reference when regulating and measuring activity. Work is supposed still to "take place" at a specific location, even in a specific room, be it a factory, an office, or a studio. In this kind of organization, the contribution of work efforts is often valued in relation to the time spent in that room, sometimes even measured as the period between arrival to and departure from it. Many rules and decrees about working conditions relate to the physical workplace. Certain activities are not permitted, such as drinking alcohol or using the Internet for personal entertainment. The employers, on the other hand, have certain obligations, including providing restrooms or safety facilities. However, the fixed relation to a specific place seems to be loosening up to some degree in permanent organizations. It is now possible for some persons to do parts of their work at home via the Internet.

There is no doubt that the project model of organizing opens up the space of economic activity even more. The factory and office gates of the industrial model have in fact been torn down. The workplace as the self-evident framework is in question when it comes to forming work-life institutions. Employment relations and institutions supporting work life are affected by this. They have to handle situations where individuals are likely to be more conspicuous than in a traditional industrial setting. The appreciation of work efforts (or lack thereof) becomes instant and communicated directly. Personal responsibility for one's future employability and for business results becomes more pronounced. However, increased personal responsibility will not automatically lead to more personal power. For project members who deliver results too late or below the expected standard, the work situation may become highly frustrating. A worker's personal health will no doubt be affected by stress, overload, or even burnout (Zika-Viktorsson 2002; Zika-Viktorsson et al. 2006; Pinto et al. 2014).

The identity of individuals and organizations becomes pronounced. Appreciated and able workers achieve higher employability than those who do not meet the demands of customers and project managers. This transformation is also likely to have an impact on the labor market and its institutions. A more polarized labor market appears, in which knowledgeable persons with experience, good connections, and the ability to work in harmony with others in a network will be the winners. But how will the educational systems of today cope with these changes of knowledge demand? Anticipating our later analysis of the impact of projectification on institutions (see Chapter 5), coworkers must certainly be prepared for situations where a lot of training and development takes place in problem-solving activities. They must be trained for continued training or in other words for lifelong learning (Lundgren 2013).

Unfortunately, a lack of research underpins our reflections on work in Project Society, especially with regard to time and space in different project-based settings. We therefore limit ourselves to describe the character of work in different settings by presenting illustrative cases from PBOs, PSOs, and PNWs, respectively. These describe the differences between the three architypes of project-based

organizing and how work differs from that in permanent organizations. Finally, with these illustrations as a background, we develop an
overall picture showing how the transformation to a Project Society
affects work practice and working life institutions.

## 4.2. WORK AND EMPLOYMENT IN PROJECT-BASED ORGANIZATIONS

By definition, most work in PBOs is performed in projects. A pure
PBO, like many construction or consultancy companies, actually has
no line production. In other words, the projects are their line. The
permanent parts of a PBO are more characteristic of an overhead
function, to take care of activity between projects and to promote
and prepare for future projects. Several studies look at the way PBOs
are organized (Lundin and Söderholm 1995; Hobday 1998, 2000;
Lindkvist 2001, 2004; Söderlund 2005; Bredin and Söderlund 2011;
Borg 2014), but remarkably few about work and working conditions
within PBOs. One exception is a recent study by Borg and Söderlund
(2014) that focuses solely on mobile project workers in one of
Scandinavia's leading technical consultancies. Even if the general
studies do not explicitly discuss working conditions, they still reveal
some features of their character.

In PBOs, the performance of each individual becomes highly
visible and, as stated earlier, the organization could by and large be
regarded as an internal market for project employment. Each time
a new project is to be staffed, the PBO has to find competent and
suitable individuals inside as well as outside its own organization.
Consequently, the PBO works as a marketplace for competence. As
the companies in construction, consulting, and elsewhere derive their
revenues from projects, the payment of the individual is often directly
connected to the type and number of projects in which he or she is
participating. If someone sells a new project, the individual may even
get an additional sales bonus. But even if wages in PBOs are based on a
fixed employment contract, it is obvious that each individual faces
a risk of not being asked to participate in future projects if he or

she cannot compete in this internal marketplace for competence (Arvidsson and Ekstedt 2006).

In the PBO model with its focus on project performance, in many cases the employees become more loyal to their project than to their home organization. In fact, a recent study shows that individuals working in projects exhibit a citizenship behavior not only toward the organization but also to the project, and this is known as "project citizenship behavior" (Braun et al. 2013). A well-adapted project member has to know and understand this orientation and the interpersonal relations on which the project is built and exhibit such behavior. Getting to know new employees quickly and making sure to not only take their specialized expertise into account but also to assert one's own are becoming key traits for a successful career in PBOs. This is important for project managers, but also for other project participants, who must demonstrate their competence to advance and be included in future projects. This places certain demands on people in terms of their social skills in relation to project managers, other project participants, customers, and outside persons and groups, as the entire group's results will be the ultimate indication of how well a project has been carried out. The PBO itself also has to be attractive (a brand name) to recruit capable new members for upcoming projects (Arvidsson and Ekstedt 2006).

The employees in the traditional industrial organization, the hierarchical bureaucracy, on the other hand, face a limited risk of losing their job if the firm or the employee does not perform, even if total job security is increasingly rare in this type of organization. The stability of employment relations will nevertheless increase if the organization invests in the training and education of its employees. In general, however, the individuals in the traditional industrial organizations only absorb a small part of the organization's overall business risk. In a PBO, the picture is quite different. If payment to the individual varies and is directly connected to the revenues and the attractiveness of the person's competence, he or she assumes a relatively large share of the organization's business risk. This is common in consulting firms, where payments may also be fully visible and variable. It is less obvious in the construction sector, where the distance between the worker and the final customer is larger and more complex. Moreover, if the organization invests less in education, the individual de facto also takes on a relatively large risk of not being employed in future projects. Quite a lot of training related to problem-solving activities in projects does take place in PBOs, which implies that those who do get assigned to projects have a good chance of developing skills and competence. As a conclusion, one may say that the individuals take a substantial share of business and employment risks in this kind of organization (Arvidsson and Ekstedt 2006).

Projects do not necessarily imply a non-bureaucratic working environment, however. Models prescribed or put forward by professional organizations (e.g. PMI) as well as industrial standards aimed at improving project efficiency and stability can in fact result in standardizing work processes even in temporary organizations. Managerial patterns as well as role-based responsibilities are well diffused and contribute to the bureaucratization of organizations, including PBOs. The search for control and efficiency, however, may harm innovativeness within the project teams (Anderson 2005). This could hypothetically lead to PBOs being characterized by "routinized" work processes and environments much in the same manner as when work in manufacturing industries became standardized in the industrial era. This type of work is not only present in construction but also in the consulting industry (Schoeneborn 2013). Standardization could be an advantage when project members do not know one another before a project starts. Projects with a routinized approach based on stable and well-known goals have been labeled "recurrent projects," which should be distinguished from "unique projects," for which the objectives are more or less unique and often of a visionary character. While PBOs may embrace both unique and recurrent projects, the latter are more common in new product development projects (Ekstedt et al. 1999). In organizations governed by standardized projects, working conditions may contain elements found in more traditional work organizations. In organizations with unique projects, however, one is more likely to find working conditions and environments that are widely different from those in traditional bureaucratic hierarchies, where the work content is often standardized and even repetitive.

As noted, the number of companies and persons working within business services has increased substantially during the past decades. Quite a few of them provide consulting on how the industrial activities should be organized and managed. Most of these companies are organized as pure PBOs. One illustration is the company Development, which works as a business development consultant (Arvidsson and Ekstedt 2006). Its consultants initiate, manage, and realize the introduction of new forms and principles concerning, for example, how an industrial company can develop its offerings. Development is a medium-size company in its industry, with some 20 employees and a strong international reputation. Its customers come from all over Europe, but mainly from Scandinavia and the UK. Revenues are generated directly from projects done for clients. Each individual project is expected to cover its own direct costs plus parts of the company's shared, non-project-related costs, and also to enhance the company's profitability. The project manager sells project ideas to customers and takes responsibility for their completion.

Each senior consultant at Development is, in practice, an income generator who sells ideas to potential customers and then creates a project to deliver the result. The consultant guarantees the future outcome through his or her role as project leader and key account manager. To a large extent, the customer buys the project based on the reputation of the company, which is manifested in its brand name; in many cases, however, the qualifications and personal contacts of the individual consultant are the decisive factors. As a result, Development has a complex structure for making decisions and allocating resources. The company is formally headed by a CEO, who is supported by a secretary. The CEO also has some right to make demands on how other consultants should use their free time – the time during which they are not working on income-generating activities. This could imply work aimed at developing and selling new projects but also internal projects, such as writing books or other forms of marketing and knowledge development. In many cases, individuals receive money from Development only for the time they work in revenue-generating projects. Any other time focused on internal projects, new sales, or other activities such as working on boards of other firms or in academia is controlled entirely by each individual. Some employees prefer to avoid non-bookable against project time because it not only may mean a lower personal wage but also sends a signal to the CEO that the person in question is not "pulling his or her weight." As a result, internal work that is not directly connected to sales tends to have lower priority and is deferred in favor of present and future customer assignments.

In practice, the top management team, which consists of senior consultants including the CEO who also are the main shareholders, is the real center of power. This group makes the critical decisions. People can become a shareholder only after having worked successfully as a senior consultant for a long time. The primary goals of the business are to deliver profitability for its consultants by providing value for its clients and to create interesting and instructive projects that develop and enhance both customers and consultants. Some projects may be taken on to improve personal learning; however, most projects are taken to maximize the financial outcome. Thus, senior consultants are primarily responsible for their own and their project group's learning, which also determines how attractive those individuals will be in the internal market for competence. This setup also makes the organization flexible in terms of the number and skills of people working in particular projects. Many of the characteristics of work in the case of Development are found in other PBOs as well. The construction sector has many similar consultants, and other kinds of companies, such as general contractors, are responsible for administering huge projects consisting of systems of various organizations. It is here where the distinction between PBOs and PNWs becomes difficult, but that has to do with the change of perspective from a focal organization to the network level of analysis. While the general contractor should be considered a PBO, this organization is not only embedded in but also the orchestrator of a wider (project) network of other organizations, many of them subcontractors or service providers. This is how a PBO is supplemented by PNWs, whose coordination is to a significant extent based on the structures of the multi-organizational networks (rather than the single organizations), that is, network rules and network resources (Sydow and Windeler 1998). In some cases, such as the Globen project in Stockholm or the Golden Terrace project in Warsaw, these companies organize projects consisting of hundreds of organizations contributing over a long period of time to the same final task.

In sharp contrast to PNWs, work in PBOs, as demonstrated by the case of Development, is carried out under the formal governance of a single hierarchy. Nevertheless, it may well take place at different physical locations. Most companies have a home office to which the coworkers are connected. But a lot of the working time is spent at the customers' facilities. This kind of work appears quite similar to the work at employment agencies. There are, however, fundamental differences in that the supervision of a worker from an agency is de facto performed by the customer, while those who work in a consultancy company and are supposed to contribute ideas or concepts emerging from the home organization or themselves are supervised by their formal employer. The presence at a specific place is of minor interest. Some consultants also work with many customers at the same time, while others may stay with the same customer and working place for a long period. In the latter case, it is natural if the relations and the loyalty to the place or the organization where the actual work takes place may become quite substantial.

Work in the construction sector is related to physical workplaces in a different way. Construction projects spread to different locations and vary in size and time frame. The projects become concrete as they are directly associated with a specific site. When working with a project, the professionals spend more or less time at the site. For some groups of professionals in the construction sector, it is not unusual to become more loyal to the project and the working site than to the management – often referred to as a place – of the company in which they are employed (Martinsson 2010). This, by the way, seems to occur also in research and development projects where staying with the customers over a longer period of time is common (Lutz 1999).

The role of the workplace is fundamentally different in PBOs as compared with that of traditional industrial organizations. In the latter, the workplace is taken for granted. The workplace is usually seen as the spatial and social arena for the work organization, closely related to its hierarchical order and decision structure. This is where the formal and informal contracts are acted out. The stability of and point of reference to a specific place is lacking when it comes to PBOs and has to be substituted with other stable structures, such as rules or roles found in professions, networks, routines, or business concepts. One problem, however, is that many formal contracts, like the legal system that includes work laws and agreements between the parties of the labor market, refer to the physical workplace as a regulative entity. The laws of the work environment often refer to the conditions at a specific place. We return to this problem when we discuss the institutions of Project Society (see Chapter 5).

We have pointed out that there are fundamental differences between PBOs and traditional industrial organizations in the relations between the organization and the market, or more precisely between its coworkers and the customers. Changes in the way each organizational type interacts with outside actors are likely to affect the relations between actors in the organization in different ways. If new patterns emerge, for instance, the preconditions for informal contracts between the actors in the organizations will change. These differences may be illustrated by the categories "exit" and "voice" once put forward by Albert O. Hirschman (1970).

Traditional industrial organizations, the role model of managerial capitalism, are designed to offer long series of standardized products and services for mass consumption. The attractiveness of the products is tested through exit mechanisms characteristic of markets (take it or leave it situations). For most economists, "exit" is seen as the main alternative when trying to understand economic interaction. In these models of industrial organizations, there are few direct contacts between the producer and the consumer; the customers are seldom aware of how the commodities have been produced. Producing commodities for stock can result in long time lags between production and consumption. Slow market signals dominate over direct contacts between actors. Industrial organizations not only are conceived as acting in these rather anonymous markets but are themselves characterized by hierarchical systems of decision making with rather clear-cut and relatively nonpermeable organizational boundaries. Efficiency is reached through economies of scale in production, despite limited interaction between levels, departments, and individuals. However, this implies high monitoring costs, as many levels of management and control are formed and professional positions are developed to handle this kind of organizational framework. Long-term formal contracts (mostly collective) have been the dominating form of employment contract.

In the PBOs, the traditional contracts – purchase and sales contracts in the market as well as employment contracts in the organization – are challenged. Activities of PBOs are generally more closely related to its customers than is the case in industrial organizations. It is not unusual for employees of both the seller and the buyer organization to work together on the same project. Here, the "exit" mechanism of the market is to a large extent replaced by "voice." In most cases, transactions are preceded by negotiations. This is as true in markets as it is in organizations or interorganizational networks. High negotiation costs in the early planning stages of a construction project, for instance, are likely to be reimbursed in terms of fewer mistakes when the whole production apparatus is involved later on (Ekstedt and Wirdenius 1995). The high level of service content in PBOs, such as consultancy companies, also contributes to closeness. Costs for monitoring and supervision are minimized, as it is in the interest of the project members to perform the assignment according to the description of the tasks to be engaged in future projects. The need for middle management is thus small. Instead, there are high upfront costs associated with contracts and negotiations (Ekstedt et al. 1999). But as a great part of the economic activity takes place with the customer, these negotiations will also influence the internal life of the PBOs. We therefore point to three aspects where one can discern important differences with the internal life of traditional industrial organizations, namely the responsibility of the individual, the industrial relations in PBOs, and the health situation of the individual.

Compared with other forms of organizations, in PBOs each individual must assume relatively high responsibility for his or her own career. Explicit elements of business contracts might also be traced in the employment contracts. Each worker must constantly arrange for his or her own supply of work by being attractive to project managers and customers. Project managers, who need competent workers, must in turn be attractive to the project workers they need for their projects. Project workers compete against one another, as do project managers for critical and scarce expertise in the PBO. Moreover, when the project model is used and salaries and compensation are tied to each person's contributions within various projects, these people become, in a sense, "self-employed" within the framework of an organization. It is said that some IT companies have explicitly called on their employees "to act as if they were self-employed." If compensation levels are tied to the time a person is employed within projects and these projects also constitute the income sources for the organization, people will assume a large part of the business risk. This situation is quite common in management and strategy consulting firms, where the individuals' risk status is considerably higher than in organizations in which employees hold permanent positions with fixed salaries.

Future employability is facilitated by individual marketing by the members of the PBO (Arvidsson and Ekstedt 2006), not unlike individuals working in project networks (see later discussion on work in PNWs). It is necessary for those working within this system to cope with the increasing internal, and sometimes also external, competition, which requires the ability to constantly improve oneself, and to have social skills to "sell" oneself within the organization. This internal sales ability is based on the success of and attention to projects in which one has participated, and on how one's contributions to the project are rated. Individual learning also occurs throughout a project, based on the problems and tasks for which each individual is responsible. Training organized outside project work consequently diminishes in favor of on-the-job training. Although the permanent structure of the PBO may well support personal development and career planning, the temporariness of projects creates noticeable obstacles to the newly employed and others who lack experience in project-based work. Entry barriers to PBOs may become high. The system obviously emphasizes the importance of personal human capital in the form of expertise in some area, and social capital in the form of a good reputation among important contact-creating people. If we take this tendency to its extreme, we see that competition will occur between individuals in various areas of specialization rather than between organizations with more or less fixed human resources. The market has entered the organization. Individual-based knowledge is favored over organization-based knowledge (Ekstedt 1988); at least, the organization of knowledge and learning on another level than that of the individual becomes a severe challenge.

The roles of employer and employee are different in PBOs compared to those of traditional industrial organizations. The delegation of responsibility to the project members impacts the formal rule system of the organization. Fulfilling the goals according to a given agreement is the central endeavor of the project team. How this is accomplished – within some boundaries – is left for the project team to decide. The way of working in project organizations could therefore be experienced as a threat to the present system of industrial relations. The employees' position and ability to negotiate will have a major impact on their working conditions. Better knowledge of what informal contracts imply, together with personal network relationships within and across the PBO, may change the power relations.

Knowledge about health issues in PBOs is limited. Research points at uncertainty and lack of security for the individuals in all kinds of organizations today. The reaction of the individual to this type of stress is connected to whether or not he or she enjoys working in this kind of organization. There seems to be a risk that work in this kind of organization (sometimes referred to as borderless work), including projects, may lead to psychological problems for workers (Zika-Viktorsson et al. 2006; Allvin et al. 2011). At the same time, PBOs with their lean permanent structures may be less equipped than traditional organizations to handle health issues. While this is a standard task in the latter type of organization, provided by the HR department, PBOs may at best source such services from external providers.

### 4.3. WORK AND EMPLOYMENT IN PROJECT-SUPPORTED ORGANIZATIONS

What will happen to work in traditional organizations when industry-related activity becomes increasingly organized in (or at least supported by) projects? What will happen to the characteristics of work in the automotive industry or the information and communication industry, for example, when project activities such as development and design are playing an increasingly important role? Formal research about this transformation with a focus on working conditions is also limited. It is, however, possible to give a rough picture of what kind of changes one can expect by illustrating the work practices in a couple of cases. We start with a case illustrating what happens to work when parts of a traditional industrial organization turn into a PSO and its work tasks become projectified. The second case illustrates the work organization in a major industrial company in the IT sector that frequently uses projects in its daily activity. We think that those examples give a fair illustration of the character of work in PSOs – of the content of work, place of work, and contracts of work.

*From assembly-line work to work in projects*

The projectification of a traditional industrial organization is likely to be an incremental process; however, in some cases, this transformation occurs in one visible, fast, and limited step. That is what happened some time ago in parts of an Ericsson factory situated in Östersund, a small city in the northern part of Sweden (Ekstedt 1991). This step turned out to be of great importance for the persons involved several decades later (Ekstedt 2013). The initiative to change direction of activity was actually local. Some of the leading actors in the factory thought that it would be more and more difficult for them to compete in the international market by the rather simple production of telephone equipment in long series with the limited supply of labor the vicinity could offer. There were also signals from the top management of Ericsson Group of a forthcoming fundamental restructuring of the company. The local managers thought that to be able to survive in the long run, they needed to start a more sophisticated activity. After a long search process, they decided to retrain some employees to become programmers. These efforts drew quite a lot of resources and commitment from the company itself, and also from the surrounding community. Subsequently, they also found a business idea in the form of serving the security of the IT systems within the Ericsson Corporation. They also hoped to perform similar activity in other organizations in the future. A new department, moving the company toward becoming a PSO, was established at the factory level.

A massive individual training program was used as a preparation to adapt the employees to totally new, much more project-oriented work tasks. Employees engaged in the production of telephone equipment were retrained to become independent programmers. People were selected to those training programs after thorough testing among interested employees in all categories of the local workforce. Quite a few of those who completed the training program previously worked on the assembly line, and many of them were females with limited formal education. The educational requirement for working on the assembly line was only an introduction course of three weeks. The work on the line followed strict routines and can be characterized as extremely monotonous. The employees had hardly any sense of responsibility for the work tasks. There was a lack of understanding of their role in the total process as well as knowledge of who would benefit from their work effort. The idea of customers was absent among those who worked on the line.

It was a huge step for these persons to become acquainted with the new organization given their background in line production. As independent programmers, they had to solve problems from the very beginning. New projects with new tasks appeared. The IT they used as a work tool improved all the time. The difficulty of the tasks increased as the new programmers became more and more confident in their new roles. They also started to ask for more education and training. When the programmers looked back to the first period of the new position, they found that the tasks they accomplished in the beginning were simple. They were learning all the time and had become part of a true "learning organization."

But other organizational matters also changed. The work became projectified. The tasks were transformed into projects of different lengths. The programmers worked directly with the internal customers and quite often as a team with other people from their own and the customer's organizations. The sense of responsibility increased when they saw that their job had a direct influence on customers as well as fellow workers. Personal empowerment increased. The role the supervisors had had in traditional assembly work was replaced by personal responsibility for what they delivered to customers.

The overhead organization for the newly founded department of programmers was limited. One leader with the assistance of one person supported more than 20 programmers. The programmers acted as their own project leaders in most cases. One important task for the leader of the department was to distribute new projects among programmers. The leadership in this part of the company was performed in a way more similar to that in PBOs than to the traditional industry organization most units of Ericsson had at that time.

The transformation from an industrial organization to a PSO also changed the relation to the workplace. The programmers spent most of their working time in the new office at the factory, but they also spent some time at the customer's location, even though not to the same extent as most people working in PBOs do. Still, the costs of traveling actually became the third-largest cost item after wages and training. The programmers experienced a fundamental difference in their relations to the world outside the factory compared to the one they had had as workers on the line. They now spent much of their time in direct contact with the customers by telephone or via the Internet. On the line, they were isolated and able to communicate with other persons only during breaks.

The psychological contracts in the organization changed in many respects, and the responsibility of the employees expanded dramatically. They had to answer directly to the customers. In a sense, they acquired more power on matters dealing with how to work, that is, how to use the time. They had frequent dialogues with the customers and other team members about how to solve different tasks. In the end, however, they had to adapt to the wishes of the customers. They also participated in the planning of their own further education. The formal contracts also changed in an obvious way. From having been members of a blue-collar union, they moved to a white-collar one.

To sum up, one may say that the case of Ericsson in Östersund illustrates the "transformation dilemma" in a nutshell. A renewal project within an industrial corporation started an entirely new projectified activity with the existing workforce, including persons with weak formal education, as a base. It was a transformation from flow-process production to project-organized production entailing abandonment of detailed rule-directed work in favor of goal- and problem-directed work. Simple, repetitive routine work was pushed into the background and development of problem-solving capability was encouraged (Ekstedt et al. 1999). The character of knowledge formation had to change in a dramatic way. In the factory, the development of the production processes was taken care of by a few well-educated technicians. The workers just followed rather simple instructions. In the new PSO, knowledge developed and was formed to a much greater extent in the working process. It was in the interest of everyone to develop knowledge to be able to handle tasks that changed and became more sophisticated over time. Besides a *widening* of knowledge to all members of the organization, there were consequently also new and high demands on the quality of knowledge (*deepening*) (Ekstedt and Forsman 1991). It was no longer enough to know how to perform a certain task. One also had to know why a specific solution should be chosen to solve arising problems.

This case has an interesting aftermath illustrating what knowledge development, including knowledge of how to work in projects, can do for people in a long-run perspective. The Ericsson factory went through many phases of reconstruction after this one with the entrance of new owners (Solectron and then Flextronics) and a final closedown in 2010. By that time, many of the programmers from the original retraining programs had already moved to other organizations, both PBOs and PSOs. Those remaining after the closedown found it easier to find new jobs than other categories of employees. This illustrates that projectified activity seems to be less vulnerable to structural change than industrial organizing. Professional knowledge and knowledge of how to run and work in a project are easily transferred to new settings. Project activity may be seen as a never-ending reconstruction process (Ekstedt 2013).

*Industry supportive work – an example from an IT company*
Many companies in industry endeavor to engage in development-oriented work, since it tends to be the most crucial for long-run survival and profitability. Such companies sometimes outsource simpler, more routine activities and service activities that are

supportive but not critical. Our IT case company is a large, publicly traded international company in a highly globalized industry that is characterized by heavy research intensity and large development projects (Arvidsson and Ekstedt 2006). Following a major crisis in the early 2000s, the company chose to focus its activities on creating systems and services ancillary to the products they had formerly manufactured. Major parts of the production process were outsourced to other companies.

At this time, most of the employees in the company generally spent 70 percent of their time on various projects. The rest of their time was spent in line functions, where they had their permanent positions. Despite this, the purpose of the projects was to support the line operations, with an emphasis on development and renewal. The company was at this time a true PSO. Line managers were, by tradition, responsible for the company's revenues and consequently decided final dates, budget sizes, and goals of the projects. The line functions were also evaluated financially, based on their contribution to overall profitability. In addition, it was executive and management experience gained in line positions that counted when top executives were to be appointed. Experience in projects did not carry the same weight.

This led to tensions resulting from the difference between the organizational logics of line functions and projects. Line functions were focused on standardized output according to predefined ideals, while projects were more prone to use dialogue between project members and with customers, leading to results that sometimes were not possible to predefine. The tensions became apparent when the two – line functions and projects – were to integrate their respective efforts, manifested in battles for resources (e.g. competent people), leadership styles, identification and loyalty, and unclear roles and responsibilities. There were internal conflicts between those who worked mainly on projects and those who worked mainly in line positions. It appeared as if the firm had developed two types of internal environments with different attitudes toward work, and internal conflicts often rose between those who preferred projects and those who preferred the line approach.

Those employees involved in the project organization usually also had a permanent line position, in which they spent 20 percent to 30 percent of their time at work. Their supervisors on the line were responsible for their learning, career, social issues, and other security and comfort-related matters. The remaining 70 percent to 80 percent of their time was spent with project managers, who were responsible only for their performance within each individual project. The project leader(s) under whom an employee worked also varied over time. This leadership was entirely performance oriented. As a result, traditional roles such as those of manager and subordinate changed in character and became more complex. Projects offered a holistic view and a performance orientation such as creating new products and services, while the line organization offered the opportunity to lead people and create a long-term perspective.

This separation between projects and lines in PSOs also entails a division among the leadership in terms of performance versus human elements, between "management of results" and "people leadership." Project managers are responsible for performance in terms of goal fulfillment, while the line managers are responsible for employee learning, competence development and career advancement, health, stress, and other personal factors. As in PBOs, stress results both from heavy workloads and from the uncertainties that result from having two parallel structures and cultures in the organization. Employees we talked with expressed deep frustration over being uncertain as to which career path was best and what sort of experience would be most useful in the long run. It seemed that a more permanent line-based organizational form produced relationships between managers and subordinates that tended to be more personal and long term, with respect to both knowledge development and employment security. The line-based organization also gave the subordinates a fairly good idea of how their own careers were likely to progress, since the career ladder and associated requirements were clearly defined and relatively enduring. Some employees seemed to identify with and feel loyalty to the line function in which they were employed, while others seemed to be loyal to the projects in which they worked. This in itself strengthened the tension between line functions and projects. The issue of identification also could be related to corporate demography; the younger generations tend to prefer working in projects, while the older ones prefer working in a line function (Arvidsson 2009).

A conclusion drawn from this case is that problems result from the use of the two organizational models within one organization at the same time. The employees are confronted with conflicts regarding prioritizations and goals, and with issues concerning who has control over critical resources, most importantly, the employees' time. Project workers often believe that they cannot simultaneously fulfill their obligations within or outside of the ongoing project, which generates stress. One way of countering this would be to develop the HR function so that it better meets the needs of individuals and manages the conflicts between the project-based and line-based organizations (Bredin and Söderlund 2011). Otherwise, projects may become pawns in internal power struggles in which managers attempt to influence project results to achieve personal goals. At the same time, project members acquire more or less unique competence by working in advanced projects and can use such knowledge as a means of advancing their own career interests. In general, one may also say that work in projects may lead to increased workloads and stress but also increased involvement as a positive factor (Zika-Viktorsson et al. 1998). Stress levels and burnout symptoms may increase as more work is done in projects, especially if the time for recuperation and rest between projects tends to become minimized.

## 4.4. WORK AND EMPLOYMENT IN PROJECT NETWORKS

In addition to PBOs and PSOs, project networks have become an increasingly important archetype for project-based organizing. This is particularly true for the construction, engineering, and film/television industries. While the notion of PNW is sometimes used for simply delineating that more than two organizations participate in a project (e.g. Hellgren and Stjernberg 1995; Jones 1996; Orr et al. 2011: 39–40), that is, for interorganizational projects (Jones and Lichtenstein 2008), we refer here to a PNW as a more than temporary organizational form that is used to coordinate network-based projects (see Chapter 2). The argument here is that PNWs provide contexts for work that are quite different from PBOs and PSOs, not least as they consist of multiple organizations whose interaction is not coordinated by hierarchical fiat, but some mixture of long-term orientation, reciprocity, and trust (Powell 1990). These coordinating mechanisms have obvious repercussions for work and working conditions in PNWs that reach far beyond the individuals or organizations that coordinate this network type of organization.

Many industry-dense areas have been hit by an extensive structural transformation during the past decades. In Germany's Ruhrgebiet, in Northern France, and in Bergslagen in Sweden, the number of employees in the steel and coal industry has been dramatically reduced as a result of rationalization and overcapacity. Many development projects with connections to local networks have been started as a response to this transformation. Alternative activities in the IT sector and the cultural industry have been promoted. Similar tendencies can be seen in the northern part of Sweden, where the tremendously fast technological development in the lumber and forest industry has resulted in a significant reduction of the labor force as production becomes more capital intensive. These industries directly or indirectly used to dominate the labor market in many villages and cities of the north. In response to such layoffs, local mobilization started to flourish in many places and projects aiming to create alternative employment and business opportunities were introduced.

During the past decade, the idea of forming and renewal of regional or local clusters has been popular among politicians, authorities, and businesspeople as a means to promote local economic development. Local authorities are often proactive in starting projects aiming to create, support, or renew regional clusters. The strength of these clusters varies, with some being no more than "wishful thinking" clusters. Many individual entrepreneurs create networks to accomplish local mobilization to develop a specific city or region. Researchers and consultants have also initiated the building of networks to stimulate economic development. Björn Gustavssen´s "democratic dialogue" and interactive research are well-known examples of this in Sweden (Svensson et al. 2002).

A network consists of different constellations of individual entrepreneurs; some of them are also entreployees of PBOs, PSOs, and other permanent organizations. The characteristics of work in PNWs are similar to those of work as already described in permanent organizations such as PBOs and PSOs. In addition, PNWs feature many of the characteristics of work in interorganizational networks: temporariness, boundary spanning, and, because of close customer or supplier involvement, triadic employment relations (Kalleberg 2000; Marchington et al. 2005, 2011; Flecker and Meil 2010). One additional type of work in PNWs is that of the people who try to make the network or the cluster endure or develop, the work of the net-brokers who engage in "nexus work" (Long Lingo and O'Mahoney 2010) requiring integration rather than communication. Net-brokers are individual persons, organizational members positioned at the boundary of an organization, or people acting within the framework of a "network administrative organization" (Human and Provan 2000). We illustrate the phenomenon by referring to the work of net-brokers in clusters of the German media sector (described in Chapter 2) and in a local mobilization case.

### Net-brokers in the German media region

Berlin, which used to be the largest industrial city in Germany, suffered from deindustrialization not only after World War II but also after reunification. Though, for different reasons, it shared this destiny with regions such as the Ruhrgebiet or Bergslagen. At the same time, the cultural and media industry developed (again) into a thriving business. Given the strong history of Berlin in this sector – typified by the Filmstudio Babelsberg in the era of Fritz Lang and the roaring 1920s – this did not come as a surprise. Local politicians, however, took advantage of the opportunity and have supported the transformation of the city into one of the largest media clusters in Germany. Based mainly on small and medium-sized firms, many "cultural entrepreneurs" (DiMaggio 1982), and also on the presence of subsidiaries of major media conglomerates such as Bertelsmann and Sony, Berlin has become again the most active region in Germany in terms of producing media content (now also for television and the Internet). About 1,100 firms are involved in the production of about 300 movies a year (Senatsverwaltung für Wirtschaft Technologie und Frauen 2008: 48). Many of them are members of media.net berlin-brandenburg (www.medianet-bb.de), the formal core of the Berlin media cluster with Universal Music, Axel Springer, Scholz & Friends, ProSiebenSat.1, Bertelsmann UFA, Studio Babelsberg, and Pixelpark among its members.

Some PBOs in the cluster initiate and organize the production of TV movies in close collaboration with major television channels (sometimes public channels, which have regained market leadership in Germany) in PNWs. While little is known about the work of net-brokers in complex networks and clusters, it is clear that the producers head and manage fairly small companies but large production teams made up of permanent and temporary employees, self-employed individuals, and employees of other firms. This implies a mixture of direct control (hierarchical fiat) and network control, that is, using the presence of others to influence and control the actions of a third party (Manning and Sydow 2007). In addition, the employment relationship may change from project to project. While a camera-woman may be a temporary employee in one project, she may be self-employed when shooting another movie. With respect to time and space, PNWs exhibit the same diverse work characteristics as PBOs. What is more, employees are very likely to work for several employers and/or customers at the same time. In consequence, the project network – at least in addition to the organization and the industry – becomes a relevant point of reference for negotiating salaries and other means of gratification, for example, by being recruited for a "hot project" (Windeler et al. 2001).

### Net-brokers in a local mobilization project

This case examines net-brokers in a much smaller cluster, Odenskog in Östersund or "The business city of Odenskog," as the Swedish region is marketing itself. The industrial area of Odenskog used to be a rather inactive network dealing with some common problems within the area such as the renting of industrial properties (Westlund and Nilsson 2003). Shortly after 2000, network members invited a researcher to talk about local development. After his enthusiastic presentation about cluster formation, some businesspeople and politicians decided to apply for funding a project from the EU structural fund. They succeeded in raising the money and engaged researchers from the National Institute for Working Life, the local university, and representatives from the local authorities and companies to participate in the project. The much discussed Triple Helix (Leydesdorff and Etzkowitz 1998; Uhlin 2001) became the role model. The core of the network consisted of the companies in the old network, but it was supported by researchers in related projects and by local authorities. A project leader and an assistant were hired. The chairman of the board of the project and the project leader became true net-brokers, but other members of the network also aided them in this capacity. An overlap between different research projects and the Odenskog project occurred. The net-brokers worked both inside the network to create a common sense of identity among the more than 200 member companies and outside the network to make it an attractive environment for new companies to join. The net-brokers arranged frequent meetings and visited many of the companies. They surveyed the members to find out what kind of support the companies expected from the Odenskog project. A lot of the activity was external. Marketing and promoting the area as an ideal place for business activity took many forms. The close relations to research and education were stressed. The net-brokers initiated projects about relations to the schools and to the university, about making the area clean and attractive, and about marketing it in general. The net-brokers themselves, as well as researchers connected to the project, participated on local radio and TV. They arranged open seminars and fair-like activities at the airport and other places that would create a lot of attention. They also became involved in the placing of a shopping center in the Odenskog area, which attracted the attention of media and even national authorities.

The project leader and his assistant had an office in the Odenskog area. The assistant had a backup function and spent a lot of time at the office, but the project leader spent most of his time in meetings in different locations. The associated net-brokers, like the researchers, spent their time in other organizations. However, the identity of the project was connected to Odenskog as an area, to which the net-brokers had relations but not in the same way as to a traditional workplace.

The work of the net-brokers took place outside traditional organizational hierarchies. The commitment of the project leader was to fulfill the visionary goals of the project. He was hired by the development project for as long as it lasted. At the end of the first three-year period, they applied for an extension of the project. The working chairman of the board of the project was also the CEO and the owner of a mid-sized member company. His economic return for representing the project at many meetings was limited, therefore demonstrating "project citizenship behavior" (Braun et al. 2013). The other net-brokers also worked in other organizations and they were committed to the project as long as it aligned with their commitments to those organizations. The only person with a traditional hierarchical position was the assistant to the project leader.

To sum up, the net-brokers were working with different means to strengthen the unity of the network by giving it an identity and thereby a better chance to promote it in a wider market or field. Even if the work of the net-workers was to promote an area or a region, they were themselves only loosely connected to a physical workplace. It is of interest to notice that the net-brokers seemed to act outside the hierarchical systems of any organization; they were only tied to a fairly independent project as a temporary organization.

## 4.5. WORKING IN PROJECT SOCIETY — SOME CONCLUSIONS

Many of the characteristics ascribed to projects actually refer to how work is performed in them. The argument is that work in projects consists of more or less specific tasks and that the complexity of the tasks demands work of a problem-solving nature. Also, the work has a clearly stated time constraint related to business-planning horizons and not to a calendar-connected bureaucracy and that the results of the work seem to be more important than how it is performed. It is also argued that work in projects is generally performed in teams consisting of different professionals from many organizations, often including the customers. Finally, projects often have the goal of leading to a transition or transformation of some kind or another. Toward this end, professional knowledge has to be paired with social capital and knowledge about the way projects function as temporary organizations embedded in more permanent structures. The latter has a technical aspect: what are the parts of the project and how are they synchronized with the needs of the customers? This kind of knowledge is hard to achieve without practical experience. The social function of the project is also vital. A certain kind and frequency of participating are expected to be considered a member of a project (Borg 2014). These general arguments are confirmed by our cases.

The cases also illustrate that the characteristics of work differ depending on not only the degree of routinization and the degree to which the individual's work situation is tied to the temporary and/or the permanent but also to the archetypal setting of projects. On-the-job training is common in all the three archetypes – PBOs, PSOs, and PNWs – often in connection to problem-solving activities of various kinds. Organized educational support to individuals is most likely to take place in PSOs where HR functions often continue to exist. Members of PBOs and net-brokers, who are important for organizing work in multi-organizational project networks, are to a great extent left to take care of their own careers, including education and training. In these latter cases, HR functions may at least sometimes be taken care of by regional institutions, as in the case of television production, more often than not supported by the regional government (Lutz et al. 2003). Industry-specific educational programs may also exist, as in the construction sector, where workers need certification to be allowed to perform certain activities in the construction process. Members of PBOs and PNWs also have high personal accountability for the results of the project, which leads to individualization of their work. They are also engaged in promoting future projects whereby their own career is hardly as boundaryless as is often assumed (DeFillippi and Arthur 1994; for a critical appraisal see Arnold and Cohen 2008). Employability is therefore directly related to personal responsibility for project performance and consequently also for personal business risks. This is perhaps stressed even more among those who work as self-employed, independent professionals. Work contracts will include elements of business contracts. However, the responsibility for business results is less pronounced in PSOs.

Places such as a factory or a hospital are central for work in traditional permanent organizations. Most activity takes place at a specific location, and the organization is often referred to by the name of the workplace. Working time is often measured and regulated by the actual time spent at this physical location. The situation is different for those who work in projects, where everything between "project as passion" (Svejenova et al. 2011) and "projects as prison" (Lindgren and Packendorff 2006a) seems possible. In PBOs and PNWs, presence at meetings at the customer's facilities is often more important than attendance at the home office – only limited parts of the working time are spent there. Being associated with a specific workplace is of less importance than belonging to a specific project team. The activity of a team is not necessarily related to a place; work may be performed at different locations and often without members' actual presence by using IT solutions. A specific place is not important for the brokers themselves, even if they work with promoting places. The role of the workplace for work in PSOs seems to be somewhere between that of traditional industrial organizations and that of PBOs/PNWs. The projects often extend their borders outside the home organization, but the project members' affiliation to the line organization provides a connection to a workplace.

In conclusion, evolving time–space arrangements of Project Society are different from those of the traditional Industrial Society. Even if the transition to a knowledge or service economy may not continue or even, as suggested by Okhuysen et al. (2013), be reversed in some industrialized countries, the importance of temporary forms of organizing is likely to stay if not grow further. Work, training, and leisure are much more intertwined in time as well as in space dimensions. The use of both local and global activity also makes it different from that of the locally bound Agrarian Society. It could be fruitful to illustrate the changed work regimes related to the projectification process by reminding ourselves of Hägerstrand's ideas of time geography (see Chapter 1). According to him, all action takes place in both time and space dimensions. The individual is introduced into the "time-room" at the point of birth and leaves it by the point of death (Asplund 1985; Hägerstrand 1991). The time-room consists of different stations.

The projectification trend has effects on careers. The term "boundary-less career" (Arthur and Rousseau 1996) has been used to describe one effect in the new organizational era opening up options for work and careers. The trend toward more frequent changes within and across organizations (including self-employment) works differently for the three archetypes. A particularly strong effect is on careers related to networks where people may find employment in several networks. The publication mentioned above on boundaryless careers contains examples from the film and television industry, which now is extremely network oriented. Currently, effects also differ in various parts of the world depending on the development of work-life institutions and industrial habits. Despite its increasing empirical relevance, more critical accounts point to the boundaries of boundaryless careers (Inkson et al. 2012).

People in the Agrarian Society both live and work at the same location. In the Industrial Society, the place and time of living and working are separated for the industrial workforce: the time-room for work is elsewhere and very different from the time-room for living. Work in the home, which still is the case for many women, especially in a country such as Germany, is not even part of employment statistics. But what will the time-room look like in the neo-industrial Project Society? The absolute separation between work and home as in the Industrial Society will probably disappear. Some work will take place at home as in the Agrarian Society, but many new stations are also likely to appear. Project work is increasingly carried out at places related to different organizations and on the move, that is, in trains and airports or at conferences, hotel rooms, and at cafes. Moreover, the lifelong learning of the old apprenticeship system may reappear in new forms (Lundgren 2013) as learning and working become more and more intertwined. Lack of practical training on how projects work may result in high entry barriers to inexperienced young people. The educational system has to prepare students both for a smooth entrance, problem solving, and flexible work situations and also for learning and relearning later on (see Chapter 5). The time-room will be extended by new dimensions. It will be possible to be at one place and still participate in working processes at other places. The new technology allows instant as well as distant project participation. A self-employed Swedish photographer may get her raw images immediately refined and edited by a Photoshop specialist in Taiwan. Even children are starting to be technically prepared for this open-room work model by early habits of using smart phones and computers.

In the next chapter, we discuss how the transitions to a Project Society challenge institutions supporting today's business and working life. How, for example, will labor laws, labor politics, educational and professional institutions, as well as market regulations be affected by projectification and the related development of information and communication technology?

# 5  Institutions and projectification

As previously argued, projectification has a profound impact on how management and work are organized. When a strong trend toward projects and other forms of temporary organizations confronts the predominant institutions of the surrounding society, friction and tensions inevitably arise because most of these are still adapted to industrial work in more permanent settings (e.g. manufacturing). Think, for instance, of the social partners (trade unions and employer associations) that are more or less consciously struggling with the transformation toward a "service society" (Fourastié 1949), "knowledge economy" (Drucker 1969), "information society" (Naisbitt 1984), or "network society" (Castells 1996), not to mention project forms of organizing. Expressed in another way: the social partners, and also many political parties, are descendants of the First and Second Industrial Revolutions, while descriptions such as those just listed as well as "Project Society" capture characteristics of a society after or in the midst of a Third Industrial Revolution (Finkelstein 1986; Magnusson 1999). We do not believe that Project Society, as an outcome related to the process of projectification on the most comprehensive level, should be conceived as a replacement of these "other" societies of the Third or Fourth Industrial Revolution, characterized by powerful information and communication technologies that can be used in most situations both instantly and at any distance. Rather, the notion of a Project Society highlights the importance of temporary forms of organizing and the understanding of management and work under those conditions; it also highlights respective demands for institutional change.

Institutions are often thought of as stabilizers, consisting of formal as well as informal rules or as North (1990: 6) puts it "constraints that structure human interaction," roles endowed with resources, and support for the functioning of organizations, temporary or otherwise, if only to legitimize or question their existence or behavior. Institutions are often taken for granted and direct or at least guide the behavior of individual and collective actors (such as organizations or interorganizational networks) and stabilize societal development (Berger and Luckmann 1966). Importantly, with imprints from the past, their often long-term existence, their ongoing reproduction through the actors, as well as their rather long-term orientation make them "carriers of history" (David 1994). This is true for more formal institutions including markets and organizations (or hierarchies), interorganizational networks, professional communities, and laws or contracts, and also for informal institutions including shared values and views, norms, and habits. Most of these formal and informal institutions, such as labor law or collective bargaining contracts on the one hand and shared interpretations and routinized behavior on the other, are certainly not made for supporting organizational change but to protect third parties' interests and, at best, to support the functioning present forms of organizing. As such, they tend to preserve existing forms rather than accommodate for expected or realized changes.

However, even if most conceive of institutions as being stable and irrefutable, the notion of institutional change has gained attention by offering new perspectives on stability and instability. Institutions can change by intended actions but also by unintended outcomes of otherwise intentional actions (Giddens 1984). Moreover, institutions may contain elements of change in themselves. But even if institutions promote change, it typically happens so slowly that, apart from very few institutions such as professional associations for project management (see Section 5.2), they cannot be regarded as contributing to the rise of a Project Society. This development is driven by economic interests and technological possibilities (see Chapter 1). Institutions and even institutional change (cf. Streeck and Thelen 2005) thus constitute a counterforce, slowing down the development toward a Project Society or even undermining it – for better or for worse. Consequently, it may be helpful to investigate their relationship to management, work, and the industrial order in more depth. For example, the regulations that are set either by labor law or collective bargaining agreements dominate working conditions that may well at least in part be obsolete, as they often are predicated on the time spent at a specific place of work. A projectified society, however, requires managers and workers to be mobile in both time and space, and most institutions are ill prepared or rather not adapted to provide the stability and security that are needed in the face of these societal changes.

Management of and working in PSOs, PBOs, and PNWs that in a Project Society are themselves likely to become institutions (and – like the stage-gate process – have already done so in fields such as consulting, construction, and content production) are affected by the ways governments and other authorities treat these organizational forms. How well are labor laws or taxation rules adapted to projectified activity? To what extent are temporary forms of organizations considered in official documents and legal texts? Institutes and schools are already training people in project management, but how is the knowledge about temporary organization spread to business education in general or even to other fields of general education? Whole professions need to be adapted to the challenges of a Project Society, and so are organizations that support project businesses. The educational system needs to prepare people for managing and working in temporary settings and ideally help create new or adapt to existing professions. This illustrates the widespread necessity of "institutional entrepreneurship" (DiMaggio 1988) or "institutional work" (Lawrence and Suddaby 2006), that is, of strategically and reflexively developing new or adapting or disrupting old institutions, taking into account the complementarities of institutions that make the institutional system inert and hard to adapt to fit managing and working in a projectified society. To what extent does research cover or even support these institutional initiatives and what are the institutional implications of managing and work in temporary organizations? What kind of organizational models are transmitted by the educational system and by the textbooks of the social science disciplines at different levels? What are major differences in this regard between countries, for example, between the EU countries and the United States? Are the actors at the EU level, whether politicians, bureaucrats, or lobby organizations such as the European Trade Union Confederation (ETUC) and BUSINESSEUROPE, aware of these changes when discussing business and work-related matters?

Starting with labor law and labor politics, in this chapter we deal with a selection of these institutions and discuss their role in the wake of a Project Society. We adopt a comparative perspective, because comparing institutions across countries or at least across different "varieties of capitalism" (Hall and Soskice 2001a), such as liberal economies of most Anglo-Saxon countries on the one hand and of coordinated market countries like Germany and Sweden on the other, will help clarify how institutions affect managing and working in a Project Society and how these institutions might have to adapt to the new circumstances. The institutional embeddedness of project activities often implies a need to manage "institutional contradictions" (Friedlander and Alford 1991) or "institutional distances" (Kostova and Zaheer 1999) that have emerged at least temporarily, not only within but across these countries. The latter, institutional distances, becomes particularly obvious in the case of "global projects," conceived as "a temporary endeavor where multiple actors seek to optimize outcomes by combining resources from multiple sites, organizations, cultures, and geographies through a combination of contractual, hierarchical, and network-based modes of organization" (Orr et al. 2011: 17). It is for this reason that we discuss this type of project, which usually involves a multiplicity of stakeholders (Aaltonen and Kujala 2010), from time to time, thereby also linking the discussion of managing and working in a Project Society to the omnipresent discourse on globalization (cf. Giddens 2002).

Globalization implies that institutions and cultures other than the European or the American need to be considered, not least those related to the successful economies of China, Japan, and Korea. Researchers, among them Fukuyama (1995, 2011), point to the importance of deeper structures other than visible institutions such as the planned economy with its roots in "political Confucianism" for the understanding of the phenomenon. He thinks that the "Confucian personal ethic" regulating day-to-day life is more important when it comes to approaching new contexts. These attitudes toward family, work, and education have proven to be most useful for modern economic activity, and they are also likely to be related to the success of overseas Chinese. In addition, the Confucian meritocratic examination system has also contributed to the recruitment of suitable persons with various social backgrounds to supply the society with personnel able to run reliable and sustainable institutions. These traditions are still part of the developments in that part of the world.

## 5.1.   LABOR LAWS AND LABOR POLITICS

Institutions related to management and work are affected in many ways by the trend to projectification. Trade unions and employer associations, together with the regulatory state, are the building blocks of any industrial relations system (Dunlop 1958). This system, more than any other institutional arrangement, has to meet new challenges in a projectified economy where employment periods may be shorter and more individualized, and participation rules and collective bargaining are losing coverage. The system of industrial relations in most developed countries has undergone significant changes (Bamber et al. 2011), largely independent and irrespective of the trend toward projectification. Major system changes concern the decreasing unionization, eroding membership of firms in employer associations, and the state taking up a less active role in this system.

Indications of decreasing *unionization*, not only in the United States but also in the EU and Asia, during recent years points to the need for trade unions to redefine their role in the system as a necessity.

Their structures and strategies are based on an employment model whereby people are related to an industry, a profession, and a company for long periods of time and benefit from a collective approach to training and wage negotiation. We believe unions must find new roles in terms of how they contribute to learning, participation, wage setting, and the work situation for employees in projectified organizations. Even their ability to collectively organize labor may be at stake if they do not adapt their policies to new circumstances. And aspects of the collective bargaining system must also be questioned when work is project based and individually performed in close contact with customers. How will institutions such as labor laws and work councils be affected when a person's work is simultaneously performed in different organizational settings and when the need for physical presence in those settings varies? Or more generally, how will they handle the "time-space" of Project Society whereby activity in permanent and temporary organizations may overlap and the borders between work and leisure time are becoming increasingly diffuse? Unions until now have only partly acknowledged the need for rethinking and redefining their role in a Project Society. Like employer associations, they are still struggling with the transformation toward more service and knowledge-intensive work without realizing that this work in practice often appears in project settings.

Not only are indications of decreasing unionization evident in many if not most developed countries, liberal and coordinated market economies alike, but employers also tend to refrain from joining or are even giving up membership in *employer associations*. In Germany in particular, employer associations have lost membership and, in consequence, control over resources, although the situation of these institutions in other European countries is less equivocal. In Sweden, where the same tendency concerning employer associations is anticipated, efforts have been made to counteract it. Institutional change on this level, however, concerns not only membership and influence but also the specific role employer associations play in coordinated market economies (Behrens 2004). In countries in which employer associations still have the capacity and will for collective bargaining as we know it, these organizations or more precisely "meta-organizations" (Ahrne and Brunsson 2005) have started to experiment with different roles and new forms. In Germany, employer associations allow more differentiated forms of interest aggregation in general and a "bargaining-free" membership with a broad variety of distinct forms in particular (Behrens 2011). Interpreting this institutional change with regard to the rise of Project Society has to take into account that in Sweden (as in other Scandinavian countries and Finland), the degree of membership of firms in employer associations is significantly higher than in Germany (Brandl 2013; see also Traxler and Huemer 2013).

Taking the construction sector as an example, institutional changes at the level of the EU have significant implications for labor and labor politics in many European countries. Companies and workers from the new low-wage economies of countries in Eastern Europe have frequently been involved in construction and building activities in the old member states. This is taking place at the same time as the use of longer and longer supply chains of subcontractors in the same project becomes more common, as illustrated on a grand scale with the 2014 Winter Olympic Games in Sochi. The contracting companies are transforming into project organizations or PBOs that are characterized by outsourcing most functions apart from the overall management. The companies and persons working at the lowest levels in these production supply chains are almost invisible to those who organize the projects. It is not unusual that persons from countries with low payments and weak employment contracts perform this work. In some states, including Norway, Germany, the Netherlands, and France, the situation has been attended to and resulted in stricter state regulations, whereby the main contractor has to make sure that the subcontractors on all levels follow actual employment contracts including minimum wage agreements. Finland has instead chosen to use inspections on the sites to prevent activity based on dubious contracts. The traditional PBO model of the construction sector has also been challenged by an increased use of self-employed individuals and personnel from employment agencies. These contractual forms are considered by the unions to make it harder to organize labor (Byggnadsarbetareförbundet 2014).

Global projects, not least those in the construction industry, most often assemble individuals and organizations from multiple sociocultural and geographical settings, possibly from liberal as well as from coordinated market economies. For many, such "grand-scale projects" (Shapira and Berndt 1997) or "megaprojects" (Flyvbjerg et al. 2003b), institutional differences matter. Despite involvement of global players and their attempts toward organizational standardization, many activities in global projects are embedded into local institutions, making management difficult. Recurrent themes in such projects, most of them touching on labor issues, are the coordination challenges that result from institutional contradictions and institutional distance; geographic dispersion and organizational interdependence; misunderstandings and misjudgments as a result of differences in values, norms, beliefs, and habits; coordination challenges that have to be considered against the benefits from different identities and historical experiences; opportunities for innovation and learning afforded by cross-fertilization of varying traditions; and exposure to new ways of thinking and doing (Orr et al. 2011: 26).

In face of the dominance of the liberal market doctrine, and hand in hand with the trend toward a more global organization of production and value creation, the *state* has in most developed countries increasingly withdrawn from intervening in national systems of industrial relations. Reformulations of labor law and accompanying labor politics by states that have remained active have almost exclusively aimed at further flexibilization of labor markets, with the Netherlands, Sweden, and Germany leading the respective change movement in the EU. Labor market reforms can be said to have supported the development of temporary forms of organization, most obviously of working for temporary work agencies (Storrie 2002). However, in the name of market liberalization, the reforms have quite deliberately adopted the employers' perspective, leading to an undermining of labor regulations whose main aim was to protect workers from unfair and unhealthy working conditions and allow for more participation or representation.

While the nation-state in many countries has withdrawn from an active regulatory role, supranational institutions such as the EU or the United Nations (UN) have not filled this space, although transnational institutional structures are on the rise and attracting increasing management and organization researchers' attention (Djelic and Quack 2003). The EU also takes on the role of a legislator with its directives in the field of labor law and labor politics. An example related to the regional development in the EU concerns rules for how EU support can be used. Until now, the influence of projectification on management and work was not considered in this context. On the transnational level, the UN and in particular the *Declaration on Fundamental Principles and Rights at Work* of the International Labour Organisation (ILO 1998) are noteworthy. However, despite their implementation in selected countries supported by the ILO with the help of resource-intensive initiatives such as the campaign for Better Work, global labor rights including the prohibition of child and forced labor or the freedom of association and collective bargaining are far from being fully implemented, particularly in those countries where they are needed most. More importantly, the temporary forms of organizing do not yet attract much attention from the regulators of these transnational institutions. Instead, the firms themselves try to fill the void by developing needed regulations, either entirely voluntarily (e.g. corporate social responsibility, CSR) with the help of private associations such as the Global Compact or the Global Reporting Initiative or with the help of bilateral Global Framework Agreements (GFA), negotiated by the management of transnational corporations on the one hand and global labor unions on the other. However, so far only around 100 such agreements have been concluded and only to a limited extent implemented in global production networks (Fichter et al. 2011). And, as far as we are aware, none of these agreements pays any attention to concepts of project-based forms of organizing.

Furthermore, the EU – probably more than other transnational actors – is also directly or indirectly supporting and even encouraging the development of a Project Society by launching an immense number of projects. Major programs such as the Framework Programs in the field of R&D or the European Regional Development Fund are executed through numerous projects run by consultancy firms, local authorities, other companies, and universities – in other words, by a mixture of PBOs, PSOs, and PNWs, including knowledge-intensive infrastructure. From 2007 to 2013, there were in total 16,930 European Regional Development Fund projects in Finland, which is a rather small country. In addition, the central actors of the EU in Brussels and elsewhere, including lobbyists, are supported by a battery of consultants performing projects with the aim to investigate or to back up different kinds of ideas and interests. This is also very much the case in the field of business and work-life issues. Specialized consultants such as Syndex, Groupe Alpha, GITP, Project Consult, WMP, IRES, Foundation Seveso, and many more are participating in developing projects but also in protecting different parts of the traditional industrial model at the same time as they themselves are organized as typical PBOs (Syndex 2013). It is a paradox that the EU, with a reputation of being a huge and cemented bureaucracy, works as an important motor in the projectification process and consequently becomes an institutional and institutionalizing part of Project Society, but in a seemingly far from conscious way.

At the firm and factory level, labor institutions that were effective in the past are likely to be undermined by the rise of temporary organizational forms. Take for instance the German Works Council, the representational and co-determination body of the employees of a manufacturing or administrative unit (Betriebsrat, Personalrat) or an entire firm (Gesamtbetriebsrat, Konzernbetriebsrat). This institution, which, contrary to the expectations of German unionists, has not spread within the EU (only in the weak form of a European Works

Council that is confined to consultancy rights), relies for effective functioning on a rather stable workforce that meets at a fixed locale like a factory or an office. As this becomes less and less the case, the capacities of works councils will almost certainly shrink in terms of membership. While PSOs, like most permanent organizations, are affected by this development, PBOs as well as PNWs, with the exception of some traditional industries such as construction or specific settings such as the U.S. movie industry in Hollywood, will never be able to rely on such labor institutions to any significant extent.

Today's business and work-life institutions in Germany, France, and Sweden were to a great extent formed by the social partners during the heyday of the industrial era. The Swedish Wage Policy Model of Solidarity, constructed by union economists in the 1950s, has been known for contributing to economic growth through structural change of the industrial sector. The policy rests on two legs. The first leg is solidarity, which means that the same kind of work should be paid equally regardless of who performs it, without consideration of gender or age, for example. This is also the part of the policy that is best known and politically promoted and advocated, not least by the Social Democratic Party. The second leg encourages structural transformation, a kind of proactive reconstruction of industrial companies. The minimum wage should be fixed by the social partners at a level high enough to force low-productive businesses to either improve their efficiency or close down. The social costs of this transformation were supposed to be paid for by the state in the form of reeducation and relocation programs – the so-called Work Line (Magnusson and Ottosson 2012). These institutions seemed to work for a couple of decades; however, as early as the 1970s, they met with problems when the expansion of work opportunities in the industrial sector leveled out and then started to decrease. This setback actually coincided with a marked expansion of employment in project-based consultancy companies predominantly supporting industry. A new division of labor in the industrial sector took shape. The expansion of those PBOs helped compensate for the decrease in employment in the traditional companies (Ekstedt and Sundin 2006). This transformation caused problems at the individual level: only in exceptional cases was it possible for individuals from the factory floor to be reeducated and end up in knowledge-intensive service activity (Ekstedt 1991). The growth of services performed by these PBOs also coincided with an externalization of production. Hardware production, formerly carried out by information and communication technology companies such as IBM or Intel were transferred to giant international production specialists including Flextronics, Solectron, and Emerson, while a company such as Ericsson was essentially transformed into a PSO concentrating on development, design, and marketing activity. This kind of activity was in turn supported by project-based consultants.

The Wage Policy of Solidarity and the Work Line institutions were able to handle extensive structural changes of the industrial sector in Sweden quite well as long as traditional companies hired more and more people. Problems occurred when the new division of labor made its entrance and the boundaries of the organizations superseded factory gates and office doors – and national territories. Demand for management and work with other kinds of training and thinking grew. Today's version of the Work Line emphasizes the matching of the labor market through instruments such as coaching but does not seem to be prepared for the new demands of Project Society. Lack of project thinking and institutions adapted to project organizing is obvious at the societal level even if many measures initiated by authorities are taken care of by the respective organizations.

Can the trade unions of today handle this situation? Are they prepared to change their role? The unions will most likely have serious problems in providing value for their members if they are stuck to the idea that organizations function like bureaucratic hierarchies. If project workers have taken over the responsibilities for employment, compensation, and learning, the unions must arguably provide new forms of service if they are to continue to exist. Perhaps they need to work to ensure that sufficient recuperation and rest between projects is enabled as well as providing for training to make their members more attractive on the project market. In Sweden, the increased activity of trade unions in handling insurance matters for individuals could perhaps be seen as a small step in this direction. But if the coverage of existing legislation and agreement of the labor market deteriorates further, it is likely that the individual coworker will look for alternative support (Ekstedt 2002).

## 5.2.   EDUCATIONAL INSTITUTIONS AND PROFESSIONS

Education has the dual function of being both the institutional cement of society and the tool to create and implement change (Sjöstrand 1993; North 2005). The first function is often strong as many educational systems have deep roots in history. This dilemma is expressed by the economist Gary Becker (1999: 40) in the following way: "Modern economies require that people invest in the acquisition of knowledge, skills, and information throughout most of their lives. Yet the basic methods of acquiring such human capital have hardly changed since the time of Socrates." However, he thinks that modern technology may make a difference: "For 2,500 years, teachers and students have met face-to-face for lectures and discussion. The growth of the Internet may revolutionize this system by allowing 'distance learning' in which teachers and students interact closely even though they are separated both physically and in time." His thoughts about distance learning are reminiscent of the way project organizations work in terms of space and time dimensions. While the historical reference to ancient times may be true for a societal elite, the institutionalization of education for the majority of the population came much later when compulsory school systems were introduced in the period of early industrialization around 150 years ago. The way schools are organized today, including their institutions, is in many respects similar to that of traditional industrial organizations, even if there are project-like exceptions such as group work, which was introduced in the 1960s and 1970s in some schools. However, in general, students are placed in classrooms that are well-defined workplaces. The teacher–student relation is similar to that of the employer–employee in working life. The calendar-planning model is also present and expressed by yearly grades, whereby students' achievements or marks can be seen as annual reports. In Sweden, the calendar-based performance and attendance of students is further reflected in the form of student grants and loans directly related to presence in school in a given semester. To be fostered in this institutional environment is probably not the best preparation for working and living in Project Society. The preparation in China with its short industrial tradition is different but still characterized by a well-educated population fostered in the Confucian meritocratic school tradition (Fukuyama 1995, 2011; Zheng and Wang 2014).

In a projectified school, solving and fulfilling tasks come in focus, no matter whether they are given to or developed by the students themselves. The practice of yearly grades and credits is a feature of the old system. In addition, the role of the classroom as a unit for communication and control can be questioned, as these functions can be replaced to a substantial degree by modern information and communication technologies – teamwork in projects and other activities may well take part over the Internet. Physical presence at a specific place can be reduced, as it used to be in evening (correspondence) schools. There are examples of educational programs in which project-like models based on IT already have an influence, but the potential for wider spread and improvements is likely to be immense (Hargreaves and Shirley 2012). Project models of learning seem to be more in line with the university tradition with its emphasis on producing papers, articles, and dissertations. The results of these learning endeavors are assessed by some kind of peer system and physical presence is reduced to seminars – a common project characteristic.

Professions and educational institutions are also affected by the described projectification of management and work. A profession is not only an important institution in many organizational fields but also an actor driving the creation and maintenance of institutions (Scott 2008), that is, an "institutional agent" performing institutional work. Professions such as medicine and law are successful in these efforts of "theorization," which is conceived as the process whereby the success and failure of structures and processes are conceptualized and linked to potential organizational solutions (Greenwood et al. 2002). These professions enjoy a particular status in society, not least because they are successful in terms of institutionalizing efforts. Following this understanding, project management, quite like management at large, though increasingly professionalized, is not a full profession (Schein 1967, 1990; Turner 1999). However, the following indicators for the increased professionalization of project management are likely to affect all forms of temporary organizations in the future:

1. The engagement of professional institutes such as the Project Management Institute (PMI) with about 470,000 members organized in 270 national chapters or the International Project Management Association (IPMA) with its 55 national associations (e.g. GPM in Germany, Swedish Project Management Association, and APM in the UK) according to their homepages. Other associations are also involved in spreading know-how and professionalism in the area in Sweden. One is the Swedish Project Academy, consisting of practicing project managers, consultants in the field, and researchers dedicated to spreading knowledge on projects in educating, training, and awarding project managers.

2. The growth of the number of so-called project management professionals who have received certification of their knowledge related to project management work from one or more of these professional institutes. Moreover, the concepts of projects and project management are also "creeping into established professional identities" (Packendorff and Lindgren 2014: 13).

3. The accreditation of educational programs at university levels in particular related to project management. The Global Accreditation Center (GAC) has thus far accredited such programs worldwide. More than 100 programs have been accredited and the number seems to be increasing, not only in the EU and the United States but also in the rest of the world, notably to a large extent in China. An unofficial PMI census, based on UNESCO's World Higher Education Database, came up with more than 900 programs at more than 450 institutions worldwide.

4. The tendency of companies hiring project managers to choose or rather require that those who are hired either have the title project management professional or come from an accredited or certified project management program. Most of these professionals are expected to be familiar with well-established guides and handbooks such as PMBOK, developed and published by the PMI in 1987, which not only has been continuously revised by the PMI Standards Committee but has also become an institution itself (Hodgson and Cicmil 2006).

5. The increased research in the field of project management in particular and temporary forms of organizing in general, not only in quantitative but also in qualitative terms: more theorizing, a greater variety of more rigorous research methods, and improved reception of results by the broader community of management and organization researchers (cf. Bakker 2010). The results of this research have a direct or at least indirect impact on educating and training professionals.

The institutes mentioned earlier engage not only in certified education and training but also in the design of the certification process itself – which is exactly what makes them *professional* institutions.

As already indicated, the educational system at large, which is still to a significant extent a reflection of the traditional industrial organization of value creation, should prepare people for work in temporary settings. This is not only true for the university system but also the vocational training system. The traditional trainee/apprenticeship system used in the construction sector, for instance, is obviously not sufficient if project organization diffuses to other parts of the economy. While some professional institutions have introduced project management even in primary and secondary schools, formal project management education and training are still confined to universities. Although the number of specialized programs in this field has increased recently at business schools and in the social sciences in general, much of the education and training in project management are still carried out in engineering departments of technological universities, where the education and training are focused on an instrumental approach to project management rather than on the processes of managing projects as an important form of temporary organization. The traditional focus on project management is, however, gradually changing into notions of managing projects and organizing for the temporary, implying a drift from focusing on the individual project to projects in context or as a set of projects in organization, network, or field contexts.

Beyond formal qualification and certification, there is reason to believe that work in some projects is characterized by fairly high entry barriers. To be able to overcome the barriers and be hired, one usually needs to have practical knowledge and extensive experience about working in projects. Professional knowledge has to be paired with project know-how and ability to function in projects (see Chapter 4), some of which is of a rather implicit or tacit nature and therefore difficult to include in formal education and training. As a rule, this kind of knowledge has always been learned via practical activity in projects through access to proper networks (Borg 2014). That is probably one of the reasons why formal educational programs that prepare students for work in the construction sector often include a lot of practical activity at the work sites. Parts of this training are consequently supervised by experienced builders (or, in the case of the film sector, film professionals) working in companies. Lately, signs of cracks are appearing in this system. The schools have problems in finding adequate places for practical training. A reason could be that when the major contractors have turned into project management companies, there is limited activity suitable for practitioners and that the subcontractors lower down in the production chain only have limited resources for this kind of activity. Still it is possible to think that the educational model used for so long in the construction and film sectors, for example, can be seen as a rough prototype for lowering the entry barriers for work in project-dense activity in general. Practical training in the project environment and reflection on how project organizations work in practice seem to be proper preparations for work in Project Society.

## 5.3.   MARKET REGULATIONS AND PROJECTIFICATION

Among the institutions having an impact on projectification, market regulations play a special role. Lawmakers in general are not too aware of the special circumstances of project businesses and what is relevant for such a context. Rather, regulation authorities are driven by a product market vision mainly inspired by not only the practice of Industrial Society but also traditional economic theory.

What appears as good practice in project management (such as front co-learning, anticipation of choice of partners, client–supplier cooperation, etc.) in the product market paradigm appears as a bias and not as good competitive behavior. The classic market rules in PBOs (especially when the client is in the public sector) generally lead to a fragmentation of the project value chain. The inefficiencies that result from this fragmentation have been largely debated, particularly in the construction and megaproject sectors. For example, these sectors are characterized by too much focus on the initial investment cost, as opposed to a value for a money perspective that takes into account the performance of the outcome of the project or for noncooperative games within the different contributors, when unplanned events have to be managed or when a problem occurs at the interface of various project actors.

In the 1990s, in the private sector and PSOs in particular, projectification was clearly connected to the transition in supply chain management and firms' purchase strategies to involve co-development or partnership relations (Garel et al. 1997; Midler and Navarre, 2004).

The case of public markets is more problematic, because of the importance of the legal system in economic regulation. Projectification of the public sector is at the center of this tension between traditional market regulation and new project management practices.

Governments spend a lot of money on behalf of their citizens – this money goes to provide infrastructure and services such as schools and teachers, hospitals, and doctors and nurses; emergency services such as ambulances and paramedics, fire stations, fire engines and firefighters, police stations, and police officers; building and maintaining roads; social services, including building and staffing prisons; and weapons systems, platforms, and the armed forces. The provision of much of this public infrastructure is delivered through projects and programs of various sorts.

A review of the first 10 volumes of the *International Journal of Project Management* from 1982 to 1992 by Betts and Lansley (1995) found few articles about project management in the public sector in spite of its importance in practice. The UK provides good examples of how public market regulation can be debated and challenged through a project performance perspective. Indeed, public sector projects are subject to far greater scrutiny than those in the private sector, and public sector project failures are featured prominently in newspapers and TV bulletins. The UK has a special institutional context: the National Audit Office (NAO) and the Public Accounts Committee (PAC), and the work is supplemented by reports from other Parliamentary Select Committees. The PAC holds public hearings in the House of Commons, where it collects evidence from a wide range of officials and managers responsible for specific areas of government spending from government department permanent secretaries and other senior officials to chief executives of hospitals, to heads of regulatory bodies, to senior military personnel, to academics. The NAO has established a high reputation for producing reports on the value for money provided by different aspects of government spending, including major public sector projects. These reports often form the basis for the enquiries undertaken by the PAC and the reports and the findings of the PAC are picked up by the media and bring problems with public sector projects to the public's attention.

There has been a trend toward seeking to utilize private sector expertise in delivering public sector projects and programs. A favorite mechanism to facilitate this has been public–private partnerships or PPPs, which represent the institutionalization of transforming the management of public projects in line with more effective project management practices.

In theory, in PPPs the public and private sectors share costs, revenues, and responsibilities. Bennett and coauthors (2000) report that PPPs span a variety of possible relationships between the public and private sectors for the cooperative provision of infrastructure services ranging from the fully public to fully private. According to Bult-Spiering and Dewulf (2006), PPPs have a long history in some countries but became much more popular in the 1980s, when some governments were pursuing policies of privatization and reviewing the role of the state in providing a range of services. The rise of "new public management" (NPM) ideas in the 1990s coupled with market-based philosophies further influenced the development of PPPs. PPPs were used by the U.S. federal government during the 1950s and 1960s to stimulate private investment in inner-city infrastructure and regional development. The Carter administration in the 1970s, the Reagan administration in the 1980s, and the Clinton administration in the 1990s continued and expanded their use, based on the premise that the private sector could more efficiently and effectively provide goods and services than the public sector. They have been used extensively in the United States for prisons, water supply, and wastewater treatment (Kwak et al. 2009). They have also been used in the United Arab Emirates (UAE), and in Asia in Korea, Hong Kong, Singapore, India, Thailand, and China.

The PPP systems are changing in the UK because of institutionalized actions. The success of the London 2012 Olympics has led to a degree of optimism about the performance of future public infrastructure projects, although some notable IT project failures remain that have hit the headlines, including the national program for IT in the National Health Service. Even more worrying, the flagship £2.4 billion welfare change program, Universal Credit, designed to consolidate six welfare payments into one single payment, which was supposed to be an example of the benefits of using evolutionary or "agile" methods, was the subject of a damning NAO report in September 2013 (NAO 2013). According to the report, the program was beset by weak management, ineffective control, and poor governance and had failed to deliver value for money. More than £30 million of the £303 million spent on IT for the program had been written off, and the systems still had limited functionality. By January 2014, the press was reporting friction between the Cabinet Office and the Department for Work and Pensions (DWP) – the owner of Universal Credit – that was causing high-level risks to the program delivery. In May 2014, it was discovered that the DWP was blocking the publication of documents – the risk register, the issues register, the milestone schedule, and a project assessment review – that would shed more light on the scale and nature of the problems faced by the program.

## 5.4.    MEGAPROJECT AND POLITICAL INSTITUTIONS

Apart from market regulation, institutions that frame public decision processes are of course key elements of the project context, especially for the megaproject. From a professional view, politics is often blamed as an irrational logic that constrains or destroys the efficiency of project management. A deeper examination of the relations between projectification of society and public institutions is clearly necessary.

Public management can be analyzed as a dual system (i.e. the civil servants and politicians) that has to juxtapose efficiency with accountability or, possibly, management with democracy. The role of projects in this context also varies: public authorities as clients were extensively treated in the previous section. Projectification of political life is another that also needs to be investigated.

On the one hand, history gives clear examples of how a political, planned economy context can align with project management rationality. A thorough analysis has shown how military policy in the World War II was an important factor in the rapid convergence of complex projects such as the Manhattan or Sidewinder Projects (Lenfle, 2011, 2014). The history of the development of project management in the 1950s and 1960s is deeply connected to the military and prestige policy efforts of the US–USSR competition of the Cold War period. In our contemporary period, the impressive development of China's construction and infrastructure investment projects cannot be interpreted without examining an alignment between advanced project management practices and public authorities working with centralized decision processes.

In the Western democratic context, the tension between projectification and political decision institutions is more uncertain. For instance, the London 2012 Olympics and – at the time of writing and most likely for the next couple of years – the still unfinished Willy Brandt Airport in Berlin can be mentioned as positive and negative examples, respectively. Discussions of such projects develop into political debates wherein the politicians tend to use the projects as arguments to make political points. The nature of politics and political parties is that opposing views are regarded as natural and as part of democracy. Megaprojects and "sensitive issues" supply arenas for political action. The political "games" are not easy though: politicians may gain or lose, and much of what is happening is connected to the political agenda and receives media attention. Initiating a project is risky because problems that become out of control lead to blame from political opponents. This type of political debate will most certainly continue in the future when expensive megaprojects catch the attention of voters, the media, and taxpayers.

It is unclear what effects these outbursts of public and political interests have on projects as such. It is to be expected that project managers in charge of efforts of this type, public administrators as much as private consultants, will work hard on how to avoid bad publicity. The project managers who perform well in these types of projects also seem to have a special skill when it comes to negotiations and discussions with politicians. Stories of project failures in terms of cost and time overruns are plentiful for such megaprojects and they tend to haunt politicians and project managers for a long time. Success stories – like the London 2012 Olympics – are less common, but the success to a significant extent might be the result of the skillfulness of the project manager in negotiating with politicians beforehand. Project managers working in close contacts with the public sector are likely to develop those skills to avoid having a project fail.

Supranational institutions such as the EU and the UN take on more and more responsibilities involving projects. The EU system for doing that is connected with support provided for activities in the EU and prescribes that the recipient country/organization adheres to a project model accepted by the EU. Since the EU supports a multitude of support programs, the projectification effect is overwhelming. These facts have been studied mostly by political scientists. In 2013, an entire issue of the *Scandinavian Journal of Public Administration* was devoted to various aspects of this grand-scale projectification. The subject of the issue was "Projectified Politics – The Role of Temporary Organizations in the Public Sector" (Löfgren et al. 2013).

The prevalence of projects in the public sector cannot be over-estimated. Even in fairly small countries, such as Finland, the number of projects in all EU programs is in fact overwhelming. The recipients of EU support, local governments, or other public organizations are expected to follow the prescribed model for handling projects resembling the one proposed by Project Management Institute in the so-called Project Management Body of Knowledge or PMBOK (PMI 2013). And since the recipients require that subcontractors also follow the prescribed model (which is appropriate when it comes to reporting back to the EU), projectification takes on a form of spreading like rings on the water. Projectification in the public sector has quantitatively taken a step forward with this. A relevant question for the future is whether this approach with a generic form of project management will continue or become diversified. A theory of projectification will have to have a component inspired by the development in the public sector and by the expanding realm vis-à-vis supranational organizations.

## 5.5.   OTHER ORGANIZATIONS SUPPORTING PROJECTS

Temporary forms of organizing, PSOs, PBOs, and PNWs, require not only well-adapted labor law and labor politics, market regulations, or professional and educational institutions but also the existence of other organizations allowing for temporary organizing. One example of temporary organizing that has often been drawn on in this book, as it may be indicative of what a Project Society means for management and work, is the film and television industry. A study of this industry in Germany, or to be more precise, in two media regions in Germany – Berlin and Cologne – shows that temporary forms of organizing rely on an institutional environment that provides all those services, including education and training, that cannot be provided within these rather lean organizational forms by the media companies themselves (Sydow and Staber 2002). Instead, regional governments and private businesses often set up respective institutions in the form of public–private partnerships. An example from the Cologne media region is the GAG Academy, which offers workshops and training for comedians and authors for respective television programs. Unsurprisingly, this academy was founded when comedy shows became popular on German television. As some of these trends are not sustainable, some business-supporting organizations may not be of a permanent but only temporary character; that is, they may themselves be projects or project networks. Projects to institutionalize projectification may be a route forward.

Consultants within the project field play an increasingly important role in countries such as France, Germany, or Sweden. And those consultants support organizations with regard to project management knowledge in various ways. Typically, together with best-selling writers and seminar organizers, consultants are considered an important mechanisms to distribute useful and, in any case, fashionable knowledge and practices in fields (Kieser 1997). Applications for EU financial support are also often handled by consultants, rather than by the applicants themselves. Universities are to an increasing degree dependent on financial support from other sources than direct transfers from the government. Most major universities in EU countries such as France, Germany, and Sweden have started to provide courses on how to apply for project money and on how to run the projects. But in practice these efforts are often run by consultants as subcontractors who contribute significantly to the diffusion of respective knowledge and practices.

In principle, business-supporting organizations can concentrate on supplying financial resources (banks, agencies), providing organizing capacities (including brokering and administration), or – as in the case of the GAG Academy in Cologne – helping develop human resources and open up career opportunities.

## 5.6.   INFORMAL INSTITUTIONS: CHANGING VALUES AND HABITS?

Even more so than formal institutions such as law, professional and educational or project business supporting organizations, values, norms, and habits usually do not change rapidly (Ingelhart 1997; Hofstede 2001). With regard to the evolving Project Society, however, some significant changes of these informal institutions of society may be noted. First, an increasing number of people, even those in coordinated market economies with a heavy emphasis on social security (e.g. Germany and Sweden), seem to accept if not prefer temporary forms of employment. The increasing number of persons working as self-employed, independent professionals, freelancers, or supertemps bears witness to this. Notwithstanding that many of these are forced to accept such employment opportunities, especially young people seem increasingly to watch out for work in projects or other forms of temporary organizations. In consequence, some of them may develop into what years ago was called a "project man" (Lundin and Hartman 2000). Second, given widespread working in projects in many different fields, not only as self-employed and so on, sometimes even starting for children at primary school, increasing numbers of individuals have gained experience with this temporary form of organizing and even enjoyed formal training for such settings. This experience may in turn and in the long run make values, norms, and habits change. Third, some fields, in particular in the cultural industries, hardly offer other than temporary employment (McKinlay and Smith 2009). Those working there are likely to have and/or develop different values, norms, and habits with regard to temporary organizations. In sum, managing and working in projects, while still new to some fields, has become an accepted way of life in many others – an institution, which means that it is a fact of life just to be accepted by many who earn their living by project work. Others experience the tensions and frictions that come with these forms of work organization.

## 5.7. INSTITUTIONAL COMPLEMENTARITIES AND INSTITUTIONAL ENTREPRENEURSHIP – CONCLUSIONS FOR ACTION

Societies are often classified according to their institutional setup. An example of such a classification is the rather coarse but nevertheless popular differentiation between liberal market economies on the one hand and coordinated market economies on the other, both of which are made up of institutions that are more or less complementary (Hall and Soskice 2001a). Institutions are conceived as complementary "if the presence (or efficiency) of one increases the returns from (or the efficiency of) the other" (Hall and Soskice 2001b: 17). In consequence, institutional complementarities not only reinforce the differences between liberal and coordinated market economies but also hinder institutional change, or at least make institutional entrepreneurship or institutional work more demanding.

The UK, a representative example of the liberal market economy model, is characterized by a dispersed system of industry associations, common contract law, small shareholdings by portfolio investors, and a single board system dominated by the CEO. Regarding informal institutions, the UK belongs to those countries classified by Hofstede (2001) as relatively individualistic, risk taking, short-term oriented, and tolerating power distances between citizens in comparison with other countries. Germany, by contrast, is often considered a prototypical example of a coordinated market economy, characterized not only by a different collective organization of business interests (see next paragraph) but also by civil rather than common law, large shareholdings by strategic investors, and a dual board system with more distributed power. Regarding informal institutions, Germany belongs to those countries classified as collectivistic and long-term oriented while fairly risk averse and critical toward large power distances (Lane and Bachmann 1997; Hofstede 2001; Vitols 2001).

The formal as well as informal institutional environments of both countries, not least because of self-reinforcing institutional complementarities (Pierson 2000), provide different conditions for interorganizational cooperation and temporary organizing. For instance, Britain is well known for its "pluralistic and lowly integrated system of business associations, with weak representation at the national level. In Germany, in contrast, the late emergence of liberalism and a strong tradition of economic self-organization provided a fertile soil for the collective organization of business interests. They have formed a very orderly and highly integrated hierarchical system, constituting an effective interlocutor for the national state" (Lane and Bachmann 1997: 234). Together with stark difference in legal regulations, these two countries provide distinct institutional environments not only for collaboration across organizational boundaries in general but for managing and working in PBOs and PNWs in particular. One important example is the trust-enhancing character of the stable and institutionally more consistent environment in Germany (Lane and Bachmann 1997). Such institutional differences obviously matter in global projects that often cut across liberal and coordinated market economies and have to take into account many specificities of institutionally diverse countries. Importantly, and as argued in the beginning of this section, institutional complementarities between industry associations, legal regulations, and also less formal institutions make a national institutional setup function more smoothly. At the same time, such complementarities, which are also manifest in the notion of "institutional thickness" (Amin and Thrift 1994), are responsible for the stability if not hyper-stability of the setup, making institutional change difficult (Streeck and Thelen 2005).

Nevertheless, management and organization research points increasingly to the fact that organizations are not only influenced by their technical and institutional environment (Meyer and Rowan

1977; Scott 2008) but are, under certain conditions at least, able to influence it via institutional entrepreneurship (DiMaggio 1988; Beckert 1999; Garud et al. 2007). Institutional entrepreneurship, now increasingly based upon Giddens's (1984) idea of a duality (rather than a dualism) of agency and structure and framed as "institutional work" (Lawrence and Suddaby 2006), is a process in which individual or collective agents create, maintain, change, or disrupt their institutional environment to an extent that makes their organization appear legitimate. Toward this end, institutional entrepreneurs, or "institutional agents" (Scott 2008) in general, may engage in elaborating, legitimating, and diffusing an institution that fits their needs and interests. With regard to temporary organizations, training and lobbying activities of professional associations such as the PMI or international consultancies such as BCG transferring knowledge about promising practices of project management are a case in point, although the homogenization via globalization in face of institutional persistencies continues to be debated (Orr et al. 2011: 79–84).

Institutional entrepreneurs or agents interestingly often use projects for influencing the institutional environment, if not for setting up new institutions. Institutional entrepreneurship or work, we argue, is by and large a project business. A case in point is social movements that often aim at institutional change. Think for instance of the environmental movement around the Green Party in some EU countries, the Clean Cloth Campaign, or organizing activities of trade unions in Europe and the United States that set out to improve the working conditions in the production networks of the global apparel industry. Although not aiming at the construction or diffusion of projects as an institution per se, such local or global movements certainly contribute to the projectification of society, paradoxically even if they are in opposition to some projects (McAdam 2011).

Under certain circumstances, such projects become institutions themselves. Think of the Olympics, which started off in ancient Athens as a project and, in the course of the centuries, became a global institution. Pretty much the same is true for the SEMATECH consortium, which was created in 1987 as a national project of the U.S. government to counter the then competitive advantage of Japanese manufacturers of semiconductors but has in the meantime become an institution with international memberships and continuous activities (Müller-Seitz and Sydow 2011). Other one-time events such as Woodstock not only became an institution but contributed significantly to the creation of an entirely new institutional field with its own rules, regulations, and expectations: live music festivals that continue for several days.

# 6   Trends and theory implications

During the past decades, scholars have started to see an end of the traditional Industrial Society or at least its dominance. Expressions such as the Third Industrial Revolution (Stine 1975; Finkelstein 1986) or the Third Wave (Toffler 1980) are trying to capture a whole societal process undergoing change, while expressions such as the Information Society (Butler 1981), the Knowledge Economy (Machlup 1962; Drucker 1969), the Second Industrial Divide (Piore and Sabel 1984), and the Control Revolution (Beniger 1986) point out aspects of what has been going on since the demise of the dominance of the Industrial Society, which is currently revived under the label of the Fourth Industrial Revolution or, in particular in Germany, Industry 4.0 (Forschungsunion and acatech 2013). Whatever the label attached to these descriptions, they share a number of common characteristics: diffusion of a revolutionizing information technology, new ways of knowledge formation, challenges to formal and informal institutions, and last but not least expansion of looser and often temporary organizational forms.

By using the expression Project Society, we are highlighting that the traditional form of industrial organization is undergoing a massive challenge from extensive projectification. This is true not only in industry and manufacturing itself, especially if the digital or smart factory becomes a reality with the help of adaptive intelligent production systems, chains, and networks, but also by expansion in project-organized sectors such as construction, consulting, engineering, media, entertainment, and information. More and more individuals, in work and in everyday life, as well as collective actors such as firms, governments, and nongovernmental organizations, are speaking and thinking in project terms. Projectification, hence, not only takes place in a substantive manner but is also, if not even to a larger extent, reflected in how people in general think and what they say – the discursive realm (Packendorff and Lindgren 2014). Internal as well as external projectification forces are driving the disintegration and replacement of the traditional industrial organization, which was dominant for more than a century. This projectification is a specification of what is happening to the ways of organizing. Ingrained roles and rules of working and business life are becoming obsolete.

In the first section of this concluding chapter, we summarize our analysis of the ongoing dynamics and the challenges of such projectification of society presented in more depth in the previous chapters of this book. In the second section, we turn to the fields of research that we believe are as yet under-explored in the wake of Project Society. This will lead us to map what could be the main research questions and conceptual frameworks that provide the theoretical and methodological tools to handle the many remaining challenges of projectification of management and work and society at large.

## 6.1. ANALYZING TRENDS – SUMMARY OF FINDINGS

Projectification of organization, management, work, and society is not only a concept but also a deep transformation trend that reshapes the organizational landscape in new contextualized patterns. In a traditional perspective of organization theory, we captured this contextual diversity through our three archetypes of the project-based organization (PBO), the project-supported organization (PSO), and the project network (PNW). Chapter 2 provided empirical evidence of this trend, as it identified the challenges it creates for the former organizing patterns. The challenges come from the inside as well as from the outside, affecting and being affected by all three archetypes of project-based organizing. The PSOs dissolve traditional permanent organizations from within when an increasing proportion of their activities takes place in projects; core activities such as R&D use temporary organizational forms often in direct conflict with those of permanent organizations. PBO projects are challenging from the outside by taking over activities and functions from permanent organizations, resulting in blurred boundaries of organizational belonging. PNWs are widening the organizational sphere even more, offering even bigger arenas and wider frameworks for organizational solutions than most other organizational forms. Together, these three archetypes drive and reflect projectification tendencies, while they overlap and penetrate former organizational territories in time as well as in space.

In face of this projectification trend, as argued in Chapter 3, the foundations of management that by and large stem from the traditional industrial organizational model are cracking. Within projects, in which a larger scope of people are involved for a major proportion of their working time, new instrumental and organizational patterns have been formalized and developed for managing projects. During half a century of development in diversified and evolving contexts, those patterns themselves have evolved and diversified. Just as one would not expect a single organizational model to fit every firm, managing projects requires quite different forms in PSOs, PBOs, and PNWs. But projectification involves transitions not only within the scope of the projects but also in the permanent settings of the organization – or networks or fields – where projects are embedded.

The third chapter also identified some key contemporary challenges that still require further research, even if they have already been identified and worked on by many researchers. The first was the importance of the strategic dimension of projects. An increasing number of projects seem to be flagged out as "strategic," that is, as relevant for the long-term success of an enterprise. This creates a dual challenge for the project management itself (because the traditional view of project as an implementation mission of a clear target is only one among several) and for the organization involved. A second problematic issue, which is not independent from the previous one, is the growing importance of the issue of multiple stakeholders in our modern socioeconomic context. Chapter 3 analyzes how the traditional view of the "project client" as the single focal interlocutor of the project vanishes, giving place to a complex fuzzy system of diversified actors that has to be "managed" in novel sophisticated governance and communication processes. Megaprojects as projects in PNWs are particularly affected by those two challenges. A third dilemma we identified as common to our three archetypes is the multiproject perspective in an innovation-based competition that requires efficient cross-project permanent creative and learning processes. Chapter 3 analyzes program and lineage notions as recent concepts that try to cope with this classic dilemma between the temporary nature of the project and the long-term knowledge creation and capitalization process. Last but not least, human resource management appears both as a central function to maintain permanent organization identity against the centrifugal forces of projects and a problematic task in organizations fragmented in various logics and time perspectives.

Two questions arise from our analysis of the projectification trend in managing organizations:

(1) After a development of half a century, has this projectification trend reached its peak, or will it go on in the future, and with it, the expansion of the challenges we just identified? All empirical evidence suggests that the ongoing global capitalist context, emphasizing intensive innovation competition and an increasingly sophisticated service economy will continue to drive an expansion of projectification in the future. Resistance will come, if it comes, from other societal spheres than the business one: the individuals who are more and more involved in project-based activities, activities that shape their working life and the different institutions that structure the multiple aspects of modern society. We developed these two issues in Chapters 4 and 5.

(2) Will the three archetypes of our typology converge with the deepening and long-lasting projectification trend? Or will they remain as the matrix of diversified organizational trajectories?

In fact, some challenges we identified in PBOs, PSOs, and PNWs share similarities: prioritizing and "making things happen" in a proliferation of projects, organizing efficient cross-project learning, managing talented people in a more complex and fragmented social scope, and so on. Looking at the answers to such issues, we also see convergences that operate within the archetypes, in a sort of hybridization of formal settings. Within PSOs, for instance, we see emergence of internal contracting practices between project teams and the firm's headquarters that mirror the client–contractor relation in PBOs. On the other hand, advanced project management in the PBO context tries to involve the client representatives closely in integrated teams (such as the PSO project teams) to develop trust among the project protagonists. PSO-stage gate tools and processes are also increasingly used to manage the project portfolio in PNWs. We see the similar development of project management offices (PMOs) in PBOs and PSOs. The diffusion of standardized tools and processes as the numerous benchmarks in the practitioner as well as academic project communities certainly plays such a convergence role.

But such convergence is more superficial than real. If some tools are common (e.g. Gannt charts, PRINCE) and if some organizational units share the same denomination (e.g. project management offices or PMOs), the practices behind the formal settings and the similar labels are generally deeply different (see e.g. Hobbs et al. 2008 for the variety of roles and statuses of PMOs). In this perspective, our three archetypes will continue to develop or unfold in the future, but certainly not to a non-contextual projectified one best way of organizing.

Chapter 4 analyzed how traditional institutions of work life are challenged by projectification. The workplace as a point of reference for the formation of rules and agreements loses its central role. In a Project Society, work may take place almost anywhere, often related to the demand of the customer. It may be at his or her facilities or even more likely in virtual space over the Internet. Projectification also influences time aspects of work. Time spent at specific workplaces loses its importance. Compensation for work becomes more and more related to the fulfillment of specified tasks. The task orientation of work in projects leads in turn to high demand of persons with the ability to work in different and rapidly changing environments. Also the traditional calendar models of planning and evaluating work are challenged and attaining specified goals comes more into focus.

204 TRENDS AND THEORY IMPLICATIONS

In other words, one may say that the combination of changed place and time regimes in work life gives work an omnibus character; it becomes possible to have instant as well as distant project participation in different settings where the borders between work, training, and leisure time may be more or less blurred.

In general, relations are different between employers and customers in project organizations compared to those of traditional industrial organizations. The employees' ties to the employer are, however, stronger in PSOs than in other project and temporary organizations. For example, it is not unusual that project workers in PSOs take part in formalized educational programs in the companies, while the members of PBOs have to take care of their own career development, including training. Members of PBOs, and naturally also those who are self-employed (independent professionals), are often and to a significant part of their working hours engaged in promoting future projects. Employability as well as employment becomes more of a personal responsibility and a business risk for these categories. They also have high personal accountability for the results of the project, which is not always matched with their ability to influence the content or aim of the activity. This in turn may lead to stress and frustration.

The project worker often engages in practices from different organizations and professions. Professional knowledge also has to be paired with knowledge about the way projects function. This knowledge has a technical aspect of the parts and ideas a project consists of and how these are synchronized with the views of the customers. This kind of knowledge is hard to develop without practical experience. But project work also demands social capability. A certain frequency of engagement and participating in project work is expected to achieve this. These two aspects of project knowledge create high entry barriers, which may confront inexperienced young people when they want to be part of a projectified labor market.

Chapter 5 discussed the role of various institutions in the wake of Project Society. It showed, on the one hand, that existing institutions such as labor law and policy, education systems, or market regulation still reflect the logics of Industrial Society. Such inertia at the institutional level is of course normal, institutions appearing as long-term stabilizers in society. The projectification transition therefore can create tensions between the level of practices and the level of institutions. The projectification creates a new social and time scope for work regulation that undermines traditional labor institutions' efficiency, which had been established at the scale of the permanent organizations. Market regulation institutions, especially in the domain of public markets where the power of regulation is more prevalent, have often been criticized as incompatible with the advanced project management practices.

On the other hand, the chapter showed that this institutional layer is also evolving to adapt to projectification. This is particularly true for the educational system, which had widely integrated elements of the project management corpus both in its engineering and business courses. Specialized institutions have also evolved that promote standards for project-based organizing and lobby for institutional change that accommodates for management and work in these arrangements. Institutional change in the wake of projectification has also been noted with regard to market regulations, where important efforts have been devoted to propose better contractual and organizational frameworks within public administration to address the classic unsatisfactory performances of complex public projects.

The level of political institutions (as opposed to public administration institutions) is more ambiguous. The historic emergence of project management in the Cold War context gives an emblematic example of the coherence between projectification and policy. On the contrary, as presented in Chapter 5, our contemporary context provides many examples of disconnection between projects and political decision-making processes. This does not mean that the political institutions do not interfere in projects. On the contrary, we see much evidence in Western countries of a greater overlap of political spheres and project activities at all levels: local, national, and supranational. Stakeholder management appears as a possible partial answer to this problematic articulation, a domain that certainly deserves more research from different disciplines.

## 6.2.   CHALLENGES FOR RESEARCH – TOPICS AND THEORY

Project management, or project-based organizing more broadly, as an academic field has some 50 years of existence, and this history is now beginning to be documented (see e.g. Morris 2013). As with many other disciplines, this history has been developed through a dialectic between practitioners and scholars. As projectification conquered new territories, practitioners found new challenges that would stimulate interaction with different academic fields. From sophisticated technical engineering challenges in the 1960s that sowed the seeds of scientific management developments, the sphere enlarged to the organizational domain leading to many new developments about temporary organizing, leadership, teams, learning, networks, and so on till the 1990s. In parallel, new issues and concepts such as project business and project strategy emerged.

The conversation between practitioners and scholars has not proceeded as smoothly as both sides had hoped, and it is far from complete. Further developments could be stimulated in at least two directions:

(1) To date, the essential academic insights on projects and project-based organizing have been produced by scholars from at least three fields: engineering, organization, and business. A first direction could be to continue this fruitful interaction on issues that are far from being totally covered by existing research. Several topics could be addressed in that perspective. One concerns the relationship between projectification and strategizing. Another is the creative aspect of projects, which could benefit from bridging with contemporary academic development in the innovation domain. The manifold relationships between projects and culture, not only with regard to organizational but also regional/national cultures, could be studied. Another topic that deserves more scholarly

attention is the increasing role of projects in the field of public management, where projectification might be understood as an important feature related to the new public management – which is not so "new" anymore. A topic of increasing concern in practice is how stakeholders related to work and business will handle projectification. How to make projects more efficient is a classic issue. Finally, the flourishing field of entrepreneurship and entrepreneurship research could profit from conceiving the founding of an organization or the spinning off of an enterprise as a project. More details on those directions are provided later in the section covering entrepreneurship.

(2) This book clearly demonstrates that projectification of society addresses issues in other fields than those covered by these three disciplines. This plea for broadening in theorizing may come as a surprise, given that the field has in recent years already turned toward theories from the wider fields of management and organization (Winter and Szczepanek 2009; Söderlund 2011), even theories such as neo-institutional theory that have the potential to connect the study of projects (and their historical and relational embeddeness) within the institutional contexts of societies at large (Kadefors 1995; Dille and Söderlund 2011). However, reality does not necessarily come in packages in line with established disciplines, so theorizing should not only connect to well-known scientific disciplines. Rather, entrepreneurial researchers can also add perspectives in an uninhibited but hopefully productive way. Regarding projects as temporary organizations definitely implies a renewal of research and thinking about the phenomenon and its contexts of a similar type.

Both approaches could and should be pursued with regard to several topics that still deserve more attention, including the nexus of project-based organizing and strategy in established firms or start-ups, for example.

## Projects and strategizing

The importance of projects for strategizing has been emphasized for a long time (see e.g. Morris and Jamieson 2004). As mentioned, an increasing number of projects seem to be flagged as "strategic," that is, as relevant for the long-term success of an enterprise. An example would be a strategic change program that is both planned and implemented as a project or the introduction of a new product range. However, there are few references to the important role of projects and programs in the strategy literature, which tends to focus on the fit between an organization and its environment (Mintzberg and Lampel 2012) and is relatively unconcerned with how strategy is implemented in projects (Grundy 1998; Morris and Jamieson 2004, 2005). It is interesting that even the more recent interest of strategy researchers in the practice of strategizing (see Jarzabkowski and Spee 2009 for a review) has resulted in neither an extensive nor intensive study of strategic projects or strategy projects.

Similarly, project researchers have rarely addressed strategic concerns and tend to define success in terms of the project coming in on time and to budget, rather than achieving appropriate organizational goals. This reflects a sharp intellectual division of labor in academic research between organizational strategy and project management, which is unfortunate as research has highlighted how many success factors for projects need to be addressed either via pre-sanctions or during the project's "front-end" definition stages (Khurana and Rosenthal 1997).

Over the years, *strategic* project management has become one of the buzz words and project management has even been claimed to be a new strategic management concept (Bea et al. 2008) that, if implemented, may lead to either a PBO or a PNW or simply a more project-oriented permanent organization such as the PSO. At the same time, project practitioners and researchers continue to complain about a systematic neglect of project management experts and expertise at the level of the top management that is typically in charge of the strategy of an organization. It is for this reason that the PMI developed arguments on how to sell project management to senior executives more than a decade ago (Thomas et al. 2002) and that the German Association of Project Management more recently organized a research conference on the importance of strategy for project management and of project management for strategizing (Wagner 2009).

One obvious reason for the disregard or even hostile relationship of strategists and project managers (that somehow seems to mirror the relationship in academia between the researchers from the respective fields) results from the formal structure common to most organizations, including PSOs: the organizational split between corporate strategic planning and development, on the one hand, and the decentralized decision making on projects, even about programs and portfolios, on the other. Recommendations to install a PMO for the entire organization (or at least a division) or of a chief project officer (CPO) only scratch at the surface of the institutional divide and cannot overcome the cognitive-normative differences required from corporate strategists and project managers. While the former focus their attention on the development of the entire organization, project managers, by the nature of their temporary task, have to concentrate on single projects or portfolios of projects at most. If projects are of strategic importance to the organization – as in many PSOs and all PBOs and PNWs – project-based organizing, however, should be conceived as a strategizing activity and vice versa.

Since one might also argue that project management knowledge emerged with a focus on operations, one should not forget that the first projects in which relevant knowledge was generated were strategic projects, not only from a historical perspective. Think for instance of the famous Manhattan or Apollo projects of the Los Alamos Laboratories and NASA, respectively. Moreover, studies of strategic organizational change (e.g. Burgelman and Grove 2007) show that some change initiatives emerged bottom-up, with the help of projects that were carried out in the shadow of the official corporate strategy. In general, as a result of recent reorientation of strategy research on everyday activities of strategists (cf. Jarzabkowski and Spee 2009), there is hope that research will provide the intellectual ground for bringing strategizing and project management closer together. Projects may constitute the action needed to realize intended strategies. The need to improve this link is strong and in light of recent publications (e.g. Wagner 2009; Manning 2010; Cattani et al. 2011; Kaplan and Orlikowski 2013), there is some hope that this will change, at least in research.

## Projects and innovation

Projects must be managed and organized to deal with the uncertainties involved in innovative activities such as creating novel products or services and constructing complex and novel infrastructure and systems.

Academics including Hayes and coauthors (1988), Clark and Fujimoto (1991), Clark and Wheelwright (1992), Cooper and coauthors (1999) and Midler (1995) have bridged the innovation and project domains especially within the context of PSOs, focusing on the product development phase of innovation processes. Portfolio management and project structures are major notions in both project and innovation academic literatures. For more than 20 years, the business context of innovation-based competition (Benghozi et al. 2000) has stimulated impressive developments in both communities, but the theorizing efforts have mainly occurred within each of the two academic domains. In particular, three theoretical frameworks appear fruitful for possible cross-fertilizing efforts with the project organizing community: the concept-knowledge design theory, the design-thinking approach, and actor network theory. All three frameworks wait to be applied for better understanding the role of projects in innovation processes, and the role of innovation in projects.

Concept-knowledge design theory was developed at École des Mines in Paris in the late 1990s (Hatchuel and Weil 2003; Le Masson et al. 2010). Its connection to the project field is rather recent (Lenfle 2008). It proposes a theoretical framework to analyze creative processes. Traditional design theory connects design activity to problem solving, which does not account for creative aspects of design: the famous "out of the box" thinking, surprises or serendipity, "unknown unknown" risks, and so on (Loch et al. 2006) that are important aspects of innovative design. Concept-knowledge design theory, in contrast, proposes an analytical framework that defines design cognitive processes as two distinct expansions: concept-expansions that may be seen as "new ideas" and knowledge-expansions that are necessary to validate these ideas or to expand them toward successful designs. Such a framework appears as a powerful analytical tool to apprehend the upstream creative phases of exploration projects (Lenfle 2008; Midler and Silberzahn 2008; Maniak and Midler 2014).

*Design thinking* has grown as a key topic in management books (Brown 2009; Verganti 2009) as well as in publications in journals such as the *Harvard Business Review* (Brown 2008). On the scholarly side, an emerging literature in the innovation management field investigates more systematically design thinking as a specific and efficient innovation approach (Liedtka 2000; Beckman and Barry 2007). As there are clearly overlaps between design-thinking processes and tools and other innovation (and project) management approaches, their integration in a comprehensive end-to-end approach proposes a specific practice that can be studied as such. Liedtka (2014) demonstrates how such a practice is valuable for reducing biases (such as projection bias, egocentric empathy gap, say/do gap, or hypothesis confirmation bias) in creative processes. Such results are surely useful for the project management community while addressing the efficiency of upstream phases of creative projects.

The development of actor network theory (ANT) started in the 1980s by Callon (1986), Law (1986), Latour (1987), and Akrich and coauthors (2006). Its connection with the project domain is not new in the French academic community (Vissac-Charles 1995; Midler 1993) and has been developing internationally more recently (Blackburn 2002; Linde and Linderoth 2006; Aubry 2011; Floricel et al. 2014). ANT focuses on social processes of innovation creation and adoption as an enrollment process of actors. This translation is the key social mechanism that ensures the enlargement and stabilization of the network. Network in the ANT theory gathers humans and nonhumans to act as a whole. The theory emphasizes the importance of project transformations to enroll new actors and stabilize the network. Such a framework is a powerful tool to analyze the political side of project manager activity (Blackburn 2002).

## Projects and culture

The interplay of projects and culture is difficult to grasp in a straight-forward way for the simple reason that both words have a multitude of meanings. Culture can be viewed as an internal project matter, that is, as shared cognitions and norms that can be managed to achieve a sense of cohesion, shared responsibilities, and so on to achieve good project results. Culture can also be a significant matter in the environment of projects. Talking about a "project culture" may also refer to the extent to which shared cognitions and norms within an organization or even an inter-organizational network support project organizing and project work. On the organizational level, this may include the culture of a department or division, on the inter-organizational level, the culture of a regional cluster or strategic network. Even more macro, on the institutional or field level, national and regional cultures may be as relevant as professional or industry cultures.

In the traditional, normative views on how to manage projects, also with respect to project culture, composition of project teams plays a role (PMI 2013: 37) and so does leadership style (PMI 2013: 20). The direct context of a project is also relevant for culture in this sense and views and norms are taken for granted (Warburton and Kanabar 2013). Shared beliefs and understanding are not always a result of attempts to influence but can be part of the wider project process and a result of what is going on in projects, possibly also unintended results. One extreme example of that is what has been labeled "groupthink" (Janis 1972), which emerges when a project group isolates itself from its environment in such a way that the members lose sight of what is happening in the environment of the project, exemplified by the Bay of Pigs case. The isolation of the "prepare an invasion of Cuba" idea allowed a special project culture to develop, including blindness to warning signals. This phenomenon, which has only recently been picked up by project researchers

(Hällgren 2010), leads to the notion of culture as something that is developing in and around a project that should be described as a temporary organization.

A culture external to a project can be of an even more macro kind, as demonstrated in various publications by Geert Hofstede and his followers (Hofstede 1980; see also Javidan et al. 2009). The questions related to this can be rephrased to cover how culture on a national or international level affects projects and temporary organizations from the outside all the way to how the culture of a PBO, a PSO, or even a PNW affects project management and project work. The signs are that PBOs and PNWs in particular develop routines for projects, since this is directly connected to revenue making. Most PBOs (but so far hardly any PNWs) have handbooks describing and prescribing how projects should be run. A popular solution has been to organize project-related matters to a PMO prescribing essentially linear procedures for how to run the project. Project members are discouraged from introducing backward loops in the project. Such backward loops are considered to be costly and should be avoided. In other words, PMO affects culture in a tangible way.

Support projects (e.g. in PSOs) tend to be more integrated with general development of the organization and its culture (Unger and al. 2014). Support projects are born within the organization, but the birth of a project might be difficult to discern in the routines and events characterizing the organization. In consequence, projects in PSOs are somewhat less likely to develop a distinct project culture; however, they do follow the general culture in the PSO. When a support project is announced, it has usually been on the minds of many before the actual announcement. However, businesses and other organizations having a PMO tend to apply the general PMO-inspired model also for support projects, thereby affecting the visibility and the culture of the support project.

PNWs, in sharp contrast to PBOs and PSOs, do not have one home but in a sense several, since a number of actors from multiple organizations are involved. In consequence, shared cognitions and norms are less likely to converge in this form of temporary organization. If the network grows older (and not necessarily bigger) and an amalgamation of several inputs occurs, potentially a network culture develops as a result of the interaction between the partners and the various interests they might have. Eventually, when the PNW gets stabilized as a result of experiences from projects carried through, a project network culture may even develop and the network becomes a stabilizing factor not only for business but also for project routines.

PNWs have at times special relationships to culture. One such case is when projects get started and a PNW is being shaped and developed in parallel with the need to carry through the project. This occurs when the network culture not only forms but is also formed in the process. Such a special case can be illustrated by peace-keeping operations initiated by the UN. These are *ad hoc* implementations formed with the intention of bringing peace to an environment where a warlike activity is taking place. The task for this kind of project is general – bring peace – and the way to accomplish that general task is virtually unknown initially. Once the project has been initiated with "bring peace" as a main rationale, formulated as a tentative "end state" (which is a military expression) for the operations, implementation including forming and reforming a PNW and learning and relearning *in situ* have to take place and when planning the next steps are guided by the experiences of the forces and the evolving forms of the network, including refining the notion of the end state as such (Lundin and Söderholm 2013).

The relationship between projects and culture becomes increasingly important for another reason. The concept of projects and project management is traveling the world via global companies going through a process of projectification. Globalization of business, not only the advent of global projects, thus plays an important role for projectification in various countries, as do professional organizations and individuals such as consultants who permeate national boundaries. All professional associations of project managers have been promoting their own models of project management education and their own ways of standardizing and certifying project management professionals (see Chapter 5). And they seem to succeed, despite all cultural differences! However, the models, standards, and certification requirements are adopted nationally. This "fit" with the cultural and institutional environment is usually made in practicing these, typically not on the formal level. Academic educational programs can be accredited for their project content via PMI and the accreditations essentially are centering on program contents based on PMBOK. The academic programs related to projects in China and in other parts of Southeast Asia are very much related to the PMI way of managing projects. The PMI reliance on the role of the appointed project manager is not only accepted but also most appreciated by the Chinese, as the PMI way is so prevalent in China. By tradition, China is a collectivity-oriented country, often expressed by phenomena such as family and personal networks (in Chinese denoted "guanxi," meaning relationship); nevertheless, individuals and organizations strive to follow the established and approved procedures that dominate in practice, perhaps because they provide orientation and guidance to those who have been so far unable to develop (or rediscover) their own practices. In any event, national cultures seem to favor a specific type of project model or, rather, a professional organization — national cultures and project models tend go together, for whatever reason.

## Projects and management in the public sector

Much of what is done in the public sector occurs in projects or under project-like circumstances, so in that sense project experiences in the public sectors have been abundant in the past. Most public infrastructure is delivered through projects and programs of various sorts. This is increasingly the case where, in the wake of outsourcing, many of these products and services are provided by private organizations or public–private partnerships (Schedler and Proeller 2011). This outsourcing creates a dynamic element in project participation that includes politicians, civil servants, and the outside providers.

Some activities occur in more or less permanent sections as PSOs; others already have characteristics more like those of PBOs and PNWs, depending on the kind of outsourcing that led or enhanced the project form. Similar processes as in the private sector approximately apply to projects run in the public sphere. However, some differences are important. Public management consists essentially of a political arena and a corresponding civil servant bureaucracy that have to work together. Decisions, not least about outsourcing and project organizing, have to be made by boards or committees to handle disagreements and often those decisions are not unanimous. This makes projects in the public sector different from other project contexts. The role of the civil part of public management is to both prepare for political decisions and take action on those decisions. Private subcontractors and/or consultants now handle much of the productive work, so the public sector consists in parts of some fairly stable PNWs in which project groups take on a stream of tasks sequentially. Hybrids of public and private actors in the PNWs are common when it comes to major projects in for example defense endeavors. This is also the case in what we earlier referred to as Triple Helix development activity. The majority of the projects carried out in connection with the public sector do not cause debates or public outrage but are handled in a routine way.

Megaprojects of the public or public–private type tend to become more controversial than others and are debated politically as part of the project process. Discussions of such projects develop into political debates wherein politicians tend to use the projects as arguments to make political points. The nature of politics and political parties is that opposing views are regarded as natural and as part of the democratic process. Megaprojects and "sensitive issues" supply arenas for political action. The political "games" are not easy though: politicians may gain but they can also lose, and much of what is happening is connected to the political agenda and to media attention. Initiating a project is risky since problems that are out of control can lead to blame from political opponents. This type of political debate will most certainly continue in the future when expensive megaprojects catch the attention of voters, the media, and taxpayers.

It is unclear what effects these outbursts of public and political interests have on projects as such. However, it is very likely that the way projects are handled and conceived of is in turmoil. The need to study and understand such projects is stressed at the same time as this field expands – projects in this context necessitate attention from political scientists of an unconventional type.

### Projectification and stakeholders

Megaprojects in the realm of public administration, as mentioned earlier, are only an extreme case pointing to the importance of what is commonly termed "stakeholder management" and are now much discussed in the project management literature (Newcombe 2003; Littau et al. 2010; Eskerod and Jepsen 2013). A challenge or a change of the institutional setting caused by projectification will no doubt influence the situation for most stakeholders in working and business life. Potential stakeholders relevant for managing and working in projects in all of our three contexts (PSOs, PBOs, and PNWs) are not only owners but also managers (CEOs, line managers, project managers), employees of other companies, suppliers, customers, financiers of projects, part of the educational system including universities, authorities, political organizations, and not least trade unions and employer associations (Rhenman 1964; Freeman 1984; Cleland 1986).

What actually will happen is hard to foresee, as many of the stakeholders take part in both the creation and the preservation of institutions, including projects. But their roles and power are definitely at stake. A likely first reaction of many stakeholders is to try to preserve the rules of the game; not until later when changes are overwhelming will they react by redefining their traditional roles. All stakeholder groups mentioned are potentially affected by projectification and will probably react to the process in line with the way they understand their own interests (Rhenman 1964). Take for instance trade unions, which will have even more increased difficulties recruiting members in a projectified environment when their strategies are adapted more to the institutional environment of the old Industrial Society with rather clear organizational and industry boundaries and an established counterpart for collective bargaining, the employee association.

To simplify, one may say that stakeholders represent three spheres of interest developed in the Industrial Society, somewhat reflecting the actors within the system of industrial relations (Dunlop 1958). The first one has its base among employers and managers; the second among the employees and their unions; and the third is an even broader institutional sphere that includes authorities, political actors, and the educational system. Management and employers need to be aware that projectification leads to new challenges in relation to time and evaluation of the activities. In a PSO, there is simultaneous planning in relation to several time dimensions – one being the calendar year, which stakeholders as owners and tax authorities tend to use for evaluating the financial performance, and another being the time horizon of project managers, which may vary dramatically, in turn causing tensions between different stakeholders.

A traditional industrial organization of course also experienced tensions between different stakeholders – such as those between owners and employees often related to the allocation of wages and profits – but we believe that the tensions and potential conflicts will become even more dramatic during the ongoing transition from an Industrial to a Project Society as the stakeholders organize their activities in relation to different views on how to relate to time and evaluation of work. In the traditional industrial context, evaluation is connected with periodic, calendar time, whereas evaluation of traditional projects is connected to the project per se when it has ended. We therefore foresee a conflict between stakeholders with a project view on management and work (top managers of PBOs, project managers, project workers, and financiers of projects on the one hand) and stakeholders governed by a traditional industrial view on management and work (top managers from industrial firms, line managers, line workers, unions, owners, investors, and tax authorities on the other hand). In the PSOs, the conflict between work in traditional industrial organizations and work in projects is clearly expressed by the tension between the line and the project way of working (Arvidsson and Ekstedt 2006; Arvidsson 2009). Practitioners as well as scholars need better insights into the potential tensions and conflicts this transformation may lead to in business activities, not least also in PBOs and PNWs.

Stakeholders such as employees and unions have to cope with many differences between the often somewhat more informal contracts of work in projects and the dominating formal rules and institutions of today's working life. More often than not, these differences give rise to conflicts and contradictions. The situation is worsened by ambivalences. In the PBOs as well as in PNWs the borders between positions as employers and employees are often rather vague and, at least in the media industry, frequently changing (Manning and Sydow 2011). Becoming an employer is actually a part of the career ladder for employees in consultancy firms. This vagueness is also illustrated by statistical definitions as illustrated in the use of the category "self-employed" in the European Labour Force Survey and "own-employers" in Swedish statistics. In some PBOs, such as project management firms in the construction industry, the contact between the managers of the contractor responsible for the project and the employees working for a subcontractor may level further out in the production chain, and sometimes may even be nonexistent. Consequently, what is commonly called corporate social responsibility (CRS) is hardly to be expected in these contexts. Work in project environments imposes specific demands on employees. The individuals are compelled to high degree of responsibility for their own negotiations, advancement, and careers. One may ask if stakeholders, such as unions, have found any measures to handle this new situation or even if they have enough knowledge about it. This social dimension of projectification is, despite first insights (see

Chapter 4), no doubt a field where scholars in the social sciences need to increase their knowledge.

Knowledge about the role of different stakeholders in the projectification process is far from developed, neither by the actors themselves nor in the research community. Political scientists, sociologists, educational researchers, historians, and others with interest in organizations and power with alternative perspectives on the transformation can contribute in many ways.

### Projects and entrepreneurship

Entrepreneurship, defined as "a dynamic and social process where individuals, alone or in collaboration, identify opportunities for innovation and act upon these by transforming ideas into practical and targeted activities" (European Commission 2006) is not far from project management, which is often conceived as "the process by which projects are defined, planned, monitored, controlled and delivered such that the agreed benefits are realized" (PMI 2013). But as Kuura et al. (2014) notice in their article about the linkage between these fields, research on these two areas has followed parallel but separate paths. Following their analysis of the two communities, we will try to map the similarities as well as the differences between the two conceptual streams and finish with a focus on potential linkages with recent developments on a convergent perspective about entrepreneurial innovative projects.

From an academic disciplinary history point of view, both entrepreneurship and project management are relatively young as academic fields, in spite of an extended existence as practice. They both appear as interdisciplinary fields. Maybe for this characteristic, both share the same critique from the established academic fields of lacking a solid theoretical basis. On the other hand, they have both grown significantly in recognition for their relevancy, not only in management and organization research but also from socioeconomic institutions, such as the United States Association for Small Business and Entrepreneurship (USASBE) or the European Council for Small

Business and Entrepreneurship (ECSB) for entrepreneurship or PMI and IPMA for project management.

Both fields have been in a significant expansion and evolution process during the past decades. Project management, as we saw earlier in this book, expanded to a multiscale approach, from an instrumental and inside view of doing projects, focused on the project manager and his or her leadership competence and tools, to a deeper approach of organizational phenomena within projects as well as to a broader analysis of project contexts: multiprojects, networks of relationships, stakeholder management, projectification and programmification of permanent organizations, project business and project strategy, project orientation, and the extension of projectification to many different domains of society. The entrepreneurship field evolved from small business or, more precisely, start-up management and from an individual focus on the entrepreneur profile to a more generic and broader approach dealing with creative processes and organizational patterns for changes in various contexts: management of start-up creation in high-tech clusters, but also entrepreneurial ventures within existing organizations to macro-level analysis of economic vitality on a regional or national level. In this perspective, "intrapreneurship" (Pinchot 1985; Bosma et al. 2010) and "entrepreneurial orientation" (Covin and Slevin 1991), to give just two examples, can be interpreted as parallel notions to projectification or project orientation in PSOs, PBOs, and PNWs. Apart from the striking similarities, Kuura et al. point out a significant difference between the two fields, concerning public support and policies. Entrepreneurship receives heavy support from international, national, and local authorities, "while project management is developing beyond its 'Cinderella' status" (Kuura et al. 2014: 219).

Such proximities call for an effort to bridge the "missing link" (Ajam 2011) between the two academic communities of project management and entrepreneurship. Kuura et al. (2014) explore various ways and scopes to implement such bridging. We insist here on innovation and/or organization creation (Hjorth 2014) as a fruitful notion to develop convergence between the two fields. Of course, all projects, as all business creations, are far from being innovative. But in the contemporary period, the innovation imperative is a key driver to projectification, including the organization of public policies supporting high-tech clusters and start-up ventures. And on the theoretic side, taking into account the specificities of creative or innovative activity is one of the main drivers of new conceptual developments in both project management and the entrepreneurial academic field.

An analysis of innovative start-up development shows indeed an evident proximity with project management. The importance of the initial "pitch" on the "opportunity" that initiates the entrepreneurial trajectory corresponds to the major role of the project target formulation in the project management paradigm. Business plans appear more and more of a key condition to engage the involvement of stakeholders in financing the investment in corporate venture processes as it appears as a condition to pass the investment decision committees in PSOs or PBOs. The high-tech start-up development from universities or research labs is generally organized in sequential go–no go phases: idea, pre-start-up, start-up, and post-start-up phases (Clarysse and Moray 2004). Such a sequential process looks very much like the stage-gate maturity-driven approach of project portfolio management (Cooper et al. 1999). Planning, cost control, and performance of the deliverable appears, in entrepreneurial venture as in projects, as key best management practices. To some extent, the project engineering of entrepreneurship is running the danger of killing the creative spirit entrepreneurial activities are – or at least should be – known for.

Analyzing Silicon Valley, where individual firms are confronted with extremely high uncertainty and volatility because of continuous changes in technology, March (1995) developed the concept of the "disposable organization." Such disposable organizations have high short-term efficiency but only modest adaptive durability. A highly efficient organization is maintained until it is dysfunctional in the changed environment; then it is discarded and another, a permanent organization, is formed. The parallel between start-up venture ecology and project portfolio management (Loch et al. 2006) is evident. As Lindgren and Packendorff (2003) argue, in particular in the extreme case of start-up in a capital venture context, entrepreneurship appears as managing an organization-creation process as a project (see also Gartner 1985; Hjorth 2014).

Some interesting theoretical as well as practical issues nevertheless remain as a platform to further fruitful connections between the two academic communities. In the entrepreneurship domain, the effectuation concept (Sarasvathy 2001) apparently reverses the goal orientation and planning (causation) approach of project management epistemology. Effectuation is a sequence of non-predictive strategies in dynamic problem solving that is primarily means driven, where goals emerge as a consequence of stakeholder commitments rather than vice versa. In the project management domain, the notions of "vanguard projects" (Brady and Davies 2004; Frederiksen and Davies 2008), "exploration projects" (Lenfle 2008), and "project lineage management" (Midler and Silberzahn 2008; Maniak and Midler 2014) propose a multiproject framework focusing on project-to-project learning. Those two theoretical frameworks share a perspective of potential expansion of opportunities as knowledge taking into account and valuing what is known as the serendipity effect (Roberts 1989).

*Project management and gender*

Project workers and even more so project managers are predominantly male, reflecting the gender bias typical of most organizations (Henderson et al. 2013; Ojiako et al. 2014). At first sight, this is quite surprising as project settings are typically described as less hierarchical, more network based, and intensively communicative – and therefore potentially less traditional when it comes to viewing skills and people. Moreover, in face of booming employment in various creative and IT industries, physically demanding project work (as in the construction and shipbuilding industries) has lost relative importance and this should eventually lead to decreasing the bias. Nevertheless, project managers continue to be overwhelmingly male, which is explained by the bias found in permanent organizations spilling over to projects, by the volatile and often unplanned character of project work that collides with family responsibilities women tend to take on, and with the mostly gendered project management techniques (Buckle and Thomas 2003; Lindgren and Packendorff 2006b). Women project managers are typically engaged in minor, less resourced projects than their male counterparts. For instance, according to one U.S. study of 563 project team members, female project members were not only nine times more likely to work with female project managers than are male project team members but also almost twice as likely to work on projects with a budget of $1 million or less than are the male project managers: "Taken together, these results indicate that both female project managers and team members may be locked in a vicious cycle of project assignments on lower-cost, smaller projects, leaving them more marginalized both geographically and culturally from power-gaining experiences in comparison to their male counterparts" (Henderson and Stackman 2010: 48).

The literature contains little about gender as a matter of feminine and masculine norms (gender as a social construction) specifically. The main concern seems to be that masculine norms linger a lot longer in project work as compared to what is happening in traditional organizations (Buckle and Thomas 2003). Moreover, gender issues in projects, in sharp contrast to some other forms of temporary organizing such as employment in temporary work agencies (e.g. Vosko 2000), have so far received little attention from management and organization scholars, not to mention any particular concern for different contexts of project-based organizing such as PBOs, PSOs, and PNWs. In addition, as projects typically are task and problem oriented, we would expect projects to have the potential to become an organizational arena wherein people are engaged and employed more on their abilities to achieve project objectives than on stereotyped attributes related to gender or some other aspect. All in all, such issues in these contexts offer ample opportunities for future project research related to gender.

## 6.3. THEORIZING PROJECT-BASED ORGANIZING IN INSTITUTIONAL CONTEXTS

The described overall organizational and institutional changes on the societal level, including discussions about transformations of technologies, which often are concrete and easy to observe, await to be fully understood by adequate theories. At the very least, these theories have to be sensitive to changes at not only the micro level of projects in their immediate contexts but also at the macro level of society, a task that so far has been addressed only by a few critical project theorists (e.g. Hodgson and Cicmil 2006). Such theories should address not only processes in general but also the importance of organizational and inter-organizational histories and how they impact project-based organizing in particular (Kieser 1994; Rowlinson et al. 2014). Only this prepares them for being sensitive to the bright as well as the dark sides of developments over time. Examples of the former are routinization and learning in and across projects, while escalating commitment and path dependence exemplify the latter. While this request is not new for the field of project management (Engwall 2003; Manning and Sydow 2011), research on temporary forms of organizing in general and on projects in particular has, in sharp contrast to organizational or inter-organizational embeddedness (cf. Bakker 2010), not yet adequately considered the historical and temporal embeddedness.

As indicated previously, there is a need for further theorizing on the components of project organizing in Project Society. One view on this matter is captured in the following sentence: "A theory is a child of its time and in need of reconsideration and reconstruction" (Lundin and Söderholm 2013: 587). The implication is that theorizing is both a matter of constructing new theories and of scrutinizing some of the taken-for-granted theories and "truths." We are reminded about that necessity to observe the notions of "faddishness" in research and in practice (Midler 1983; Abrahamson 1991; Abrahamson and Fairchild

1999; Starbuck 2009; Bort and Kieser 2011). The observation is that research themes and special practices tend to come in clusters, which should make us aware of the need to scrutinize, revise, and reconstruct in line with suggestions made by Morris (2013), especially since we are in the social sciences.

One way of understanding the wave of current interest in projects in practice and the concomitant expansion of research efforts in the area of projects and temporary organizations is to label the matter a "fad." Traditionally, the notion of a fad is connected with something regarded as detrimental, possibly more so when it comes to management fads than for fads in research. We do not share that negative view when it comes to research for the simple reason that as a whole the phenomenon of massive expansion in a research area not only reflects, at least in most cases, real changes in practice but also offers expectations and promises for major advances in research. To put it personally, we feel proud of being part of the project organizing research wave and will do our best to continue to contribute by doing empirical and theoretical research.

Finally, let us just indicate an avenue for further research in the area of project management and temporary organizing more generally that appears to us particularly promising at the present time. However, let us start by saying that we very much appreciate the increased efforts of project researchers to overcome empiristic methods and, instead, base their research efforts on sound theoretical reasoning. This has over the years resulted in a multiplicity of theories considered relevant for research on temporary organizations (see overviews by Winter and Szczepanek 2009 or Söderlund 2011). Although we agree that the potential of several of these approaches has not yet been fully exploited by project researchers, we wish to point to two theorizing efforts that, from our perspective at least, seem particularly promising and can potentially even inform each other.

The recent turn toward practice theory in social science (Giddens 1984; Schatzki et al. 2001) has already had a strong impact on management and organizations research, in particular on strategy research (see recent reviews Jarzabkowski and Spee 2009; Vaara and

Whittington 2012; Erden et al. 2014; Seidl and Whittington 2014). Practice theory, we are convinced, can provide the methodological background for renovating project management theory or concepts of temporary organizing more broadly. Comprising approaches such as activity, actor-network, social capital, or structuration theory (cf. Nicolini 2013), practice theory shares enough assumptions to be considered as a stream of theorizing "the social" that provides a sound methodological basis to overcome many useless dualisms (most prominently that between agency and structure). Moreover, practice theory offers a more holistic and yet analytical understanding of social praxis constituted not only by socially embedded human agents with their cognitions and emotions but also by material artifacts, though not necessarily attributing agency to the latter (see, however, Orlikowski and Scott 2008). Research based on practice theory promises to help revitalize the conversation between practitioners and scholars, also in the field of project management and temporary organizing.

Few studies have hitherto tried to apply an "as-practice" approach to temporary organizations (e.g. Blomquist et al. 2010; Hällgren and Söderholm 2010; Manning 2010; Manning and Sydow 2011). Based on Nicolini's (2013) *Practice Theory, Work and Organization*, Floricel and coauthors (2014) list five dimensions of practice theory useful for research on temporary organizations. These dimensions follow (in a simplified form):

1) It points to the *work and efforts* involved in project work rather than plans and decisions.
2) It stresses the *material aspects and conditions* for managing and working in projects.
3) It focuses on *creativity and entrepreneurship* for project implementation.
4) It offers a *transformation of traditional views on knowledge.*
5) It highlights how *diversity of interests and power* transform as part of project processes.

Not unlike studies in the strategy-as-practice stream, we expect such studies to be extremely effective at capturing what is going on in praxis in detail. However, research that adopts a project-as-practice lens runs into two tightly connected dangers: first, being too descriptive, that is, stopping short of analytical rigor; second, capturing only the immediate context of projects such as those distinguished in this book – PBOs, PSOs, and PNWs – with little concern for the wider context of society. In consequence, a practice turn in project research has to take the institutional context seriously. Increasing our knowledge about the "actuality" of managing and working in project settings of different kinds is indeed not sufficient (Cicmil et al. 2006).

For this reason, and in particular with an eye on Project Society – and how it influences what is going on in temporary organizations and how respective organizing efforts in turn impact the further development of society – we welcome recent attempts of project researchers to give neo-institutional theory more prominence (e.g. Jones and Liechtenstein 2008; Bresnen and Marshall 2011; Dille and Söderlund 2011; Morris and Geraldi 2011; Orr et al. 2011). In the meantime, neo-institutional theory dominates management and organization theory and should, in particular in face of the need to link project and organizational research, be picked up more widely in research on temporary organizations. More importantly, with concepts such as institutional entrepreneurship and, in particular, institutional work (see Chapter 5), institutionalists have given more prominence to strategic agency in institutionalization processes. Initiated by Scott (2008) in his second edition of *Organizations and Institutions*, and based upon Giddens's (1984) conception of agency as "knowledgeable" and his conceptualization of the relationship between agency and structure as a "duality" (rather than a dualism), neo-institutionalism is better prepared than ever to inform research on projects and other forms of temporary organization. For research on these forms, for a long time and for what, at that time, seemed good reasons, was action oriented. It took project researchers a while to become more sensitive toward contexts in terms of relations (and structures) in structuration processes – not to mention the time–space relations that are so central to Hägerstrand's (1974) work and have let project researchers take at least the time dimension more seriously (Maaninen-Olsson and

Müllern 2009; Dille and Söderlund 2011). Like other advanced theories in the realms of management and organization, project research has to seriously consider the paradox of "embedded agency," which is much debated among institutionalists (cf. Battilana and D'Aunno 2009). That is, agency is on the one hand socially embedded in different contexts; at the same time, it is considered as potentially strategic, that is, able to influence the context in which it is embedded. Without losing its concern for institutions and institutional changes, this conceptual modification makes it significantly easier for project researchers to connect with this kind of theory that, for a long time, has only provided an outside-in view for organizing; that is, it has emphasized the influence of the organizational or institutional field on organizations (Meyer and Rowan 1977; DiMaggio and Powell 1983).

The practice turn would, for instance, allow studying the "normalization of deviance" (Vaughan 1996) in the context of projects, not only within but also across organizations, an important research gap identified recently by Pinto (2014), who makes clear that this phenomenon is distinct and can derail projects very much like competence or decision traps, political conflict, or overbureaucratization do. Researchers adopting a project-as-practice lens have for a long time investigated deviations in projects with respect to project goals and rules (e.g. for global projects: Hällgren and Söderholm 2010) but, apart from Pinto, have not yet paid attention to this subtle phenomenon at the interface between organizing as a routinized activity and organizing as a reflexive, possibly innovative practice. Project researchers should, however, be sensitive to the importance of institutional contexts for explaining how normalization of deviance occurs in reality; institutions not only within and across organizations but also in the wider society that have an impact on unintended consequences of intentional actions are produced, most likely enhanced by the hidden dynamics of some self-reinforcing processes in an institutionally vicious problem context (cf. Masuch 1985).

The themes mentioned are directly in line with the main areas of research covered in this book. In this way, we stress the idea that continuity in research should be aspired to and involve trying to find loose ends in what is available. This goes for research themes as well as for the methodological development of empirical research. Research on projects or temporary forms of organizing more generally now uses a wide range of methods, ranging from the quantitative analysis of secondary data to the collection of primary data with the help of either quantitative or qualitative methods. What is still rare in this field of research is a mixed-method approach, combining qualitative and quantitative methods for data collection and analysis in creative ways (cf. Creswell and Plano Clark 2011), starting for instance with a quantitative approach to detect interesting cases before studying these with ethnographic and other qualitative methods. In particular, the practice perspective favored by us and other project researchers (e.g. Blomquist et al. 2010) would profit from the use of mixed methods not only but also as it requires a process methodology.

In this book, we have essentially analyzed and illustrated a number of "transformation dilemmas" that are challenging conceptions of management, work, and supporting institutions on the development paths as we are entering Project Society. As a final indication of direction for the future, we advocate an expansion of research related more explicitly to Project Society involving a wide range of methods; a lively discussion among researchers with related interests; a wide set of disciplines, not only the traditional ones such as management and engineering but also nontraditional ones such as ethnography; and junior researchers with an open mind. Last but certainly not least, we advocate involvement with practitioners and others "out there" to inspire researchers with "empirical disturbances" and talk about what we need and how things really are.

# References

Aaltonen, K. and Kujala, J. (2010) A project lifecycle perspective on stakeholder influence strategies in global projects. *Scandinavian Journal of Management*, 26(4): 381–397.

Abrahamson, E. (1991) Managerial fads and fashion: The diffusion and rejection of innovations. *Academy of Management Review*, 16(3): 586–612.

Abrahamson, E. and Fairchild, G. (1999) Management fashion: Lifecycles, triggers and collective learning processes. *Administrative Science Quarterly*, 44: 708–740.

Ackroyd, S., Batt, R., Thompson, P., and Tolbert, P. S. (eds.) (2004) *The Oxford Handbook of Work and Organisation*. Oxford: Oxford University Press.

Ahola, T., Russka, I., Artto, K., and Kujula, J. (2014) What is project governance and what are its origins? *International Journal of Project Management*, 32: 1321–1332.

Ahrne, G. and Brunsson, N. (2005) Organizations and meta-organizations. *Scandinavian Journal of Management*, 21(4): 429–449.

Ajam, M. (2011) Entrepreneurship and project management – The missing link. *PM World Today*, XIII(IV).

Akrich, M., Callon, M., and Latour, B. (2006) *Sociologie de la traduction: Textes fondateurs (Sociology of Translation: Seminal Texts)*. Paris: Presses des Mines.

Allertz, W. (2009) Cross-border organisation development and its consequences for industrial relations. In Moreau, M. A. (ed.) with the collaboration of Negrelli, S. and Pochet, P. *Building Anticipation in Restructuring Europe*. Frankfurt: Peter Lang, 87–112.

Allvin, M., Aronsson, G., Hagström, T., Johansson, G., and Lundberg, U. (2006) *Gränslöst arbete – Socialpsykologiska perspektiv på det nya arbetslivet (Work Without Borders – Socio-psychological Perspectives on the New Working Life)*. Malmö: Liber.

Allvin, M., Aronsson, G., Hagström, T., Johansson, G. and Lundberg, U. (2011) *Work without Boundaries – Psychological Perspectives on the New Work Life*. Oxford: Wiley-Blackwell.

Amabile, T. M., Conti, R., Coon, H., Lazenby, J., and Herron, M. (1996) Assessing the work environment for creativity. *Academy of Management Journal*, 39(5): 1154–1184.

Amabile, T. M., Schatzel, E. A., Moneta, G. B., and Kramer, S. J. (2004) Leader behaviors and the work environment for creativity: Perceived leader support. *Leadership Quarterly*, 15(1): 6–32.

Amin, A. and Thrift, N. (1994) Living in the global. In Amin, A. and Thrift, N. (eds.), *Globalization, Institutions and Regional Development in Europe*. Oxford: Oxford University Press, 1–22.

Anderson, H. (2005) Projektorganisation – stöder eller kväver innovation? (Project organization – supports or chokes innovations?) In Fjaestad, B. and Wolvén, L-E. (eds.), *Arbetsliv och samhällsförändringar*. Lund: Studentlitteratur.

Andriani, P., Jones, C., Perkmann, M., De Propris, L., Sena, V., Delbridge, R., Möslein, K., and Neely, A. 2005. *Challenging Clusters: The Prospects and Pitfalls of Clustering for Innovation and Economic Development*. London: Advanced Institute of Management (AIM) Research.

Apleberger, L., Jonsson, R., and Åhman, P. (2007) *Byggandets industrialisering: Nulägesbeskrivning (Industrialization of Building: Description of the Current Development)*. Göteborg: Sveriges byggindustrier, Rapport/FoU-Väst, nr 0701.

Archer, N. P. and Ghasemzadeh, F. (1999) An integrated framework for project portfolio selection. *International Journal of Project Management*, 17(4): 207–216.

Archibald, R. D. (2004) A global system for categorizing projects. *Management in Government*: 1–11.

Arnold, J. and Cohen, L. (2008) The psychology of careers in industrial and organizational settings: A critical but appreciative analysis. *International Review of Industrial and Organizational Psychology*, 23: 1–42.

Arthur, M. B. and Rousseau, D. M. (1996) *The Boundaryless Career – A New Employment Principle for a New Organizational Era*. New York: Oxford University Press.

Artto, K. and Wikström, K. (2005) What is project business? *International Journal of Project Management*, 23(5): 343–353.

Artto, K., Kujala, J., Dietrich, P., and Martinsuo, M. (2008) What is project strategy? *International Journal of Project Management*, 26(1): 4–12.

Artto, K., Martinsuo, M., and Kujala, J. (2011) *Project Business*. Helsinki: http://pbgroup.tkk.fi/en/.

Artto, K., Martinsuo, M., Gemünden, H. G., and Murtoaro, J. (2009) Foundations of program management: A bibliometric view. *International Journal of Project Management*, 27(1): 1–18.

Arvidsson, N. (2009) Exploring tension in projectified matrix organizations. *Scandinavian Journal of Management*, 25(1): 97–107.

Arvidsson, N. and Ekstedt, E. (2006) The growth of project organisation and its effects on working conditions. In Olofsson, J. and Zavisic, M. (eds.), *Routes to a*

*More Open Labour Market*, Yearbook 2006. Stockholm: National Institute for Working Life, 88–102.

Asplund, J. (1985) *Tid, rum, individ och kollektiv (Time, Room, Individual and Collective)*. Stockholm: Liber förlag.

Aubry, M. (2011) The social reality of organisational project management at the interface between networks and hierarchy. *International Journal of Managing Projects in Business*, 4(3): 436–457.

Axelsson, B. and Easton, G. (1992) (eds.) *Industrial Networks. A New View of Reality*. London: Routledge.

Bäckström, H. (1999) *Den krattade manegen – Svensk arbetsorganisatorisk utveckling under tre decennier. (Swedish development of work organization during three decades)* (diss.). Uppsala Universitet.

Baines, T. S., Lightfoot, H. W., Benedettini, O., and Kay, J. M. (2009) The servitization of manufacturing: A review of literature and reflection on future challenges. *Journal of Manufacturing Technology Management*, 20(5): 547–567.

Bakker, R. M. (2010) Taking stock of temporary organizational forms: A systematic review and research agenda. *International Journal of Management Reviews*, 12(4): 466–486.

Bakshi, H., Hargreaves, I., and Mateos-Garcia, J. (2013) *A Manifesto for the Creative Economy*. London: Nesta.

Bamber, G., Lansbury, R., and Wales, N. (2011) *International and Comparative Employment Relations*. 5th edn. Crows Nest, NSW: Allen & Unwin.

Banerjee, M., Tolbert, P. S., and DiCiccio, T. (2012) Friend or foe? The effects of contingent employees on standard employees' work attitudes. *International Journal of Human Resource Management*, 23(11): 2180–2204.

Barczak, G. and Wilemon, D. (1989) Leadership differences in new product development teams. *Journal of Product Innovation Management*, 6(4): 259–267.

Barley, S. and Kunda, G. (2001) Bringing work back in. *Organization Science*, 12(1): 76–95.

Barney, J. (1991) Firm resources and sustained competitive advantage. *Journal of Management*, 17(1): 99–120.

Bathelt, H., Malmberg, A., and Maskell, P. (2004) Clusters and knowledge: Local buzz, global pipelines and the process of knowledge creation. *Progress in Human Geography*, 28: 31–56.

Battilana, J. and D'Aunno, T. (2009) Institutional work and the paradox of embedded agency. In Lawrence, T. B., Suddaby, R., and Leca, B. (eds.), *Institutional Work: Actors and Agency in Institutional Studies of Organizations*. Cambridge: Cambridge University Press, 31–58.

Bea, F. X., Scheurer, S., and Hesselmann, S. (2008) *Projektmanagement* (*Project Management*), Stuttgart: Haupt.

Beaume, R., Midler, C., and Maniak, R. (2013) Renewing project management in mature industries: An analysis of innovation and advanced engineering efforts. In Lundin, R. A. and Hällgren, M. (eds.), *Advancing Research on Projects and Temporary Organizations*. Copenhagen: Copenhagen Business School Press, 150–168.

Beck, U. (1992) *The Risk Society: Towards a New Modernity*. London: Sage.

Becker, G. S. (1999) How the web is revolutionizing learning. *Business Week* (*Industrial/technology edition*), December 27 (3661): 40.

Beckert, J. (1999) Agency, entrepreneurs, and institutional change. The role of strategic choice and institutionalized practices in organizations. *Organization Studies*, 20(5): 777–799.

Beckert, J. (2010) How do fields change? The interrelations of institutions, networks, and cognition in the dynamics of markets. *Organization Studies*, 31(5): 605–627.

Beckman, S. and Barry, M. (2007) Innovation as a learning process: Embedding design thinking. *California Management Review*, 50(1): 25–56.

Behrens, M. (2004) New forms of employers' collective interest representation? *Industrielle Beziehungen – The German Journal of Industrial Relations*, 11(1–2): 77–91.

Behrens, M. (2011) *Das Paradox der Arbeitgeberverbände: Von der Schwierigkeit, durchsetzungsstarke Unternehmensinteressen kollektiv zu vertreten* (*The Paradox of Employer Associations: About the Difficulties to Represent Corporate Interests in an Effective Manner*). Berlin: Sigma.

Benghozi, P. J., Charue, F., and Midler, C. (2000) *Innovation Based Competition and Design Systems*. Paris: L'Harmattan.

Bengtsson, M. and Kock, S. (2000) "Coopetition" in business networks – To cooperate and compete simultaneously. *Industrial Marketing Management*, 29(5): 411–426.

Bengtsson, M., Mullern, T., Söderholm, A., and Wåhlin, N. (2009) *A Grammar of Organizing*. Cheltenham: Edgar.

Beniger, J. R. (1986) *The Control Revolution. Technological and Economic Origins of the Information Society*. Cambridge, MA: Harvard University Press.

Bennett, E., James, S., and Grohmann, P. (2000) *Joint Venture Public-Private Partnerships for Urban Environmental Services*. New York: Public Private Partnerships for the Urban Environment.

Berger, P. L. and Luckmann, T. (1966) *The Social Construction of Reality: A Treatise in the Sociology of Knowledge*. Garden City, NY: Anchor Books.

Betts, M. and Lansley, P. (1995) International Journal of Project Management: A review of the first ten years. *International Journal of Project Management*, 13(4): 207–217.

Blackburn, S. (2002) The project manager and the project-network. *International Journal of Project Management*, 20(3): 199–204.

Blomquist, T., Hällgren, M., Nilsson, M., and Söderholm, A. (2010) Project-as-practice: In search of project management research that matters. *Project Management Journal*, 41(1): 5–16.

Borg, E. (2014) *Liminality at work. Mobile project workers in-between.* Linköping University: Linköping Studies in Arts and Science No. 614.

Borg, E. and Söderlund, J. (2014) Moving in, moving on: Liminality practices in project-based work. *Employee Relations*, 36 (2): 182–197.

Bort, S. and Kieser, A. (2011) Fashion in organization theory: An empirical analysis of the diffusion of theoretical concepts. *Organization Studies*, 32(5): 655–681.

Bosma, N., Stam, E., and Wennekers, S. (2010) *Intrapreneurship – An International Study.* Zoetermeer: SCALES.

Bourdieu, P. (1977) *Outline of a Theory of Practice.* Cambridge: Cambridge University Press.

Bourne, L. and Walker, D. H. T. (2005) Visualizing and mapping stakeholder influence. *Management Decisions*, 43(5): 649–660.

Boutinet, F. (2004) *Anthropologie du projet (Project Anthropology).* Paris: Puf Rééd.

Bower, J. L. and Christensen, C. M. (1995) *Disruptive Technologies: Catching the Wave* (pp. 506–520). Cambridge, MA: Harvard Business Review Video.

Bower, J. L. and Hout, T. (1988) Fast cycle capability for competitive power. *Harvard Business Review*, 66: 110–118.

Brady, T. and Davies, A. (2004) Building project capabilities: From exploratory to exploitative learning. *Organization Studies*, 25(9): 1601–1621.

Brady, T. and Davies, A. (2011) Learning to deliver a mega-project: The case of Heathrow Terminal 5. In Howard, M. and Caldwell, N. (eds.), *Procuring Complex Performance.* London: Routledge, 174–198.

Brady, T., Davies, A., and Gann, D. (2005) Creating value by delivering integrated solutions. *International Journal of Project Management*, 23: 360–365.

Brady, T., Davies, A., and Nightingale, P. (2012) Dealing with uncertainty in complex projects: Revisiting Klein and Meckling. *International Journal of Managing Projects in Business*, 5(4): 718–736.

Brandenburger, A. M. and Nalebuff, B. J. (1996) *Co-opetition.* New York: Doubleday.

Brandl, B. (2013) Die Repräsentativität von Arbeitgeberverbänden in Europa: Eine Standortbestimmung des „deutschen Modells" (Representativity of employer associations in Europe: Localization of the „German Model"). *WSI Mitteilungen*, 66(7): 510–518.

Braun, T., Ferreira, A., and Sydow, J. (2013) Citizenship behavior and effectiveness in temporary organizations. *International Journal of Project Management*, 31(6): 862–876.

Braun, T., Müller-Seitz, G., and Sydow, J. (2012) Project citizenship behavior? – An explorative analysis at the project-network-nexus. *Scandinavian Journal of Management*, 28(4): 271–284.

Bredillet, C. (2010) Blowing hot and cold on project management. *Project Management Journal*, 41(3): 4–20.

Bredin, K. and Söderlund, J. (2011) *Human Resource Management in Project-Based Organizations: The HR Quadriad Framework*. London: Palgrave Macmillan.

Bresnen, M., Goussevskaia, A., and Swan, J. (2004) Embedding new management knowledge in project-based organizations. *Organization Studies*, 25(9): 1535–1555.

Bresnen, M. and Marshall, N. (2011) Projects and partnerships: Institutional processes and emergent practices. In Morris, P. W. G., Pinto, J. K., and Söderlund, J. (eds.), *The Oxford Handbook of Project Management*. Oxford: Oxford University Press, 154–174.

Bröchner, J., Ekstedt, E., Lundin, R. A., and Wirdenius, H. (1991) *Att bygga med kunskap. Förnyelseförmåga i byggsektorn. (To Build with Knowledge. Renewal Capacity in the Construction Sector.)* Stockholm: Byggforskningsrådets förlag.

Brown, S. L. and Eisenhardt, K. M. (1995) Product development: Past research, present findings, and future directions. *Academy of Management Review*, 20(2): 343–378.

Brown, S. L. and Eisenhardt, K. M. (1998) *Competing on the Edge – Strategy as Structured Chaos*. Boston: Harvard Business School Press.

Brown, T. (2008) Design thinking. *Harvard Business Review*, 86 (June): 1–9.

Brown, T. (2009) *Change by Design: How Design Thinking Transforms Organizations and Inspires Innovation*. New York: HarperCollins.

Brulin, G., and Ekstedt, E. (2007) Towards a new work organisation contract in Sweden – The need for a legitimising process. In Garibaldo, F. and Telljohann, V. (eds.), *New Forms of Work Organisation and Industrial Relations in Southern Europe*. Frankfurt: Peter Lang, 109–117.

Brunsson, N. (1989) *The Organization of Hypocrisy: Talk, Decisions and Actions in Organizations*. Chichester: Wiley.

Bryman, A., Bresnen, M., Beardsworth, A. D., Ford, J., and Keil, E. T. (1987) The concept of the temporary system: The case of the construction project. *Research in the Sociology of Organization*, 5: 253–283.

Buckle, P. and Thomas, J. (2003) Deconstructing project management: A gender analysis of project management guidelines. *International Journal of Project Management*, 21: 433–441.

Bult-Spiering, M. and Dewulf, G. (2006) *Strategic Issues in Public-Private Partnerships: An International Perspective*. Oxford: Blackwell Publishing.

Burgelman, R. A. and Grove, A. S. (2007) Let chaos reign, then rein in chaos – repeatedly: Managing strategic dynamics for corporate longevity. *Strategic Management Journal*, 49(3): 6–26.

Butler, D. (1981) *Britain and the Information Society*. London: Heyden.

Byggnadsarbetareförbundet (2014) *Report from the program committee of the Construction Workers Union in Sweden*. Stockholm: Byggnadsarbetarförbundet.

Caldwell, N. and Howard, M. (eds.) (2011) *Procuring Complex Performance, Studies of Innovation in Product-Service Management*. New York: Routledge.

Callon, M. (1986) Some elements of a sociology of translation; domestication of the scallops and the fishermen of St Brieuc Bay. In Law, J. (ed.), *Power, Action and Belief – A New Sociology of Knowledge?* London: Routledge and Kegan Paul, 196–123.

Cameron, R. and Neal, L. (2003) *A Concise Economic History of the World. From Paleolithic Times to the present*. 4th edn. Oxford: Oxford University Press.

Cantarelli, C. C., Flyvbjerg, B., Molin, E. J. E., and van Wee, B. (2010) Lock-in and its influence on the project performance of large-scale transportation infrastructure projects: Investigating the way in which lock-in can emerge and affect cost overruns. *Environment and Planning B: Planning and Design*, 37(5): 792–807.

Capelli, P. and Keller, J. R. (2013) Classifying work in the new economy. *Academy of Management Review*, 38(4): 575–596.

Carlile P. R. (2002) A pragmatic view of knowledge and boundaries: Boundary objects in new product development. *Organization Science*, 6(4): 350–372.

Carlsson, S. (1951) *Executive Behaviour. A Study of Work Load and Working Methods of Managing Directors*. Stockholm: Strömbergs förlag.

Castells, M. (1996) *The Rise of the Network Society*. Oxford: Blackwell.

Cattani, G., Ferriani, S., Frederiksen, L.,and Täube, F. (eds.) (2011). *Project-Based Organizing and Strategic Management*. Bingley: Emerald.

Chandler, A. D. (1962) *Strategy and Structure: Chapters in the History of the Industrial Enterprise*. Cambridge, MA: MIT Press.

Chandler, A. D. (1977) *The Visible Hand: The Managerial Revolution in American Business*. Cambridge, MA: Belknap Press of Harvard University Press.

Chandler, A. D. (1991) The functions of the HQ unit in the multibusiness firm. *Strategic Management Journal*, 12(S2): 31–50.

Charue, F. (2000) Innovative projects and the construction of new expertise in research and market analysis: The case of chemical specialities. In Benghozi, C. and Midler, C. (eds.) *Innovation Based Competition and Design Systems Dynamics*. Paris: l'Harmattan, pp. 239:257.

Charue-Duboc, F. (2006) A theoretical framework for understanding the organization of the RD function. An empirical illustration from the chemical and pharmaceutical industry. *International Journal of Innovation Management*, 10(4): 455–476.

Chesbrough, H. W. (2003) *Open Innovation: The New Imperative for Creating and Profiting from Technology*. Boston: Harvard business School Press.

Christénsen, S. and Kreiner, K. (1991) *Projektledelse i løst koblede systemer: ledelse og læring i en ufuldkommen verden (Project Management in Loosely Coupled Systems: Management and Learning in an Imperfect World)*. Copenhagen: Jurist-og Okonomforbundets Forlag.

Cicmil, S., Williams, P., Thomas, J., and Hodgson, D. (2006) Rethinking project management: Researching the actuality of projects. *International Journal of Project Management*, 24: 675–686.

Ciett (2013) *The agency work industry around the world. Economic report*. Brussels: Ciett.

Clark, K. B. and Fujimoto, T. (1991) *Product Development Performance. Strategy, Organization and Management in the World Auto Industry*. Boston: Harvard Business School Press.

Clark, K. B. and Wheelwright, S. C. (1992) *Revolutionizing Product Development*. New York: Free Press.

Clarysse, B. and Moray, N. (2004) A process study of entrepreneurial team formation: The case of a research-based spin-off. *Journal of Business Venturing*, 19(1): 55–79.

Cleland, D. I. (1986) *Project Stakeholder Management*. Hooboken, NJ: Wiley.

Clegg, S. and Courpasson, D. (2004) Political hybrids: Tocquevillean views on project organizations. *Journal of Management*, 41(4): 525–547.

Coase, R. (1988) *The Firm, the Market, and the Law*. Chicago: University of Chicago Press.

Cohendet, P. and Simon, L. (2007) Playing across the playground: Paradoxes of knowledge creation in the videogame firm. *Journal of Organizational Behavior*, 28(5): 587–605.

Cooke-Davis, T. (2004) The "real" success factors on projects. *International Journal of Project Management*, 20(3): 185–190.

Cooper, R. G., Edgett, S. J., and Kleinschmidt, E. J. (1999) New product portfolio management: Practices and performance. *Journal of Product Innovation Management*, 16(4): 333–351.

Cova, B., Ghauri, P. N., and Salle, R. (2002) *Project Marketing: Beyond Competitive Bidding*. New York: Wiley.

Covin, J. G., and Slevin, D. P. (1991) A conceptual model of entrepreneurship as firm behavior. *Entrepreneurship Theory & Practice*, 16(1): 7–25.

Crawford, L., Cooke-Davis, T., Hobbs, B., Labuschagne, L., Remington, K., and Chen, P. (2008) Governance and support in the sponsoring of projects and programs. *Project Management Journal*, 39 (supplement): S43–S55.

Creswell, J. W. and Plano Clark, V. (2011) *Designing and Conducting Mixed Methods Research*. Los Angeles: Sage.

Cusumano, M. A. and Nobeoka, K. (1998) *Thinking beyond Lean: How Multi-project Management Is Transforming Product Development at Toyota and Other Companies*. New York: Free Press.

Cyert, R. M. and March, J. G. (1963) *A Behavioral Theory of the Firm*. Englewood Cliffs, NJ: Prentice Hall.

Czarniawska, B. (2005) *En teori om organisering (A theory of organizing)*. Lund: Studentlitteratur.

David, P. (1994) Why are institutions the "carriers of history"? Path dependence and the evolution of conventions, organizations and institutions. *Structural Change and Economic Dynamics*, 5(2): 205–220.

Davies, A. (1997) The life cycle of a complex product system. *International Journal of Innovation Management*, 1(3): 229–256.

Davies, A. (2003) Integrated solutions: The changing business of systems integration. In Prencipe, A., Davies, A., and Hobday, M. (eds.), *The Business of Systems Integration*. Oxford: Oxford University Press, 333–368.

Davies, A. (2004) Moving base into high-value integrated solutions: A value stream approach. *Industrial and Corporate Change*, 13(5): 727–756.

Davies, A. and Brady, T. (2000) Organisational capabilities and learning in complex product systems: Towards repeatable solutions. *Research Policy*, 29: 931–953.

Davies, A., Brady, T., and Hobday, M. (2006) Charting a path toward integrated solutions. *Sloan Management Review*, 47(3): 39–48.

Davies, A., Brady, T., and Hobday, M. (2007) Organizing for solutions: Systems seller vs. systems integrator. *Industrial Marketing Management*, 36: 183–193.

Davies, A. and Hobday, M. (2005) *The Business of Projects: Managing Innovation in Complex Products and Systems*, Cambridge: Cambridge University Press.

Davies, A., Gann, D., and Douglas, T. (2009) Innovation in megaprojects: Systems integration at Heathrow Terminal 5. *California Management Review*, 51(2): 101–125.

Declerck, R. P., Debourse, J. P., and Navarre, C. (1983) *La Méthode de Direction générale: Lemanagement stratégique* (*The Method for CEO: Strategic Management*). Paris: Hommes et Techniques.

DeFillippi, R. J. and Arthur, M. B. (1994) The boundaryless career: A competency-based perspective. *Journal of Organizational Behavior*, 15(4): 307–324.

Delmestri, G., Montanari, F., and Usai, A. (2005) Reputation and strength of ties in predicting commercial success and artistic merit of independents in the Italian feature film industry. *Journal of Management Studies*, 42 (5): 975–1002.

Deutsche Bank Research (2007) *Deutschland im Jahr 2020: Neue Herausforderungen für ein Land auf Expedition* (*Germany in 2020: New Challenge for a Country on Expedition*). Frankfurt: Deutsche Bank.

Diamond, J. (1999) *Guns, Germs and Steel. The Fates of Human Societies*. New York: Norton.

Diamond, J. (2011) *Collapse. How Societies Choose to Fail or Succeed*. New York: Penguin.

Dille, T. and Söderlund, J. (2011) Managing inter-institutional projects: The significance of isochronism, timing norms and temporal misfits. *International Journal of Project Management*, 29(4): 480–490.

DiMaggio, P. (1982) Cultural entrepreneurship in nineteenth-century Boston. *Media, Culture and Society*, 4: 33–50.

DiMaggio, P. J. (1988) Interest and agency in institutional theory. In Zucker, L. G. (ed.), *Institutional Patterns and Organizations*. Cambridge, MA: Ballinger, 3–21.

DiMaggio, P. J., and Powell, W. W. (1983) The iron cage revisited: Institutional isomorphism and collective rationality in organizational fields. *American Sociological Review*, 48: 147–160.

Dischner, S., Sieweke, J., and Süß, S. (2013) Regeln in interorganisationalen Projekten: Eine qualitative Studie (Rules in interorganizational projects: A qualitative study). *Managementforschung*, 23: 157–192.

Dittrich, K. and Duysters, G. (2007) Networking as a means for strategy change: The case of open innovation in mobile telephony. *Journal of Product Innovation Management*, 24(6): 510–521.

Dittrich, K., Duysters, G., and de Man, A. (2007) Strategic repositioning by means of alliance networks: The case of IBM. *Research Policy*, 36: 1496–1511.

Djelic, M.-L. (1998) *Exporting the American Model*. Oxford: Oxford University Press.

Djelic, M.-L. and Quack, S. (eds.) (2003) *Globalization and Institutions: Redefining the Rules of the Economic Game.* Cheltenham: Edward Elgar.

Dohse, D. (2000) Technology policy and the regions – The case of the BioRegio contest. *Research Policy,* 29(9): 1111–1133.

Dougherty, D. (1992) Interpretive barriers to successful product innovation in large firms. *Organization Science,* 3(2): 179–202.

Drucker, P. F. (1968) *The Age of Discontinuity.* New York: Harper & Row.

Drucker, P. F. (1969) The knowledge society. *New Society,* 13(343): 629–631.

Dunlop, J. T. (1958) *Industrial Relations System.* New York: Holt.

Dyer, J. H. and Nobeoka, K. (2000) Creating and managing a high-performance knowledge-sharing network: The Toyota case. *Strategic Management Journal,* 21(3): 345–367.

ECOSIP (1993) *Gestion industrielle et mesure économique.* Paris: Economica.

Eisenhardt, K. M. and Martin, J. A. (2000) Dynamic capabilities: What are they? *Strategic Management Journal,* 21: 1105–1121.

Ekstedt, E. (1988) *Humankapital i brytningstid. Kunskapsuppbyggnad och förnyelse för företag (Human Capital in a Period of Transition. Building Knowledge and Renewal for Companies).* Stockholm: Allmänna förlaget.

Ekstedt, E (1991) *Ericsson i Östersund. Att utnyttja kompetensreserven. Arbetsorganisation och produktivitet (Ericson in Östersund. To Utilize the Reserve of Competences. Work Organization and Productivity).* Expertrapport nr 5 till Produktivitetsdelegationen (*Report of experts to the Swedish State Delegation on Productivity*). Stockholm: Allmänna förlaget.

Ekstedt, E. (2002) *Ekonomins omvandling och arbetskontrakten (Economic development and contracts of work),* i DS 2002:56 (Bilaga) Hållfast arbetsrätt för ett föränderligt arbetsliv (*Sustainable Labour Law for a Changeable Working Life: Appendix to the Government Report on Labour Law*). Stockholm: Norstedt and Näringsdepartementet.

Ekstedt, E. (2013) *The Swedish case. How can the issue of work be linked when considering the impact of restructuring on the role of work group as a factor in the (re)building of professional expertise?* Brussels: Syndex and ETUC.

Ekstedt, E. and Forsman, A. (1991) To deepen or to widen. Knowledge formation in the post-industrial rconomy. In Ullenhag, K. (ed.), *Hundred Flowers Bloom.* Uppsala: Acta Universitatis Upsaliensis.

Ekstedt, E. and Sundin, E (eds.) (2006) *Den nya arbetsdelningen. Arbets- och näringslivets organisatoriska omavandling i tid, rum och tal (The New Division of Labour. Organizational Change in Time, Space and Rhetoric in Working Life and Business).* Stockholm: Arbetslivsinstitutet.

Ekstedt, E. and Wirdenius, H. (1995) Renewal projects: Sender target and receiver competence in ABB "T50" and Skanska "3T." *Scandinavian Journal of Management*, 11(4): 409–421.

Ekstedt, E., Lundin, R. A., Söderholm, A., and Wirdenius, H. (1999) *Neo-industrial Organising. Renewal by Action and Knowledge Formation in a Project-intensive Economy*. London: Routledge.

Elvander, N. and Elvander-Seim A. (1995) *Gränslös samverkan. Fackets svar på företagens internationalisering (Borderless Cooperation. The Union Answers to the Internationalization of Enterprises)*. Stockholm: SNS förlag.

Engwall, L. and Zamagni, V. (eds.) (1998) *Management Education in Historical Perspective*. Manchester: Manchester Business School Press.

Engwall, M. (1995) *Jakten på det effektiva projektet (In Search of the Effective Project)*. Stockholm: Nerenius & Santérus förlag.

Engwall, M. (2003) No project is an island: Linking projects to history and context. *Research Policy*, 32(5): 789–808.

Enright, M. J. (2003) Regional clusters: What we know and what we should know. In Bröcker, J., Dohse, D., and Soltwedel, R. (eds.), *Innovation Clusters and Interregional Competition*. Berlin: Springer, 99–129.

Ericksen, J. and Dyer, L. (2004) Right from the start: Exploring the effects of early team events on subsequent project team development and performance. *Administrative Science Quarterly*, 49(3): 438–471.

Erden, Z., Schneider, A., and von Krogh, G. (2014) The multifaceted nature of social practices: A review of the perspectives on practiced-based theory building about organizations. *European Management Journal*, 32(5): 712–722.

Ernst, D. and Kim, L. (2002) Global production networks, knowledge diffusion, and local capability formation. *Research Policy*, 31(9): 1417–1429.

Eskerod, P. (1997) *Nye perspektiver på fordeling af menneskelige ressourcer i et projektorganiseret multiprojekt-miljø (New Perspectives on the Allocation of Human Resources in a Project Organized Multi-Project Context)*. Sønderborg, Denmark: Handelshøjskole Syd.

Eskerod, P. and Jepsen, A. L. (2009) Stakeholder analysis in projects: Challenges in using current guidelines in the real world. *International Journal of Project Management*, 27(4): 335–343.

Eskerod, P. and Jepsen, A. L. (2013) *Project Stakeholder Management*. Aldershot: Gower.

Etzkowitz, H. and Leydesdorff, L. (2000) The dynamics of innovation: From National Systems and "Mode 2" to a Triple Helix of university–industry–government relations. *Research Policy*, 29: 109–123.

European Commission (2006) Entrepreneurship education in Europe: Fostering entrepreneurial mindsets through education and learning. Final proceedings of the Conference on Entrepreneurship Education. Oslo.

Fayol, H. (1949) *General and Industrial Management*. London: Pitman. First edition published 1916.

Fichter, M., Helfen, M., and Sydow, J. (2011) Employment relations in global production networks – Initiating transfer of practices via union involvement. *Human Relations*, 63 (4): 599–624.

Finkelstein, J. (1986) *The Third Industrial Revolution – Questions and Implications for Economic Historians*. New York: Economic Historic World Congress Bern.

Fizel, J and D'Itri, M. (1997) Managerial efficiency managerial succession and organizational performance. *Managerial and Decision Economics*, 18(4): 295–308.

Flecker, J. and Meil, P. (2010) Organisational restructuring and emerging service value chains. Implications for work and employment. *Work, Employment and Society*, 24(4): 680–698.

Fligstein, N. and MacAdam, D. (2012) *A Theory of Fields*. Oxford: Oxford University Press.

Floricel, S., Bonneau, C., Aubry, M., and Sergi, V. (2014) Extending project management research: Insights from social theories. *International Journal of Project Management*, 32(7): 1091–1107.

Flyvbjerg, B. (2011) Over budget, over time, over and over again: Managing major projects. In Morris, P. W. G., Pinto, J. K., and Söderlund, J. (eds.), *The Oxford Handbook of Project Management*. Oxford: Oxford University Press, 321–344.

Flyvbjerg, B. (ed.) (2014) *Megaproject Planning and Management: Essential Readings*. Cheltenham: Edward Elgar.

Flyvbjerg, B., Skamris Holm, M. K.,and Buhl, S. L. (2003a) How common and how large are cost overruns in transport infrastructure projects? *Transport Reviews*, 23(1): 71–88.

Flyvbjerg, B., Bruzelius, N., and Rothengatter, W. (2003b) *Megaprojects and Risk: An Anatomy of Ambition*. Cambridge: Cambridge University Press.

Ford, R. C. and Randolph, W. A. (1992) Cross-functional structures: A review and integration of matrix organization and project management. *Journal of Management*, 18(2): 267–294.

Forschungsunion and acatech (eds.) (2013) *Umsetzungsempfehlungen für das Zukunftsprojekt Industrie 4.0*. Abschlussbericht des Arbeitskreises Industrie 4.0. Frankfurt.

Forsell, A. and Jansson, D. (2000) *Idéer som fängslar – Recept för offentlig reformation (Ideas which attract – Recipes for reforming the public sector)*. Malmö: Liber Ekonomi.

Fourastié, J. (1949) *Le grand espoir du XXe siècle: Progrès technique, progrès économique, progrès social (The Great XX Century Hope: Technological Progress, Economic Growth and Social Development)*. Paris: Presses Universitaires de France.

Fourcade, F. and Midler, C. (2004) Modularization in the auto industry: Can manufacturer's architectural strategies meet supplier's sustainable profit trajectories? *International Journal of Automotive Technology and Management*, 4(2/3): 240–260.

Fourcade, F. and Midler, C. (2005) The role of 1st tier suppliers in automobile product modularisation: The search for a coherent strategy. *International Journal of Automotive Technology and Management*, 5(2): 146–165.

Frederiksen, L. and Davies, A. (2008) Vanguards and ventures: Projects as vehicles for corporate entrepreneurship. *International Journal or Project Management*, 26(5): 487–496.

Freeman, R. E. (1984). *Strategic Management – A Stakeholder Approach*. Boston: Harvard Business School Press.

Friedlander, R. and Alford, R. R. (1991) Bringing society back in: Symbols, practices, and institutional contradictions. In Powell, W. W., and DiMaggio, P. (eds.), *The New Institutionalism in Organizational Analysis*. Chicago: University of Chicago Press, 232–266.

Fukuyama, F. (1995) Confucianism and democracy. *Journal of Democracy* 6(2): 20–33.

Fukuyama, F. (2011) *The Origins of Political Order. From Prehuman Times to the French Revolution*. London: Profile Books.

Ganesan, S., Malter, A. J., and Rindfleisch, A. (2005) Does distance still matter? Geographic proximity and new product development. *Journal of Marketing*, 69(4): 44–60.

Gann, D. M. and Salter, A. J. (2000) Innovation in project-based, service-enhanced firms: The construction of complex products and systems. *Research Policy*, 29(7–8): 955–972.

Gareis, R. (1990) Management by projects. *Proceedings, Vol 1 of the 10th INTERNET World Congress on Project Management*. Vienna: Manz, 1–14.

Garel G., Giard, V., and Midler, C. (2003) Management de projet et gestion des ressources humaines (Project management and human resource management). In Allouche, R. (ed.), *L'encyclopédie de la gestion des ressources humaines (Human Resource Management Encyclopedia)*. Paris: Vuibert, 818–843.

Garel, G. (1996) L'entreprise sur un plateau: un exemple d'ingénierie concourante dans l'industrie automobile (The colocalized firm: A case of concurrent engineering in auto industry). *Gestion* 2000, 3: 111–134.

Garel, G., Kesseler A., and Midler, C. (1997) Le co-développement, définitions, enjeux et problèmes (Codevelopment, definition, issues and challenges). *Education Permanente*, 95–108.

Gartner, W. B. (1985) A conceptual framework for describing the phenomenon of new venture creation. *Academy of Management Review*, 10(4): 696–706.

Garud, R., Hardy, C., and Maguire, S. (2007) Institutional entrepreneurship as embedded agency: An introduction to the special issue. *Organization Studies*, 28: 957–969.

Gastaldi, L. and Midler, C. (2005) Exploration concourante et pilotage de la recherche (Concurrent exploration and management of research). *Revue Française de Gestion* 2(155): 173–189.

Gastaldi, L. and Midler, C. (2010) Concurrent exploration and research management: Case study featuring a specialty chemicals company. In Midler, C., Minguet, G., and Vervaeke, M. (eds.), *Working on Innovation*. Abington, UK: Routledge, 72–90.

Geels, F. W. (2004) From sectoral systems of innovation to socio-technical systems: Insights about dynamics and change from sociology and institutional theory. *Research Policy*, 33(6–7): 897–920.

Geraldi, J., Maylor, H., and Williams, T. (2011) Now, let's make it really complex (complicated): A systematic review of the complexities of projects. *International Journal of Operations & Production Management*, 31(9): 966–990.

Gerstner, L. V. (2002) *Who Said Elephants Can't Dance? Inside IBM's Historic Turnaround*. London: Harper & Collins.

Giard, V. and Midler, C. (eds.) (1993) *Pilotages de projets et entreprises, diversités et convergences (Project Management and Firms, Variety and Convergencies)*. Paris: Economica.

Giddens, A. (1984) *The Constitution of Society: Outline of the Theory of Structuration*. Cambridge: Polity.

Giddens, A. (2002) *Runaway World: How Globalisation Is Reshaping Our Lives*. 2nd edn. London: Profile Books.

Glete, J. (2002) *Navies and Nations; Warships, Navies, and State Buildings in Europe and America, 1500–1860*. Stockholm: Almquist and Wiksell international.

Göransson, A. (1988) *Från familj till fabrik (From Family to Factory)*. Lund: Arkiv

Gomes-Casseres, B. (1996) *The Alliance Revolution*. Cambridge, MA: Harvard University Press.

Grabher, G. (1993) The weakness of strong ties: The lock-in of regional development in the Ruhr area. In Grabher, G. (ed.), *The Embedded Firm. On the Socioeconomics of Industrial Networks*. London: Routledge, 253–277.

Grabher, G. (2004) Temporary architectures of learning: Knowledge governance in project ecologies. *Organization Studies*, 25(9): 1491–1514.

Grabher, G. (2005) Switching ties, recombining teams: Avoiding lock-in through project organization? In Fuchs, G. and Shapira, P. (eds.), *Rethinking Regional Innovation and Change*. Berlin: Springer, 63–83.

Grabher, G. and Powell, W. W. (eds.) (2004) *Networks*. Cheltenham: Elgar.

Granovetter, M. (1979) *The Theory-gap in Social Network Analysis*. New York: Academic Press.

Greenwood, R., Suddaby, R., and Hinings, C. R. (2002) Theorizing change: The role of professional associations in the transformation of institutionalized fields. *Academy of Management Journal*, 25(1): 58–80.

Grönroos, C. (2011) Value co-creation in service logic: A critical analysis. *Marketing Theory*, 11(3): 279–301.

Grundy, T. (1998) Strategy implementation and project management. *International Journal of Project Management*, 16(1): 43–50.

Gustavsson, T. K. and Hallin, A. (2014) Rethinking dichotomization: A critical perspective on the use of "hard" and "soft" in project management research. *International Journal of Project Management*, 32(4): 568–577.

Habakkuk, H. J. (1962) *American and British Technology in the Nineteenth Century – The Search for Labour-saving Inventions*. Cambridge: Cambridge University Press.

Hägerstrand, T. (1974) *Tidsgeografiska beskrivningar: Syfte och postulat (Time Geographical Descriptions: Aim and Postulate)*. Lund: Svensk geografisk årsbok.

Hägerstrand, T. (1991) *Om tidens vidd och tingens ordning: Texter (About the Width of Time and the Orderniless of Things)*. Stockholm: Statens råd för byggnadsforskning.

Hällgren, M. (2010) Groupthink in temporary organizations. *International Journal of Managing Projects in Business*, 3(1): 94–110.

Hällgren, M. and Söderholm, A. (2010) Orchestrating deviations in global projects: Project-as-practice observations. *Scandinavian Journal of Management*, 26: 352–367.

Hall, P. A. and Soskice, D. (eds.) (2001a) *Varieties of Capitalism. The Institutional Foundations of Comparative Advantage*. Oxford: Oxford University Press.

Hall, P. A. and Soskice, D. (2001b) An introduction to varieties of capitalism. In Hall, P. A., and Soskice, D. (eds.), *Varieties of Capitalism. The Institutional Foundations of Comparative Advantage*. Oxford: Oxford University Press, 1–68.

Hansen, M. T., Nohria, N., and Tierney, T. (1999) What's your strategy for managing knowledge? *Harvard Business Review*, 77(2): 106–116.

Hargadon, A. (1998) Firms as knowledge brokers: Lessons in pursuing continuous innovation. *California Management Review*, 40(3): 209–227.

Hargadon, A. (2003) *How Breakthroughs Happen: The Surprising Truth about How Companies Innovate*. Boston: Harvard Business School Press.

Hargreaves, A. and Shirley, D. (2012) *The Global Fourth Way: The Quest for Educational Excellence*. Thousand Oaks, CA: Corwin Press.

Hatchuel, A. and Weil, B. (2003) A new approach of innovative design: An introduction to C-K theory. Proceedings of the international conference on engineering design (ICED'03). Stockholm, 109–124.

Hayes, R. H., Wheelwright, S. C.,and Clark, K. B. (1988) *Dynamic Manufacturing: Creating the Learning Organization*. New York: Free Press.

Hedlund, G. (1986) The hyper-modern MNC – A heterarchy? *Human Resource Management*, 25(1): 9–35.

Hedlund, G. (1993) Assumptions of hierarchy and heterarchy, with applications to the management of the multinational corporation. In Ghoshal, S. and Westney, D. E. (eds.), *Organization Theory and the Multinational Corporation*. New York: St. Martin's Press, 211–236.

Hedlund, G. (1994) A model of knowledge management and the N-form corporation. *Strategic Management Journal*, 15(2): 73–90.

Hellgren, B. and Stjernberg, T. (1995) Design and implementation in major investments – A project network approach. *Scandinavian Journal of Management*, 11(4): 377–394.

Henderson, R. M. and Clark, K. B. (1990) The reconfiguration of existing product technologies and the failure of established firms. *Administrative Science Quarterly*, 35(1): 9–30.

Henderson, L. S. and Stackman, R. W. (2010) An exploratory study of gender in project management: Interrelationships with role, location, technology, and project cost. *Project Management Journal*, 41, 37–55.

Henderson, L. S., Stackman, R. W., and Koh, C. Y. (2013) Women project managers: The exploration of their job challenges and issue selling behaviors. *International Journal of Managing Projects in Business*, 6(4): 761–791.

Hirschman, A. O. (1970) Exit, *Voice and Loyalty. Responses to Decline in Firms, Organizations, and States*. Cambridge MA: Harvard University Press.

Hjorth, D. (2014) Entrepreneurship as organization-creation. In Sternberg, R. and Krauss, G. (eds.), *Handbook of Research on Entrepreneurship and Creativity*. Cheltenham, UK: Edward Elgar.

Hobbs, B. and Aubry, M. (2010) *The Project Management Office (PMO): A Quest for Understanding*. Newtown Square, PA: PMI.

Hobbs, B., Aubry M., and Thuillier, D. (2008) The project management office as an organisational innovation. *International Journal of Project Management*, 26(5): 547–555.

Hobday, M. (1998) Product complexity, innovation and industrial organization. *Research Policy*, 26: 689–710.

Hobday, M. (2000) The project-based organisation: An ideal form for managing complex products and systems? *Research Policy*, 29(7–8): 871–893.

Hodgson, D. (2004) Project work: The legacy of bureaucratic control in the post-bureaucratic organization. *Organization*, 11(1): 81–100.

Hodgson, D., and Cicmil, S. (2006) Are projects real? The PMBOK and the legitimation of project management knowledge. In Hodgson, D. and Cicmil, S. (eds.), *Making Projects Critical*. Houndsmill: Palgrave Macmillan, 29–50.

Hodgson, G. (1993) *Economics and Evolution. Bringing Life back into Economics*. Cambridge: Polity Press.

Hoegl, M. and Gemuenden, H. G. (2001) Team work quality and success of innovative projects: A theoretical concept and empirical evidence. *Organization Science*, 12(4): 435–449.

Hofstede, G. (1980) *Culture's Consequences: International Differences in Work-related Values*. Thousand Oaks, CA: Sage.

Hofstede, G. (2001) *Culture's Consequences: Comparing Values, Behaviors, Institutions and Organizations across Nations*. 2nd edn. London: Sage.

Human, S. E. and Provan, K. G. (2000) Legitimacy building in the evolution of small-firm networks: A comparative study of success and demise. *Administrative Science Quarterly*, 45(2): 327–365.

Huxham, C. and Vangen, S. (2000) Leadership in the shaping and implementation of collaboration agendas: How things happen in a (not quite) joined up world. *Academy of Management Journal*, 43(6): 1159–1175.

Huxham, C. and Vangen, S. (2005) *Managing to Collaborate*. London: Routledge.

ILO (1998) *ILO Declaration on Fundamental Principles and Rights at Work*. Geneva: International Labour Organisation.

Ingelhart, R. (1990) *Cultural Shift in Advanced Industrial Society*. Princeton: Princeton University Press.

Ingelhart, R. (1997) *Modernization and Postmodernization: Cultural, Economic, and Political Change in 43 Societies*. Princeton: Princeton University Press.

Inkson, K., Gunz, H., Ganesh, S., and Roper, J. (2012) Boundaryless careers: Bringing back boundaries. *Organization Studies*, 33 (3): 323–340.

Isaksen, A. (2003) "Lock-in" of regional clusters: The case of offshore engineering in the Oslo region. In Fornahl, D. and Brenner, T. (eds.), *Cooperation, Networks and Institutions in Regional Innovation Systems*. Cheltenham: Edward Elgar: 247–273.

Isidorsson, T. (2001) *Striden om tiden: Arbetstidens utveckling i Sverige under 100 år i ett internationellt perspektiv (The battle about working time in Sweden during 100 years in an international perspective)* (diss.). Gothenburg: University of Gothenburg.

Itasaki, H. (1999) *The Prius that Shook the World*. Tokyo: Nikkan Kogyo Shimbun.

Ivory, C. and Vaughan, R. (2008) The role of framing in complex transitional projects. *Long Range Planning*, 41: 93–106.

Jacobsson, M., Burström, T., and Wilson, T. L. (2013a) The role of transition in temporary organizations: Linking the temporary to the permanent. *International Journal of Managing Projects in Business*, 6(3): 576–586.

Jacobsson, M., Lundin, R. A. and Söderholm, A. (2013b) Researching and theorizing the temporary organization and project families. *Proceedings of the 22nd Nordic Academy of Management Conference (NFF)*. Reykjavik, Island, August 21–23, 2013.

Janis, I. L. (1972) *Victims of Groupthink: A Psychological Study of Foreign-policy Decisions and Fiascoes*. Boston: Houghton Mufflin.

Jarillo, J. C. (1988) On strategic networks. *Strategic Management Journal*, 9(1): 31–41.

Jarzabkowski, P. and Spee, A. P. (2009) Strategy-as-practice: A review and future directions for the field. *International Journal of Management Reviews* 11(1): 69–95.

Javidan, M., House, R. J., Dorman, P. W., Hanges, P. J. and de Luque, M. S. (2009) Conceptualizing and measuring cultures and their consequences: A comparative review of GLOBE's and Hofstede's approaches. *Journal of International Business*, 37: 897–914.

Jeantet, A. (1996) La coordination par les objets dans les équipes intégrées de conception de produit (Object based coordination in product development integrated teams). Coopération et Conception: Octares publisher.

Johanson, J. and Vahlne, J.-E. (1977) The internationalization process of the firm – A model of knowledge development and increasing foreign market commitments. *Journal of International Business Studies*, 8(1): 23–32.

Johanson, J. and Vahlne, J.-E. (1990) The mechanism of internationalization. *International Marketing Review*, 7(4): 11–24.

Johansson, A. O. (1977) *Den effektiva arbetstiden: Verkstäderna och arbetsintensitetens problem 1900–1920 (The efficient work time: The problem of work intensity at the shop floors)* (diss.). Uppsala: Uppsala Universitet.

Johansson, A. (2010) *Hyrt går hem. Historien om den svenska bemanningsbranschen (The History of the Employment Agencies in Sweden)*. Stockholm: Informationsförlaget.

Johnson, R. A., Kast, F. E., and Rosenzweig, J. E. (1963) *Theory and Management of Systems*. New York: McGraw-Hill.

Jolivet, F. (2003) *Manager l'entreprise par projets (Managing the Company through Projects)*. Paris: EMS.

Jolivet, F. and Navarre, C. (1993) *Grand projets, auto-organisation, métarègles: Vers de nouvelles formes de management des grands projets* (Mega projects, auto-organization and metarules : Toward new mega project management practices). *Gestion 2000*: 191, 200.

Jones, C. 1996. Careers in project networks: The case of the film industry. In Arthur, M. B. and Rousseau, D. M. (eds.), *The Boundaryless Career*. Oxford: Oxford University Press, 58–75.

Jones, C. and Lichtenstein, B. B. (2008) Temporary inter-organizational projects: How temporal and social embeddedness enhance coordination and manage uncertainty. In Cropper, S., Ebers, M., Huxham, C., and Ring, P. S. (eds.), *The Oxford Handbook of Inter-Organizational Relations*. Oxford: Oxford University Press: 231–255.

Jones, G. (2005) *Multinationals and Global Capitalism. From the Nineteenth to the Twenty-first Century*. Oxford: Oxford University Press.

Jönsson, S. (1995) *Goda utsikter – Svenskt management i perspektiv (Good Prospects – Swedish Management in Perspective)*. Stockholm: Nerenius & Santerus.

Jönsson, S. and Lundin, R. A. (1977) Myths and wishful thinking as management tools. In Nystrom, P. and Starbuck, W. (eds.), *Prescriptive Models of Organizations*. Amsterdam: North Holland, 157–170.

Junginger, S. (2007) Learning to design: Giving purpose to heart, hand and mind. *Journal of Business Strategy*, 28(4): 59–65.

Junginger, S. (2008) Product development as a vehicle for organizational change. *Design Issues*, 24(1): 26–35.

Kadefors, A. (1995). Institutions in building projects: Implications for flexibility and change. *Scandinavian Journal of Management*, 11(4): 395–408.

Kalleberg, A. L. (2000) Nonstandard employment relations: Part-time, temporary and contract work. *Annual Review of Sociology*, 26: 341–365.

Kalleberg, A. L. (2011) *Good Jobs, Bad Jobs: The Rise of Polarized and Precarious Employment Systems in the United States, 1970s-2000s*. New York: Russell Sage Foundation.

Kaplan, S. and Orlikowski, W. (2013) Temporal work in strategy making. *Organization Science*, 24(4): 965–995.

Karlsen J. T. (2002) Project stakeholder management. *Engineering Management Journal*, 14(4): 19–24.

Keegan, A. and Turner, J. R. (2002) The management of innovation in project-based firms. *Long Range Planning*, 35(4): 367–388.

Keller, R. T. (1992) Transformational leadership and the performance of research and development project groups. *Journal of Management*, 18(3): 489–501.

Kenis, P. and Knoke, D. (2002) How organizational field networks shape interorganizational tie-formation Rates. *Academy of Management Review*, 27(2): 275–293.

Kenis, P., Janowicz-Panjaitan, M., and Cambré, B. (eds.) (2009) *Temporary Organizations – Prevalence, Logic and Effectiveness*, Cheltenham, UK: Elgar.

Kesseler, A. (1998) *The creative supplier* (diss.) Paris: Ecole Polytechnique.

Ketels, C. H. M, Lindqvist, G., and Sölvell, Ö. (2006) *Cluster Initiatives in Developing and Transition Economies*. Stockholm: Center for Strategy and Competitiveness.

Khanna, T. (1998) The scope of alliance. *Organization Science*, 9(3): 340–355.

Kieser, A. (1994) Why organization theory needs historical analysis – And how these should be performed. *Organization Science*, 5: 608–620,

Kieser, A. (1997) Rhetoric and myth in management fashion. *Organization*, 4(1): 49–74.

Kim, J. and Wilemon, D. (2002) Strategic issues in managing innovation's fuzzy front-end. *European Journal of Innovation Management*, 5(1): 27–30.

Kim, T. Y., Oh, H., and Swaminathan, A. (2006) Framing interorganizational network change: A network inertia perspective. *Academy of Management Review*, 31: 704–720.

Khurana, A. and Rosenthal, S. R. (1997) Integrating the fuzzy front end of new product development. *Sloan Management Review*, 38: 103–120.

Klein, B. H. and Meckling, W. (1958) Application of operations research to development decisions. *Operations Research*, 6: 352–63.

Kogut, B. and Zander, U. (1992) Knowledge of the firm, combinative capabilities, and the replication of technology. *Organization Science*, 3(3): 383–397.

Kostova, T., and Zaheer, S. (1999) Organizational legitimacy under conditions of complexity: The case of the multinational enterprise. *Academy of Management Review*, 24: 64–81.

Kotter J. P. (2001) What leaders really do. *Harvard Business Review*, 79 (December): 2–11.

Kreiner, C. (1995) In search of relevance: Project management in drifting environments. *Scandinavian Journal of Management*, 11(4): 335–346.

Kuura, A., Blackburn, R. A., and Lundin, R. A. (2014) Entrepreneurship and projects – Linking segregated communities. *Scandinavian Journal of Management*, 30: 214–230.

Kwak, Y. H. and Anbari, F. T. (2009) Analyzing project management research: Perspectives from top management journals. *International Journal of Project Management*, 27(5): 435–446.

Kwak, Y. H., Chih, Y .Y., and Ibbs, C .W. (2009) Towards a comprehensive understanding of public private partnerships for infrastructure development. *California Management Review*, 51(2): 51–78.

Labour Force Survey Database (2013) *European Commission Eurostat*. Version November, 2013.

Lampel, J., Scarbrough, H., and Macmillan, S. (2008) Managing through projects in knowledge-based environments: Special issue introduction. *Long Range Planning*, 41: 7–16.

Lane, C. and Bachmann, R. (1997) Co-operation in inter-firm relations in Britain and Germany: The role of social institutions. *British Journal of Sociology*, 48(2): 226–254.

Larson, E. W. and Gobeli, D. H. (1987) Matrix management: Contradictions and insights. *California Management Review*, 29 (4): 126–138.

Larson, M. and Wikström, E. (2007) Relational interaction process in project networks: The consent and negotiation perspectives. *Scandinavian Journal of Management*, 23: 327–352.

Latour, B. (1987) *Science in Action: How to Follow Scientists and Engineers through Society* Milton Keynes, UK: Open University Press.

Law, J. (1986) On power and its tactics: A view from the sociology of science. *Sociological Review*, 34: 1–38.

Lawrence, T. B. and Suddaby, R. (2006) Institutions and institutional work. In Clegg, S. R., Hardy, C., Lawrence, T. B., and Nord, W. R. (eds.), *The Sage Handbook of Organization Studies*. 2nd edn. London: Sage, 215–254.

Le Masson, P., Weil, B., and Hatchuel, A. (2010) *Strategic Management of Innovation and Design*. Cambridge: Cambridge University Press.

Lefebvre, P., Roos, P., and Sardas, J. C. (2010) Redynamizing trades: A case study in the aeronautic industry. In Midler, C., Minguet, G., and Vervaeke, M. (eds.), *Working on Innovation*. London: Routledge, 180–203.

Leighton, P. and Brown, D (2013) *Future Working: The Rise of the Independent Professionals (iPros)*. London: European Forum of Independent Professionals.

Lenfle, S. (2008) Exploration and project management. *International Journal of Project Management*, 26(5): 469–478.

Lenfle, S. (2011) The strategy of parallel approaches in projects with unforeseeable uncertainty: The Manhattan case in retrospect. *International Journal of Project Management*, 29(4): 359–373.

Lenfle, S. (2014) Toward a genealogy of project management: Sidewinder and the management of exploratory projects. *International Journal of Project Management*, 32(6): 921–931.

Lenfle, S. and Loch, C. (2010) Lost roots: How project management came to emphasize control over flexibility and novelty. *California Management Review*, 53(1): 32–55.

Lenfle, S. and Midler, C. (2001) Innovation-based competition and the dynamics of design in upstream supplier. *International Journal of Automotive Technology & Management*, 2(3): 269–286.

Leonard-Barton, D. (1995) *Wellsprings of Knowledge: Building and Sustaining the Sources of Innovation*. Boston: Harvard Business School Press.

Lewin, A. Y., Massini, S., and Peeters, C. (2009) Why are companies offshoring innovation? The emerging global race for talent. *Journal of International Business*, 40: 901–925.

Lewin, K. (1951) *Field Theory in Social Science: Selected Theoretical Papers*. New York: Harper.

Leydesdorff, L. and Etzkowitz, H. (1998) The triple Helix as a model for innovation studies. *Science and Public Policy*, 25(3): 195–203.

Liedtka, J. (2000) In defense of strategy as design. *California Management Review*, 42(3): 8–30.

Liedtka, J. (2014) Linking design thinking to innovation outcomes: The role of cognitive bias reduction. *Annual Meeting of the Academy of Management*, Philadelphia, August, 2014.

Linde, A. and Linderoth, H. C. J. (2006) An actor network theory perspective on IT projects. In Cicmil, S. and Hodgson, D. (eds.), *Making Projects Critical*. Houndmills: Palgrave Macmillan, 155–170.

Lindgren, M., and Packendorff, J. (2003) A project-based view of entrepreneurship: Towards action-orientation, seriality and collectivity. *Entrepreneurship: New Movements*, 86–102.

Lindgren, M., and Packendorff, J. (2006a) Projects and prisons. In Hodgson, D. and Cicmil, S. (eds.), *Making Projects Critical*. Houndsmill: Palgrave Macmillan, 111–131.

Lindgren, M., and Packendorff, J. (2006b) What's new in new forms of organizing? On the construction of gender in project-based work. *Journal of Management Studies*, 43: 841–866.

Lindgren, M., and Packendorff, J. (2009) Project leadership revisited: Towards distributed leadership perspectives in project research. *International Journal of Project Organisation and Management*, 1(3): 285–308.

Lindgren, M., Packendorff, J., and Sergi, V. (2014) Thrilled by the discourse, suffering through the experience: Emotions in project-based work. *Human Relations*, 67(10): 1–30.

Lindkvist, L. (2001) Det projektbaserade företaget – Om styrning i ett distribuerat kunskapssystem (The project-based company – About steering in a distributed knowledge system). In Berggren, C. and Lindkvist, L. (eds.), *Projekt – Organisation för målorientering och lärande*. Lund: Studentlitteratur, 258–291.

Lindkvist, L. (2004) Governing project-based firms: Promoting market-like processes within hierarchies. *Journal of Management and Governance*, 8: 3–25.

Littau, P., Jujagiri, N. J., and Adlbrecht, G. (2010) 25 years of stakeholder theory in project management literature (1984–2009). *Project Management Journal*, 41(4), 17–29.

Loch, C., DeMeyer, A., and Pich, M. (2006) *Managing the Unknown. A New Approach to Managing High Uncertainty and Risks in Projects*. Hoboken, NJ: Wiley.

Löfgren, K., Sjöblom, S., and Godenhjelm, S. (2013) Projectified politics. The role of temporary organisations in the public sector. *Scandinavian Journal of Public Administration*, 17(2): 1–146.

Long Lingo, E. and O'Mahoney, S. (2010) Nexus work: Brokerage on creative projects. *Administrative Science Quarterly*, 55: 47–81.

Luhmann, N. (1979) *Trust and Power*. Chichester: Wiley.

Luhmann, N. (1995) *Social Systems*. Stanford: Stanford University Press.

Lundgren, K. (2013) *Kan landet Lagom bli bäst (Is It Possible for the Country "Lagom" to Be Best?)*. Stockholm: SNS förlag.

Lundin, R. A. (1998) Temporära organizationer – Några perspektivbyten *(Temporary organizations – Some changes in perspectives)*. In Czarniawska, B. (ed.), *Organizationsteori på Svenska (Organization Theory in Swedish)*. Copenhagen: Liber, 194–214.

Lundin, R. A. (2008) The beauty and the beast – On the creativity/project management encounter. *International Journal of Managing Projects in Business*, 1(2): 206–215.

Lundin, R. A. and Hällgren, M. (eds.) (2014) *Advancing Research on Projects and Temporary Organizations*. Copenhagen: Liber.

Lundin, R. A. and Hartman, F. T. (2000) Pervasiveness of projects in business. In Lundin, R. A. and Hartman, F. T. (eds.), *Projects as Business Constituents and Guiding Motives*. London: Kluwer Academic Publishers, 1–10.

Lundin, R. A. and Midler, C. (eds.) (1998) *Projects as Arenas for Renewal and Learning Processes*. Norwell, MA: Kluwer.

Lundin, R. A. and Norbäck M. (2009) Managing projects in the TV production industry – The case of Sweden. *Journal of Media Business Studies*, 6(4): 103–122.

Lundin, R. A. and Packendorff, J. (eds.) (1994) *Proceedings from the IRNOP Conference on Temporary Organizations and Project Management* in Lycksele, Sweden, March 22–25, 1994. Umeå, Sweden: Umeå Business School.

Lundin, R. A. and Söderholm, A. (1995) A theory of the temporary organization. *Scandinavian Journal of Management*, 11(4): 437–455.

Lundin, R. and Söderholm, A. (2013) Temporary organizations and end states: A theory is a child of its time and in need of reconsideration and reconstruction. *International Journal of Managing Projects in Business*, 6(3): 587–594.

Lutz, A., Sydow, J., and Staber, U. (2003) TV content production in media regions: The necessities and difficulties of public policy support for a project-based industry. In Brenner, T. and Fornahl, D. (eds.), *Cooperation, Networks and Institutions in Regional Innovation Systems*. Aldershot: Elgar, 194–219.

Lutz, S. (1999) Learning through intermediaries: The case of inter-firm research collaborations. In Ebers, M. (ed.), *The Formation of Inter-organizational Networks*. London: Routledge, 220–237.

Maaninen-Olsson, E. and Mähring, M. (2008) *Boundary work across project life cycle*. Paper presented at the 24th EGOS Colloquium, Free University of Amsterdam, July 10–12, 2008.

Maaninen-Olsson, E. and Müllern, T. (2009) A contextual understanding of projects – The importance of space and time. *Scandinavian Journal of Management*, 25: 327–339.

Machlup, F. (1962) *The Production and Distribution of Knowledge in the United States*. Princeton, NJ: Princeton University Press.

MacMillan, K. and Farmer, D. (1979) Redefining the boundaries of the firm. *Journal of Industrial Economics*, 27(3): 277–285.

Magnusson, L. (1999) *Den tredje industriella revolutionen – Och den svenska arbetsmarknaden (The Third Industrial Revolution – And the Swedish Labor Market)*. Stockholm: Prisma.

Magnusson, L. and Ottosson, J. (2012) *Den hållbara svenska modellen. Innovationskraft och förnyelse effektivitet (A Sustainable Swedish Model. Efficiency in Innovation and Renewal)*. Stockholm: SNS förlag.

Mahmoud-Jouini, S. B., Midler, C., Cruz, V., and Gaudron, N. (2014) *Objects in Projects*. Euram Conference, Valencia, June.

Malerba F. (2002) Sectoral systems of innovation. *Research Policy*, 31(2): 247–264.

Malmberg, A. (2001) Lokala miljöer för industriell innovations-och utvecklingskraft (Local settings for industrial innovation and development). In Ekstedt, E. (ed.), *Kunskap och handling för företagande och regional utveckling (Knowledge and Action for Entrepreneurship and Regional Development)*. Stockholm: Arbetslivsinstitutet:13–36.

Malmberg, A., and Power, D. (2006) True clusters. A severe case of conceptual headache. In Asheim, B., Cooke, P., and Martin, R. (eds.), *Clusters and Regional Development. Critical Reflexions and Explorations*. London: Routledge, 50–68.

Maniak, R. and Midler, C. (2014) Multiproject lineage management: Bridging project management with design-based innovation strategy. *International Journal of Project Management*, 32(7): 1146–1156.

Maniak, R., Midler, C., and Beaume, R. (2014) Featuring capability: How carmakers organize to deploy innovative features across products. *Journal of Product Innovation Management*, 31(1): 114–127.

Maniak, R., Midler, C., Beaume, R., and von Pechmann, F. (2014) Featuring capability: How carmakers organize to deploy innovative features across products. *Journal of Product Innovation Management*, 31(1): 114–127.

Maniak, R., Midler, C., Lenfle, S., and Le Pellec, M. (2014) Value management for exploration projects. *Project Management Journal*, 45(4): 44–66.

Manning, S. (2010) The strategic formation of project networks: A relational practice perspective. *Human Relation*, 63(4): 551–574.

Manning, S. (2005) Managing project networks as dynamic organizational forms: Learning from the TV movie industry. *International Journal of Project Management*, 23: 410–414.

Manning, S. and Sydow, J. (2007) Transforming creative potential in project networks: The case of TV production. *Critical Sociology*, 33(1–2): 19–42.

Manning, S. and Sydow, J. (2011) Projects, paths, practices: Sustaining and leveraging project-based relationships. *Industrial and Corporate Change*, 20(5): 1369–1402.

March, J. G. (1995) The future, disposable organizations and the rigidities of imagination. *Organization*, 2(3–4): 427–440.

March, J. G. and Simon, H. A. (1958) *Organizations*. New York: Wiley.

Marchington, M., Grimshaw, D., Rubery, J., and Willmott, H. (eds.) (2005) *Fragmenting Work. Blurring Organizational Boundaries and Disordering Hierarchies*. Oxford: Oxford University Press.

Marchington, M., Rubery, J., and Grimshaw, D. (2011) Alignment, integration and consistency in HRM across multi-employer networks. *Human Resource Management*, 50(2): 313–339.

Marshall, A. (1890) *Principles of Economics: An Introductory Volume*. London: Macmillan.

Martin, R. and Sunley, P. (2003) Deconstructing clusters: Chaotic concept or policy panacea? *Journal of Economic Geography*, 3: 5–35.

Martinsson, I. (2010) *Standardized knowledge transfer: A study of project-based organizations in the construction and IT sectors* (diss.). Stockholm: Stockholm University.

Maskell, P., Bathelt, H., and Malmberg, A. (2006) Building global knowledge pipelines: The role of temporary clusters. *European Planning Studies*, 14(8): 997–1013.

Masuch, M. (1985) Vicious circles in organizations. *Administrative Science Quarterly*, 29: 14–33.

Maylor, H., Brady, T., Cooke-Davis, T., and Hodgson, D. (2006) From projectification to programmification. *International Journal of Project Management*, 24(8): 663–674.

MBOpartners (2013) *Third Annual Independent Workforce Report*. USA: MBOpartners.

McAdam, D. (2011) Social movements and the growth in opposition to global projects. In Scott, R. W., Levitt, R. E., and Orr, R. J. (eds.), *Global Projects – Institutional and Political Challenges*. Cambridge: Cambridge University Press, 86–110.

McCraw, T. K. (ed.) (2005) *Creating Modern Capitalism. How Entrepreneurs, Companies, and Countries Triumphed in Three Industrial Revolutions*. Boston: Harvard University Press.

McKinlay, A. and Smith, C. (eds.) (2009) *Creative Labour. Working in the Creative Industries*. New York: Palgrave Macmillan.

McLaughlin, K., Osborne, S. P., and Ferlie, E. (2002) *New Public Management: Current Trends and Future Prospects*. London: Psychology Press.

Ménard, C. (2004) The economics of hybrid organizations. *Journal of Institutional and Theoretical Economics*, 160(3): 345–376.

Metcalfe, C. H. (1885) *The Cost of Manufactures and the Administration of Workshops, Public and Private*. 3rd edn. (1907) New York: Wiley.

Meyer, J. W. and Rowan, W. (1977) Institutionalized organizations: Formal structure as myth and ceremony. *American Journal of Sociology*, 83(2): 340–363.

Meyerson, D., Weick, K. E., and Kramer, R. M. (1996) Swift trust and temporary groups. In Kramer, R. M. and Tyler, T. R. (eds.), *Trust in Organizations: Frontiers of Theory and Research.* Thousand Oaks, CA: Sage, 166–195.

Midler, C. (1986) Logique de la mode managériale (The logic of managerial fashion). *Gérer et Comprendre,* 3: 74–85.

Midler, C. (1993) *L'Auto qui n'existait pas, management des projets et transformation de l'entreprise (The Car That Did Not Exist, Management of Projects and the Transformation of the Firm).* Paris: Interéditions, Dunod (New editions 1996 and 2012).

Midler, C. (1995) "Projectification" of the firm: The Renault case. *Scandinavian Management Journal,* 11(4): 363–375.

Midler, C. (2013) Implementing low-end disruption strategy through multi-project lineage management: The Logan Case. *Project Management Journal,* 44(5): 24–35.

Midler, C. and Beaume, R. (2009) Project-based learning patterns for dominant design renewal: The case of electric vehicle. *International Journal of Project Management,* 28(2): 142–150.

Midler C. and Silberzahn, P. (2008) Managing robust development process for high-tech startups through multi-project learning: The case of two European start-ups. *International Journal of Project Management,* 26(5): 479–486.

Midler, C., Maniak, R., and Beaume, R. (2012) *Réenchanter l'industrie par l'innovation (Reenchant Industry through Innovation).* Paris: Dunod.

Midler, C., Minguet, G., and Vervaeke, M. (2010) *Working on Innovation.* London: Routledge.

Midler, C. and Navarre, C. (2004) Project management in automotive industry. In Morris, P. W. G. and Pinto, J. K. (eds.), *The Wiley Guide to Managing Projects.* Hoboken, NJ: Wiley, 1368–1388.

Miller, R. and Hobbs, B. (2005) Governance regimes for large complex projects. *Project Management Journal,* 36(3): 42–50.

Miller, R. and Lessard, D. (2000) *The Strategic Management of Large Engineering Projects – Shaping Institutions, Risks, and Governance.* Boston: MIT Press.

Miller, R., Hobday, M., Leroux-Demers, T., and Olleros, X. (1995) Innovation in complex system industries: The case of flight simulators. *Industrial and Corporate Change,* 4(2): 363–400.

Mintzberg, H. (1976) *The Nature of Managerial Work.* New York: HarperCollins.

Mintzberg, H. and Lampel, J. (2012) Reflecting on the strategy process. *MIT Sloan Management Review*, 40(3): 21–30.

Moreau, M.-A., Negrelli, S., and Pochet, P. (eds.) (2009) *Building Anticipation of Reconstruction in Europe*. Bruxelles: Peter Lang.

Morris, P. and Jamieson, A. (2004) *Translating Corporate Strategy into Project Strategy: Realizing Corporate Strategy through Project Management*. Newtown Square, PA: PMI.

Morris, P. W. G. (1994) *The Management of Projects*. London: Telford.

Morris, P. W. G. (2013) *Reconstructing Project Management*. Chichester: Wiley-Blackwell.

Morris, P. W. G. and Geraldi, J. (2011) Managing the institutional context for projects. *Project Management Journal*, 42(6): 20–32.

Morris, P. W. G. and Jamieson, A. (2005) Moving from corporate strategy to project strategy. *Project Management Journal*, 36(4): 5–18.

Morris, P. W. G., Pinto, J. K., and Söderlund, J. (eds.) (2011) *The Oxford Handbook of Project Management*. Oxford: Oxford University Press.

Müller-Seitz, G. and Sydow, J. (2011) Terminating institutionalized termination – Why Sematech became more than a temporary organization. *Advances in Strategic Management*, 28: 147–186.

Müller, R. (2009) *Project Governance*. Farnham: Gower.

Müller, R. (2011) Project governance. In Morris, P. W. G., Pinto, J. K., and Söderlund, J. (eds.), *The Oxford Handbook of Project Managemen.*, Oxford: Oxford University Press, 483–499.

Muller, L. (2003) Swedish East India trade and international markets: Re-export of tea 1731–1813. *Scandinavian Economic History Review*, 51: 28–44.

Mumford, M. D., Scott, G. M., Gaddis, B., and Strange, J. M. (2002) Leading creative people: Orchestrating expertise and relationships. *Leadership Quarterly*, 13(6): 705–750.

Naisbitt, J. (1984) *Megatrends*. New York: Warner.

Nalebuff, B. J. and Brandenburger, A. M. (1996) *Co-opetition*. New York: Doubleday.

NAO (2013) *Universal Credit: Early Progress*. London: National Audit Office.

Newcome, R. (2003) From client to project stakeholders: A stakeholder mapping approach. *Construction Management and Economics*, 21(8): 841–848.

Newell, S., Goussevskaia, A., Swan, J., Bresnen, M., and Obembe, A. (2008) Interdependencies in complex project ecologies: The case of biomedial innovation. *Long Range Planning*, 41: 33–54.

Nicolini, D. (2013) *Practice Theory, Work, and Organization*. Oxford: Oxford University Press.

Nightingale, P. and Brady, T. (2011) Projects, paradigm and predictability. Project-based organizing and strategic management. *Advances in Strategic Management*, 28: 83–112.

Nonaka, I. (1991) The knowledge-creating company. *Harvard Business Review*, 69(6): 96–104.

Nonaka, I. (1994) A dynamic theory of organizational knowledge creation. *Organization Science*, 5(1): 14–37.

Normann, R. (2001) *Reframing Business – When the Map Changes the Landscape*. London: Wiley.

North, D. (1981) *Structure and Change in Economic History*. New York: Norton.

North, D. (1990) *Institutions, Institutional Change and Economic Performance*. Cambridge: Cambridge University Press.

North, D. (2005) *Understanding the Process of Economic Change*. Princeton, NJ: Princeton University Press.

Obstfeld, D. (2005) Social networks, the tertius jungens orientation, and involvement in innovation. *Administrative Science Quarterly*, 50: 100–130.

Ojiako, U., Chipulu, M., Gardiner, P., Williams, T., Mota, C., Maguire, S., Shou, Y., and Stamati, T. (2014) Effect of project role, age and gender differences on the formation and revision of project decision judgments, *International Journal of Project Management* 32: 556–567.

Okhuysen, G. A., Lepak, D., Ashcraft, K. L., Labianca, G., Smith, V., and Steensma, H. K. (2013) Theories of work and working today. *Academy of Management Review*, 38(4),491–502.

Olofsdotter, G. (2008) *Flexibilitetens främlingar: Om anställda i bemanningsföretag (Strangers of flexibility: Hired in employment agencies)* (diss.). Sundsvall: Mid Sweden.

Olofsson, P. (2013) Skall bemanningsföretagen ta över världen? (Will temporary agencies take over the world?) Stockholm: Laborantes förlag.

Ordanini, A., Rubera, G., and Sala, M. (2008) Integrating functional knowledge and embedding learning in new product launches: How project forms helped EMI Music. *Long Range Planning*, 41: 17–32.

Orlikowski, W. J. and Scott, S. (2008) Sociomateriality: Challenging the separation of technology, work and organization. *Academy of Management Annals*, 2(1): 433–474.

Orlikowski, W. J. and Yates, J. (2002) It's about time: Temporal structuring in organizations. *Organization Science*, 13(6): 684–700.

Orr, R. J., Scott, W. R., Levitt, R. E., Artto, K., and Kujala, J. (2011) Global projects: Distinguishing features, drivers, and challenges. In Scott, R. W., Levitt, R. E., and Orr, R. J. (eds.), *Global Projects – Institutional and Political Challenges.* Cambridge: Cambridge University Press, 15–51.

Overtrup, L. (2006) The new knowledge region: From simple to complex innovation theory. In Cooke, P. and Piccaluga, A. (eds.), *Regional Development in the Knowledge Economy.* London: Routledge, 246–271.

Packendorff, J. (1995) Inquiring into the temporary organization: New directions for project management research. *Scandinavian Journal of Management,* 11(4): 319–333.

Packendorff, J. (2002) The temporary society and its enemies: Projects from an individual perspective. In Sahlin-Andersson, K. and Söderholm, A. (eds.), *Beyond Project Management.* Copenhagen: Copenhagen Business School Press, 39–58.

Packendorff, J. and Lindgren, M. (2014) Projectification and its consequences: Narrow and broad conceptualizations. *South African Journal of Economic and Management Sciences,* 17: 7–21.

Padgett, J. F. and Powell, W. W. (eds.) (2012) *The Emergence of Organizations and Markets.* Princeton, NJ: Princeton University Press.

Patanakul, P. and Shenhar, A. J. (2011) What project strategy really is: The fundamental building block in strategic project management. *Project Management Journal,* 43(1): 4–20.

Petit, Y. (2012) Project portfolios in dynamic environments: Organizing for uncertainty. *International Journal of Project Management,* 30(5): 539–553.

Petit Y. and Hobbs, B. (2010) Project portfolios in dynamic environments: Sources of uncertainty and sensing mechanisms. *Project Management Journal,* 41(4): 46–58.

Pierson, P. (2000) Increasing returns, path dependence, and the study of politics. *American Political Science Review,* 94: 251–267.

Piketty, T. (2014) *Capital in the Twenty-First Century.* Cambridge, MA: Belknap Press of Harward University Press.

Pinchot, G. (1985) *Intrapreneurship.* New York: Harper & Row.

Pine II, B. J. (1993) *Mass Customization – The New Frontier in Business Competition.* Boston: Harvard Business School Press.

Pinney, B. (2001) Projects, management, and protean times: Engineering enterprise in the United States, 1870–1960 (diss.). Boston: MIT.

Pinto, J. K., Thoms P., Trailer, J., Palmer, T., and Govekar, M. (1998) *Project Leadership: From Theory to Practice.* Newton Square, PA: PMI.

Pinto, J. K. (2002) Project management 2002. *Research-Technology Management,* 45(2): 22–37.

Pinto, J. K. (2014) Project management, governance, and the normalization of deviance. *International Journal of Project Management*, 32: 376–387.

Pinto, J. K. and Slevin, D. P. (1998) Critical success factors. In Pinto, J. K. (ed.), *Project Management Handbook*. San Francisco, CA: Jossey-Bass, 379–395.

Pinto, J. K., Dawood, S., and Pinto, M. B. (2014) Project management and burnout: Implications of the demand-control-support model on project-based work. *International Journal of Project Management*, 32(4): 578–589.

Piore M. and Sabel, C. F. (1984) *The Second Industrial Divide: Possibilities for Prosperity*. New York: Basic Books.

PMI (2013) *PMBOK GUIDE*. Newton Square, PA: PMI.

Polanyi, M. (1967) *The Tacit Dimension*. London: Routledge.

Pongratz, H. J. and Voß, G. G (2003) From employee to "entreployee": Towards a "self-entrepreneurial" work force? *Concepts and Transformations*, 8(3): 239–254.

Porter, M. E. (1980) *Competitive Strategy: Techniques for Analyzing Industries and Competitors*. New York: Free Press.

Porter, M. E. (1985) *Competitive Advantage: Creating and Sustaining Superior Performance*. New York: Free Press.

Porter, M. E. (1990) *The Competitive Advantage of Nations*. New York: Free Press.

Porter, M. E. (2000) Local competition and economic development: Local clusters in a global economy. *Economic Development Quarterly*, 14(1): 15–34.

Powell, W. W. (1990) Neither market nor hierarchy: Network forms of organization. *Research in Organizational Behavior*, 12: 295–336.

Prahalad, C. K. and Hamel, G. (1990) The core competence of the corporation. *Harvard Business Review*, 68(3): 79–93.

Prahalad, C. K. and Ramaswamy, V. (2004) *The Future of Competition: Co-creating Unique Value with Customers*. Boston: Harvard Business School Press.

Prencipe, A. and Tell, F. (2001) Inter-project learning: Processes and outcomes of knowledge codification in project-based firms. *Research Policy*, 30: 1371–1394.

Priemus, H. (2010) Mega-projects: Dealing with pitfalls. *European Planning Studies*, 18(7): 1023–1039.

Provan, K. G. (1983) The federation as an interorganizational linkage network. *Academy of Management Review*, 8(1): 79–89.

Provan, K. G. and Kenis, P. (2008) Modes of network governance: Structure, management, and effectiveness. *Journal of Public Administration Research and Theory*, 8: 229–252.

Provan, K. G., Fish, A., and Sydow, J. (2007) Interorganizational networks at the network level: A review of empirical literature on whole networks. *Journal of Management*, 33(3): 479–516.

Putnam, R. D. (1992) *Making Democracy Work: Civic Traditions in Modern Italy*. Princeton, NJ: Princeton University Press.

PWC (2004) *Boosting Business Performance through Programme and Project Management*. London: PricewaterhouseCoopers.

Räisänen, C. and Linde, A. (2004) Technologizing discourse to standardize projects in multi-project organizations: Hegemony by consensus? *Organization*, 11(1): 101–121.

Rhenman, E. (1964) *Företagsdemokrati och företagsorganisation (Industrial Democracy and Organization)*. Stockholm: PAN/Norstedts.

Roberts, R. M. (1989) *Serendipity: Accidental Discoveries in Science*. New York: Wiley.

Romanelli, E. and Khessina, O. (2005) Regional industrial identity: Cluster configurations and regional economic development. *Organization Science*, 16(4): 344–358.

Rosengren, C. (2009) *Arbetstidens symbolvärde. Om historisk kontinuitet och förändring i synen på arbetstid samt normers inverkan på arbetstidens gestaltning (The symbolic value of working time. About historical continuity and change in viewpoints on working time, the importance of norms and effect on work setup)* (diss.). Stockholm: RIT.

Rowlinson, M., Hassard, J., and Decker, S. (2014) Research strategies for organizational history: A dialogue between historical theory and organizational theory. *Academy of Management Review*, 39(3): 250–274.

Sahlin-Andersson, K. (2002) Project management as boundary work. In Sahlin-Andersson, K. and Söderholm, A. (eds.), *Beyond Project Management. New Perspectives on the Temporary-permanent Dilemma*. Malmö: Liber, 241–260.

Sahlin-Andersson, K. and Söderholm, A. (2002) The Scandinavian school of project studies. In Sahlin-Andersson, K. and Söderholm, A. (eds.) *Beyond Project Management. New Perspectives on the Temporary-permanent Dilemma*. Malmö: Liber, 11–24.

Sandberg, Å. (ed.) (2013) *Nordic Lights: Work, Management and Welfare in Scandinavia*. Stockholm: SNS förlag.

Sapsed J., Nightingale, P., Mateos-Garcia, J., Camerani, R., Byford, J., and Miles, S. with Docherty, D. and Jones, P. (2013) The Brighton Fuse Report available at http://www.brightonfuse.com/wp-content/uploads/2013/10/The-Brighton-Fuse-Final-Report.pdf.

Sarasvathy, S. D. (2001) Causation and effectuation: Toward a theoretical shift from economic inevitability to entrepreneurial contingency. *Academy of Management Review*, 26(2): 243–263.

Saundry, R. (1998) The limits of flexibility: The case of UK television. *British Journal of Management*, 9(2): 151–162.

Sawyer, P. (ed.) (1997) *The Oxford Illustrated History of the Vikings*. Oxford: Oxford University Press.

Saxenian, A. (1994) *Regional Advantage*. Cambridge, MA: Harvard University Press.

Schatzki, T., Knorr-Cetina, K., and von Savigny, E. (eds.) (2001) *The Practice Turn in Contemporary Theory*. London: Routledge.

Schein, E. H. (1967) Organizational socialization and the profession of management. *Sloan Management Review*, 30(1).

Schein, E. H. (1990) Organizational culture. *American Psychologist*, 45(2): 109–119.

Schedler, K. and Proeller, I. (2011) *New Public Management*. 5th edn. Berne: Haupt.

Schoeneborn, D. (2013) PowerPoint und die Einkapselung von Prozessualität im projektübergreifenden Lernen (PowerPoint and the encapsulation of processuality in cross-project learning). *Managementforschung*, 23: 127–156.

Schön, D. (1983) *The Reflective Practitioner*. New York: Basic Books.

Schreyögg, G. and Geiger, D. (2007) The significance of distinctiveness: A proposal for rethinking organizational knowledge. *Organization*, 14(1): 77–100.

Schüßler, E., Decker, C., and Lerch, F. (2013) Networks of clusters: A governance perspective. *Industry and Innovation*, 20(4): 357–377.

Schüßler, E., Wessel, L., and Gersch, M. (2012) Taking stock: Capability development in interorganizational projects. *Schmalenbach Business Review*, 64: 171–186.

Schumpeter, J. A. (1947) The creative response in economic history. *Journal of Economic History*, 7(2): 149–159.

Schwab, A. and Miner, A. S. (2008) Learning in hybrid-project systems: The effects of project performance on repeated collaboration. *Academy of Management Journal*, 51(6): 1117–1149.

Scott, R. W. (2008) *Organizations and Institutions*. 3rd edn. Thousand Oaks, CA: Sage.

Sedström O. (2007) *Stress and conflict in project management. A mixed research study of a Swedish energy company* (diss.). Gothenburg: Chalmers University of Technology.

Seidl, D. and Whittington, R. (2014) Enlarging the strategy-as-practice research agenda: Towards taller and flatter ontologies. *Organization Studies*, 35(10): 1407–1421.

Senatsverwaltung für Wirtschaft Technologie und Frauen (2008) *Kulturwirtschaft in Berlin – Entwicklungen und Potenziale*. Berlin.

Shapira, Z. and Berndt, D. J. (1997) Managing grand-scale construction projects: A risk-taking perspective. *Research in Organizational Behavior*, 19: 303–360.

Shenhar, A. J. (2004) Strategic project leadership: Toward a strategic approach to project management. *R&D Management*, 34(5): 569–578.

Simon, H. A. (1947) *Administrative Behavior*. New York: Free Press.

Singelman, J. (1978) *From Agriculture to Dervices*. London: Sage.

Sjöstrand, S-E. (ed.) (1993) *Institutional Change – Theory and Empirical Findings*. Armonk, NY: Sharpe.

Slevin, D. P. and Pinto, J. K. (2007) An overview of behavioral issues in project management. In Morris P. and Pinto J. K. (eds.), *The Wiley Guide to Project Management Competencies*. Chichester: Wiley, 1–19.

Snickare, L. (2012) *Makt utan magi – En studie av chefers yrkeskunnande (Power without Magic – A study of Executive Skills)*. Stockholm: KTH.

Snow, C. C., Miles, R. E., and Coleman, Jr., H. J. (1992) Managing 21st century network organizations. *Organizational Dynamics*, 20(3): 5–20.

Söderlund, J. (2005) *Projektledning and projektkompetens – Perspektiv på konkurrenskraft (Project management and project competence – Perspective on competitive capacity)*. Malmö: Liber.

Söderlund, J. (2011) Pluralism in project management: Navigating the crossroads of specialization and fragmentation. *International Journal of Management Reviews*, 13: 153–176.

Söderlund, J. and Bredin, K. (2005) *Perspektiv på HRM – Nya organisationsformer, nya utmaningar (Perspectives on HRM – New Organizational Forms, New Challenges)*. Malmö: Liber.

Söderlund, J. and Tell, F. (2009) The P-form organization and the dynamics of project competence: Project epochs in Asea/ABB, 1950–2000. *International Journal of Project Management*, 27: 101–102.

Söderlund, J. and Tell, F. (2011) Strategy and capabilities in the P-form corporation: Linking strategic direction with organizational capabilities. *Advances in Strategic Management*, 28: 235–262.

Sorenson, O. and Waguespack, D. M. (2006) Social structure and exchange: Self-confirming dynamics in Hollywood. *Administrative Science Quarterly*, 51: 560–589.

Star, S. L. and Griesemer, J. R. (1989) Institutional ecology, "translations" and boundary objects: Amateurs and professionals in Berkeley's Museum of Vertebrate Zoology. *Social Studies of Science*, 19(3): 387–420.

Starbuck, W. H. (2009) The constant causes of never-ending faddishness in the behavioral and social sciences. *Scandinavian Journal of Management*, 25(1): 108–116.

Starkey, K., Barnatt, C., and Tempest, S. (2000) Beyond networks and hierarchies: Latent organizations in the U.K. television industry. *Organization Science*, 11: 299–305.

Stine, G. H. (1975) *The Third Industrial Revolution*. New York: G.P. Putnam's Sons

Storper, M. and Christopherson, S. (1987) Flexible specialization and regional industrial agglomerations: The case of the U.S. motion picture industry. *Annals of the American Association of Geographers*, 77: 104–117.

Storrie, D. (2002) *Temporary Agency Work in the European Union*. Dublin: European Foundation for the Improvement of Living and Working Conditions.

Streeck, W. (1992) *Social Institutions and Economic Performance-Studies of Industrial Relations in Advanced Capitalist Economies*. London: Sage.

Streeck, W. and Thelen, K. (eds.) (2005) *Beyond Continuity: Explorations in the Dynamics of Advanced Political Economies*. Oxford: Oxford University Press.

Sturgess, G. L. (2011) Commissions and concessions: A brief history of contracting for complexity in the public sector. In Caldwell, N. and Howard, M. (eds.), *Procuring Complex Performance: Studies of Innovation in Product-Service Management*. New York: Routledge, 41–58

Svejenova, S., Strandgaard Petersen, J., and Vives, L. (2011) Projects as passion: Lessons for strategy from temporary art. *Advances in Strategic Management*, 28: 501–517.

Svensson, L., Brulin, G., Ellström, P-E., and Widegren, Ö. (2002) *Interaktiv forskning – För utveckling av teori och praktik (Interactive Research – For the Development of Theory and Practice)*. Stockholm: Work Life in Transition.

Sydow, J. (2005) Managing interfirm networks – Towards more reflexive network development? In Theurl, T. (ed.), *Economics of Interfirm Networks*. Tübingen: Mohr Siebeck, 217–236.

Sydow, J. and Lerch, F. (2007) *Developing Photonics Cluster – Commonalities, Contrasts and Contradictions*. London: Advanced Institute of Management (AIM) Research.

Sydow, J. and Manning S. (2004) *Projects, paths, and relationships: Binding processes in TV production*. Paper presented at the SAM/IFSAM VIIth World Congress, July 5–7, Gothenburg.

Sydow, J. and Schreyögg, G. (eds.) (2013) *Self-reinforcing Processes in and among Organizations*. London: Palgrave Macmillan.

Sydow, J. and Staber, U. (2002) The institutional embeddedness of project networks: The case of content production in German television. *Regional Studies*, 36 (3): 223–235.

Sydow, J. and Windeler, A. (1998) Organizing and evaluating interfirm networks – A structurationist perspective on network management and effectiveness. *Organization Science, 9* (3): 265–284.

Sydow, J. and Windeler, A. (1999) Projektnetzwerke: Management von (mehr als) temporären Systemen (Project networks: Management of (more than) temporary systems). In Engelhard, J. and Sinz, E. (eds.), *Kooperation im Wettbewerb.* Wiesbaden: Gabler, 211–235. Reprinted in Sydow, J. and Windeler, A. (eds.) (2004) *Organization von Content-Produktion.* Wiesbaden: Westdeutscher Verlag, 37–55.

Sydow, J. and Windeler, A. (2003) Knowledge, trust and control: Managing tensions and contradictions in a regional network of service firms. *International Studies of Management & Organization,* 33: 69–100.

Sydow, J., Lindkvist, L., and DeFillippi, R. (2004) Project-based organizations, embeddedness and repositories of knowledge – Editoral. *Organization Studies,* 25(9): 1475–1489.

Syndex (2013) *How Can the Issue of Work Be Linked When Considering the Impact of Restructuring on the Role of Work Group as a Factor in the (Re)Building of Professional Expertise?* Brussels: ETUC.

Tarique, I. and Schuler, R. S. (2010) Global talent management: Literature review, integrative framework, and suggestions for further research. *Journal of World Business,* 45(2): 105–196.

Taylor, F. (1911) *The Principle of Scientific Management.* New York: Harper & Row.

Teece, D., Pisano, G., and Shuen, A. (1997) Dynamic capabilities and strategic management. *Strategic Management Journal,* 18(7): 509–533.

Teller, J., Kock, A., and Gemünden, H. G. (2014) Risk management in project portfolios is more than managing project risks: A contingency perspective on risk manangement. *Project Management Journal,* Special issue: International Research Network on Organizaing by Projects (IRNOP), 45(4): 67–80.

Temin, P. (1964) *Iron and Steel in Nineteenth-Century America: An Economic Inquiry.* Cambridge, MA: MIT Press.

Tengblad, S. (2006) Is there a "new managerial work"? A comparison with Mintzberg's classic study 30 years later. *Journal of Management Studies,* 43(7): 1437–1461.

Thamhain, H. J. (2004) Linkages of project environment to performance: Lessons for team leadership. *International Journal of Project Management,* 22(7): 533–544.

Thomas, J., Delisle, C., and Jugdev, K. (2002) *Selling Project Management to Senior Executives: Framing the Moves That Matter.* Newton Square, PA: PMI.

Thomke, S. H. (1998) Simulation, learning and R&D performance: Evidence from automotive development. *Research Policy*, 27(1): 55–74.

Toffler, A. (1980) *The Third Wave*. New York: William Morrow & Company.

Tracey, P., Heide, J. B., and Bell, S. J. (2014) Bringing "place" back in: Regional clusters, project governance, and new product outcomes. *Journal of Marketing*, 78(6): 1–26.

Traxler, F. and Huemer, G. (eds.) (2013) *Handbook of Business Interest Associations and Governance: A Comparative Analytical Approach*. London: Routledge.

Turner, J. R. (1999) Project management: A profession based on knowledge or faith? *International Journal of Project Management*, 17(6): 329–330.

Turner, J. R. and Müller, R. (2003) On the nature of the project as a temporary organization. *International Journal of Project Management*, 21(1): 1–8.

Tyssen, A. K., Wald, A., and Spieth, P. (2013) Leadership in temporary organizations: A review of leadership theories and a research agenda. *Project Management Journal*, 44(6): 52–67.

Uhlin, Å. (2001) Om regionala innovationssystem, lärande, komplexitet och tillit (Regional innovation systems, learning, complexity and trust). In Ekstedt, E. (ed.), *Kunskap och handling för företagande och regional utveckling (Knowledge and Action for Entrepreneurship and Regional Development)*. Stockholm: Work Life in Transition, 37–76.

Unger, B. N., Rank, J. and Gemünden, H.G. (2014, 2015) *Corporate Innovation Culture and Dimensions of Project Portfolio Success: The Moderating Role of National Culture, Project Management Journal* Volume 45, Issue 6, pages 38–57, December 2014/January 2015.

Unger, C. (2006) *Industrialized house building – Fundamental change or business as usual?* (diss.). Stockholm: RIT.

Uzzi, B. (1997) Social structure and competition in interfirm networks: The paradox of embeddedness. *Administrative Science Quarterly*, 42(1): 35–67.

Vaara, E. and Whittington, R. (2012) Strategy-as-practice: Taking social practices seriously. *Academy of Management Annals*, 6(1): 285–336.

Van de Ven, A. H., Polley, D., Garud, R., and Venkatraman, S. (1999) *The Innovation Journey*. New York: Oxford University Press.

Vanhaverbeke, W. and Nooderhaven, N. G. (2001) Competition between alliance blocks: The case of the RISC microprocessor technology. *Organization Studies*, 22(1): 1–30.

Vaughan, D. (1996) *The Challenger Launch Decision: Risky Technology, Culture and Deviance at NASA*. Chicago: University of Chicago Press.

Verganti, R. (2009) *Design-Driven Innovation: Changing the Rules of Competition by Radically Innovating What Things Mean*. Boston: Harvard Business School Press.

Vissac-Charles, V. (1995) *Dynamique des réseaux et trajectoire de l'innovation: application à la gestion de projet (Dynamics of networks and innovation trajectory: Application to project management)* (diss.). Paris: Ecole des Mines de Paris.

Vitols, S. (2001) Varieties of corporate governance: Comparing Germany and the UK. In Hall, P. A. and Soskice, D. (eds.), *Varieties of Capitalism. The Institutional Foundations of Comparative Advantage*. Oxford: Oxford University Press, 337–360.

Von Hippel, E. (1998) Economics of product development by users: The impact of "sticky" local information. *Management Science*, 44(5): 629–644.

Vosko, L. F. (2000) *Temporary Work. The Gendered Rise of a Precarious Employment Relationship*. Toronto: University of Toronto Press.

Wagner, R. (ed.) (2009) *Projekt als Strategie – Strategie als Projekt*. Nürnberg: GPM.

Wakabayashi, N., Yamashita, M., and Yamada, J. (2009) Japanese networks for top-performing films: Repeated teams preserve uniqueness. *Journal of Media Business Studies*, 6(4): 31–48.

Warburton, R. and Kanabar, V. (2013) *The Art and Science of Project Management*. Newport, RI: RW Press.

Weick, K. E. (1995) *Sensemaking in Organizations*. Newbury Park, CA: Sage.

Welch, J. with Bryne, J. A. (2001) *Jack: What I've Learned Leading a Great Company and Great People*. London: Headline Book.

Westlund, H. and Nilsson, E. (2003) Företagens sociala kapital – I teorin och i Odenskogs företagspark (The social capital of companies – in theory and in the Industrial Park of Odenskog). In Ekstedt, E. and Wolvén, L-E. (eds.), *Relationsbyggande för ekonomisk utveckling (Building Relations for Economic Development)*. Stockholm: Work Life in Transition, 103–124.

Whitley, R. (2006) Project-based firms: New organizational form or variations on a theme? *Industrial and Corporate Change*, 15(1): 77–99.

Whittington, R., Pettigrew, A., Peck, S., Fenton, E., and Conyon, M. (1999) Change and complementarities in the new competitive landscape: A European panel study, 1992–1996. *Organization Science*, 10(5): 583–600.

Wikman, A. (2002) *Temporära kontrakt och inlåsningseffekter (Temporary Contracts and Lock- in Effects)*. Stockholm: Work Life in Transition.

Wikström, K., Artto, K., Kujala, J., and Söderlund, J. (2010) Business models in project business. *International Journal of Project Management*, 28: 832–841.

Wikström, S., Normann, R., Anell, B., Ekvall, G., Forslin, J., and Skärvad, P-H. (1992) *Kunskap och värde. Företaget som ett kunskapande och värdeskapande system (Knowledge and Value: The Company as a Knowledge and Value Creating System)*. Stockholm: FA rådet & Norstedts juridik.

Wilhelm, M. (2011) Managing coopetition through horizontal supply chain relations: Linking dyadic and network levels of analysis. *Journal of Operations Management*, 29(7–8): 663–676.

Williamson, O. E. (1985) *The Economic Institutions of Capitalism*. New York: Free Press.

Williamson, O. E. (1991) Comparative economic organization: The analysis of discrete structural alternatives. *Administrative Science Quarterly*, 36(2): 269–296.

Winch, G. (2013) Escalation in major projects: Lessons from the Channel Fixed Link. *International Journal of Project Management*, 31: 724–734.

Winch, G. (2014) Three domains of project organising. *International Journal of Project Management*, 32: 721–731.

Windeler, A. and Sydow, J. (2001) Project networks and changing industry practices – Collaborative content production in the German television tndustry. *Organization Studies*, 22(6): 1035–1061.

Windeler, A., Wirth, C., and Sydow, J. (2001) Die Zukunft in der Gegenwart erfahren. Arbeit in Projektnetzwerken der Fernsehproduktion (Experiencing the future in the present: Working in project networks of television production). *Arbeitsrecht im Betrieb*, 22(12): 12–18.

Winter, M. and Szczepanek, T. (2009) *Images of Projects*. Farnham: Gower.

Wirdenius, H. (1958) *Supervisors at Work*. Stockholm: Swedish Council for Personnel Administration.

Wolvén, L. and Ekstedt, E. (eds.) (2004) *Företagande och gemenskap (Entrepreneurship and Solidarity)*. Stockholm: Arbetslivsinstitutet.

World Bank (2009). World Development Indicators CD-ROM. Washington, DC: World Bank Publications.

Zheng, J. and Wang, L. (2014) *Institutions and development: The case of China in comparative perspective*. University of Gothenborg and Irish Institute for Chinese Studies, University College, Dublin (unpublished manuscript).

Zika-Viktorsson, A. (2002) *Det industriella projektet. Studier av projektmedlemmars arbetssituation (The industrial project. Studies of the work situation of project members)* (diss.). Stockholm: KTH.

Zika-Viktorsson, A., Nordqvist S., and Hovmark, S. (1998) *Psykosocial arbetsmiljö, ledning och effektivitet i projektgrupper (Psycho-social work environments, leadership, and efficiency in project groups)*. Rapport nr 99, Psykologiska institutionen, Stockholms Universitet.

Zika-Viktorsson, A., Sundström, P., and Engwall, M. (2006) Project overload: An exploratory study of work and management in multi-project settings. *International Journal of Project Management*, 24: 385–394.

Zuboff, S. (1988) *In the Age of the Smart Machine. The Future of Work and Power.* New York: Basic Books.

Zuboff, S. and Maxmin, J. (2002) *The Support Economy. Why Corporations Are Failing Individuals and the Next Episode of Capitalism.* London: Penguin.

# Index

Printed in the United States
By Bookmasters